"This insightful and timely book deals with the formidable post-COVID challenges facing Asia. The fresh perspective of two prominent Asian economists outlines the critical challenge of achieving sustainable development at a time of growing deglobalization pressures. The book is well written and offers illuminating case studies as well as constructive, concrete guidance for a better future. It is essential reading for policy-makers, scholars, and practitioners."

Joshua Aizenman
Robert R. and Katheryn A. Dockson Chair in Economics and International Relations and Professor of International Relations and Economics
University of Southern California

"The though-provoking book by Professor Lee and Dr Park takes a strategic geopolitical look at Asia, its place in the world, and its prospects at a time of ever-accelerating digital transformation amid the unprecedented global shock of the COVID-19 pandemic. Their timely book offers Asia a clear blueprint for coping with game-changing trends such as deglobalization (a trend likely reinforced by COVID-19) and the Fourth Industrial Revolution. Against this turbulent background, the authors examine how the region can address the global challenge of climate change and the related imperative of sustainable development. This book is a must-read for all strategic thinkers interested in the most transformative forces shaping the Pale Blue Dot we all share!"

Erkko Autio
Professor in Technology Venturing and Entrepreneurship
Imperial College London

"COVID-19 changes everything, or so it is said. In this important book, Lee and Park ask how it will change the global economic landscape and how Asian countries should respond. New thinking about the effects of the pandemic is crucial, and the authors are quick off the mark."

Barry Eichengreen
George C. Pardee Professor of Economics and Political Science
University of California, Berkeley

"This important contribution by Professor Lee and Dr Park explores how Asian economies can prosper in the post-COVID world. Deglobalization is a serious concern for the region. However, if Asian economies assume a leading role in the Fourth Industrial Revolution, they can bring about a Pax Asiana that will benefit not only Asia but the whole world. The authors' views may challenge conventional wisdom, but they nevertheless provide a plausible blueprint for Asia's sustainable development in these troubling times."

Shin-ichi Fukuda
Professor, Economics Department
University of Tokyo

"Hyun-Hoon Lee and Donghyun Park present a comprehensive, credible, and forward-looking examination of the global and regional implications of the pandemic. They advance a wide range of policy options to take advantage of the opportunities brought by the pandemic. Their book is a valuable reference for policy-makers, academics, and general readers who would like to better understand the post-COVID world economic challenges and what they mean for Asia."

M. Ayhan Kose
Director, Prospects Group, Equitable Growth,
Finance and Institutions
World Bank Group

"COVID-19 has profound ramifications for Asia and the world. The pandemic is likely to accelerate deglobalization, which is bad news for a region that benefited hugely from globalization. However, Lee and Park argue that Asian countries can turn this daunting crisis into promising opportunities. To do so, they must further strengthen their economic links with each other while keeping their doors open to the wider world. In addition, they will have to be leaders, not just bystanders, of the Fourth Industrial Revolution, which is reshaping the global technological landscape. Working closely together, Asian countries can spearhead a new golden age of globalization. If successful, they have every chance of leading the global fight against climate change, poverty, and other challenges to achieve sustainable development and prosperity in the post-COVID-19 world."

Justin Yifu Lin
Dean, Institute of New Structural Economics, Peking University
Former Chief Economist, The World Bank

"A timely and comprehensive account of the challenges and opportunities facing Asia in these uncertain times. This book is a must-read for anyone pondering the critical choices Asia must make to adjust to COVID-19, ride the next wave of globalization, take advantage of new technologies, and invest in the livelihood of its people. It is time for Asia to be in the driver's seat and Hyun-Hoon Lee and Donghyun Park lay out how."

Changyong Rhee
Director of the Asia and Pacific Department,
International Monetary Fund
Former Chief Economist, Asian Development Bank

"This perceptive and illuminating book by Professor Lee and Dr Park takes an in-depth look at the challenges and opportunities facing Asia in the post-COVID world. The risk of deglobalization, which has been heightened significantly since the outbreak of the pandemic, poses a major threat to Asia's economic success. However, the on-going Fourth Industrial Revolution will give rise to a new, more digital wave of globalization, which offers plenty of exciting opportunities. The authors make a cogent case that Asian countries are fully capable of leveraging the new opportunities to achieve sustainable development. But to do so, they must assume a stronger leadership role on the global stage."

Yasuyuki Sawada
Chief Economist
Asian Development Bank

POST-COVID ASIA

Deglobalization, Fourth Industrial Revolution, and Sustainable Development

POST-COVID ASIA

Deglobalization, Fourth Industrial Revolution, and Sustainable Development

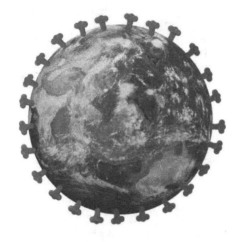

Hyun-Hoon Lee
Kangwon National University, South Korea

Donghyun Park
Asian Development Bank, Philippines

NEW JERSEY · LONDON · SINGAPORE · BEIJING · SHANGHAI · HONG KONG · TAIPEI · CHENNAI · TOKYO

Published by

World Scientific Publishing Co. Pte. Ltd.
5 Toh Tuck Link, Singapore 596224
USA office: 27 Warren Street, Suite 401-402, Hackensack, NJ 07601
UK office: 57 Shelton Street, Covent Garden, London WC2H 9HE

Library of Congress Cataloging-in-Publication Data
Names: Yi, Hyŏn-hun, 1959– author. | Park, Donghyun, author.
Title: Post-COVID Asia : deglobalization, fourth industrial revolution, and
    sustainable development / Hyun-Hoon Lee, Kangwon National University,
    South Korea, Donghyun Park, Asian Development Bank, Philippines.
Description: Singapore ; Hackensack, NJ : World Scientific, [2021] |
    Includes bibliographical references and index.
Identifiers: LCCN 2020042484 (print) | LCCN 2020042485 (ebook) |
    ISBN 9789811228971 (hardcover) | ISBN 9789811230233 (paperback) |
    ISBN 9789811228988 (ebook) | ISBN 9789811228995 (ebook other)
Subjects: LCSH: COVID-19 (Disease)--Economic aspects--Asia. | Globalization--Asia. |
    Asia--Economic conditions--21st century | Asia--Economic policy--21st century.
Classification: LCC HC412 .Y54 2021 (print) | LCC HC412 (ebook) | DDC 330.95--dc23
LC record available at https://lccn.loc.gov/2020042484
LC ebook record available at https://lccn.loc.gov/2020042485

British Library Cataloguing-in-Publication Data
A catalogue record for this book is available from the British Library.

For any available supplementary material, please visit
https://www.worldscientific.com/worldscibooks/10.1142/12062#t=suppl

Desk Editors: Aanand Jayaraman/Yulin Jiang

Typeset by Stallion Press
Email: enquiries@stallionpress.com

About the Book

Coronavirus disease (COVID-19) has been an unprecedented, once-in-a-century gamechanger for the world. The central focus of *Post-COVID Asia* is the new world that will emerge after the coronavirus. In particular, this book explores how deglobalization will proceed in the post-COVID world and what kind of impact deglobalization will have on Asian economies. After all, in the last few decades, Asia has leveraged globalization to become the world's fastest-growing, most dynamic region. Therefore, an urgent challenge facing Asian economies is to figure out how to survive and thrive when the globalization which served them so well is giving way to deglobalization.

Opportunities have emerged for Asian economies amid the winding down of the third wave of globalization. In fact, the next wave of globalization is already beginning to take shape, in tandem with the Fourth Industrial Revolution, which is full of exciting new technologies. This book offers insights that would help governments, companies and people in Asia to ride the next wave of globalization to power their prosperity.

Preface

The coronavirus disease (COVID-19) has been an unprecedented, once-in-a-century gamechanger for the world. The pandemic, which first emerged in Wuhan, China, in December 2019, spread like a wildfire across the world and will fundamentally reshape global politics, economy, culture, society, and all other fields of human activity. Former US Secretary of State Henry A. Kissinger wrote in *The Wall Street Journal* that COVID-19 will permanently alter the world order and predicted it may revive the walled city, an anachronism in a world where mankind's prosperity depends on global movement of goods and services, capital, and people.[1]

According to *The New York Times* columnist Thomas Friedman, the impact of this pandemic may be so far-reaching that human history may now be divided into Before Coronavirus (BC) and After Coronavirus (AC). It remains to be seen whether we will see BC and AC in the

---

[1] H. A. Kissinger (2020). *"The coronavirus pandemic will forever alter the world order,"* The Wall Street Journal, April 3.

history textbooks of our children and grandchildren. What is beyond doubt that none of us have experienced and suffered anything like COVID-19 in our lifetime.

The central focus of our book is the new world that will emerge after the coronavirus. In particular, we want to explore how deglobalization will proceed in the post-COVID world and what kind of impact it will have on Asian economies. After all, in the last few decades, Asia has leveraged integration into the world economy and financial system to become the fastest-growing, most dynamic region. That is, globalization enabled Asia to transform itself from a group of typical stagnant Third World economies to the third center of gravity of the world economy, along with the US and Europe. Therefore, an urgent challenge facing Asian economies is to figure out how to survive and thrive when the globalization which served them so well is giving way to deglobalization.

The golden age of globalization which dominated the global landscape in the postwar period has already been in retreat since a few years ago. COVID-19 is not kicking off deglobalization. However, the global nature of COVID-19 will exacerbate, intensify, and accelerate the ongoing retreat from globalization. In this book, we will examine how COVID-19 will speed up deglobalization and how the hegemonic power struggle between America and China — the incumbent superpower and the rising challenger superpower — will play out. The superpower rivalry puts other Asian countries on the edge of a precipice.

The current wave of globalization, the third golden age of globalization, began with the end of the Second World War. The first wave of globalization began in early 19th century while the second wave took place during the interwar period, ending as the Second World

War began. Each wave of globalization accompanied an industrial revolution. The first wave of globalization was preceded by the First Industrial Revolution, the second wave preceded by the Second Industrial Revolution, and the third wave of globalization evolved in tandem with the Third Industrial Revolution.

The defining characteristic of the third golden age is the cost minimization of manufacturing through deepening of the global value chain. The basic logic behind the global value chain is to produce each part and component of a manufactured product at its lowest-cost location. In this process, China, which was endowed with an abundance of hard-working, low-wage workers, became the Workshop of the World and industrialized and grew with extraordinary speed. Never before had such a large economy grown so rapidly for so long.

However, COVID-19 highlighted the fact that the global value chain is extremely vulnerable to external shocks. If any country in the chain suffers a big coronavirus outbreak and its factories are shut down, then the entire production process is severely disrupted. Indeed Wuhan, a large city in central China that was the original epicenter of the pandemic, is a key hub in the global value chain. As a result, global multinational companies from US, Japan, Western Europe, Korea, and other advanced economies will start to shift production back home. This is a process known as reshoring, or the reversal of offshoring. Companies will also shift production to safer, politically more stable countries.

While the physical relocation of manufacturing to home countries and stable countries is significant, even more significant will be the fundamental reshaping of the global value chain due to technological revolution. More specifically, physical global value chain will be replaced by the virtual, digital global value chain. The world will experience a new wave of globalization, the fourth wave of globalization. This next wave of globalization will go hand in hand with the Fourth Industrial Revolution.

That technological revolution is being defined by exciting new technologies such as artificial intelligence, 3D printing, smart sensors, big data, and robotics. Intensive use of digital technology in the post-COVID world, evident in working from home and online shopping, will precipitate a shift from physical globalization to virtual globalization. Even as the world economy retreats from physical globalization, it may enter into a new golden era of virtual globalization, based on rapid flow of ideas across borders. After all, the internet has no borders. For example, the scientific race to find a vaccine to stop COVID-19 has encouraged unprecedented international collaboration.[2]

Herein lies the opportunity for Asian economies. The bigger the crisis, the bigger the opportunity. For sure, the end of the third wave of globalization is a big setback for Asian economies, its biggest beneficiaries. However, the next wave of globalization is already beginning to take shape, in tandem with the emerging Fourth Industrial Revolution. The next wave of globalization offers a great opportunity for Asian economies. We hope that our book will help Asia's governments, companies, and people ride the next wave of globalization to power their prosperity and sustainable development.

In fact, Asia is well-positioned to lead the next wave of globalization, which will be accompanied by the Fourth Industrial Revolution. After all, Asia is now the world's largest economy and its leadership position will loom even larger in the coming years. Furthermore, Asia is no longer technologically backward but increasingly challenging the West

---

2   I. Goldin (2020). "Covid-19 proves globalization is not dead," Financial Times, August 26.

for global technological supremacy. As the biggest beneficiary of globalization, we can expect Asia to become the new global champion of globalization. If Asian countries collectively become a benign leader of the fourth wave of globalization, then the Pax Americana of the third wave of globalization will give way to a new Pax Asiana.

Lastly, we acknowledge that this book draws partly from a Korean-language book authored by Professor Lee, one of the co-authors of this book. That book is entitled *New World after Coronavirus* (2020, Seoul: Haenam Publishing Co.) and it focuses mostly on Korea.

About the Authors

**Hyun-Hoon LEE** is Professor of International Economics at Kangwon National University (KNU), Korea. He is also President of International Urban Training Center (IUTC), Korea, which provides a wide range of capacity building programs for government officials and policy-makers as well as non-governmental organization (NGO) leaders of developing countries in the Asia-Pacific region. He was Senior Analyst at the Asia-Pacific Economic Cooperation (APEC) Secretariat and was Senior Environmental Affairs Officer at the United Nations Economic and Social Commission for Asia and the Pacific (UN ESCAP). He has also been Visiting Professor/Scholar/Fellow at the University of British Columbia, the University of Melbourne, Keio University, and the Bank of Korea. He has a Ph.D. in Economics from the University of Oregon, USA. His research areas include international trade and finance, environmental economics,

development economics, the Korean economy, and regional economic cooperation in East Asia and the Pacific. He has published a large number of articles in many leading international journals, as well as a number of books.

 **Dr. Donghyun PARK** is currently Principal Economist at the Economics Research and Regional Cooperation Department (ERCD) of the Asian Development Bank (ADB), which he joined in April 2007. Prior to joining ADB, he was a tenured Associate Professor of Economics at Nanyang Technological University in Singapore. Dr. Park has a Ph.D. in Economics from UCLA, and his main research fields are international finance, international trade, and development economics. His research, which has been published extensively in journals and books, revolves around policy-oriented topics relevant for Asia's long-term development, including innovation, entrepreneurship, and financial sector development. Dr. Park plays a leading role in the production of *Asian Development Outlook*, ADB's biannual flagship publication on macroeconomic issues, and leads the team that produces *Asia Bond Monitor*, ADB's quarterly flagship report on emerging Asian bond markets.

Contents

66 ━━━━━━━━━━━━━━━━━━━━━━━━━━━━━━━━

In the midst of every crisis, lies great opportunity.

Albert Einstein

━━━━━━━━━━━━━━━━━━━━━━━━━━━━━━ 99

Chapter 1

COVID-19 Will Accelerate Deglobalization

1.1. Another Great Depression?

The coronavirus disease (COVID-19) which emerged in Wuhan, China, in December 2019 is shaking the world to its core. The pandemic spread like a wildfire from China to other Asian countries to Europe and the US, and on to Africa and Latin America. Although some countries and regions were hit harder than others, virtually no country or region was immune from the virus. As of October 20, 2020, the number of confirmed cases and deaths due to COVID-19 stands at over 40 million and 1.1 million, respectively, and both numbers show no sign of receding any time soon. COVID-19 has turned out to be a once-in-a-lifetime pandemic (Figure 1.1).

The global spread of the coronavirus put a sudden stop to everything. The movement of people stopped. Unemployment rose sharply as the economy was paralyzed. Due to the highly contagious

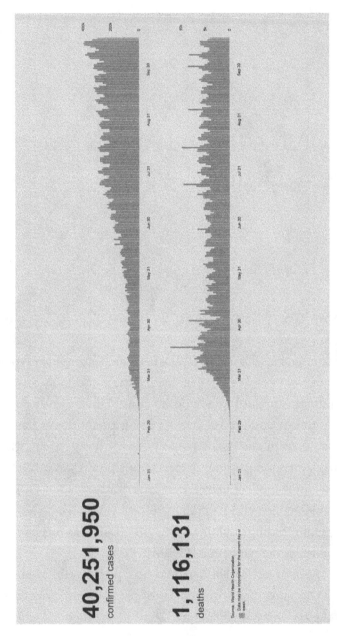

Figure 1.1. Trend of the numbers of confirmed cases and deaths due to COVID-19 (as of 20 October 2020).
Source: World Health Organization, Coronavirus Disease (COVID-19) Dashboard.

nature of the coronavirus, for the first time in living memory, the world will have to live with social distancing restrictions and lockdowns for some time to come. The world had experienced other coronavirus outbreaks before, most notably SARS in 2002–2003 and MERS in 2012–2015. However, the negative global impact of COVID-19 is of an altogether different magnitude, with profound effects on economy, society, culture, and all other spheres of human life.

In an interview with UK newspaper *The Guardian*, the Nobel-Prize–winning economist Joseph E. Stiglitz warned that a second Great Depression may be on its way.[1] The Great Depression was a severe worldwide economic depression that occurred mostly during the 1930s. It was the longest and deepest global economic downturn of the 20th century. Between 1929 and 1932, global income fell by an estimated 15%. By way of comparison, the Great Recession that followed the global financial crisis of 2008–2009 shaved off 1% of global income. Professor Nouriel Roubini, who gained fame by presciently predicting the Asian financial crisis of 1997–1998, pessimistically wrote in *The Guardian* that COVID-19 may result in a worldwide Greater Depression, even worse than the Great Depression of the 1930s.[2]

At a conference call of G20 finance ministers and central bank governors (March 31, 2020), the Managing Director of the International Monetary Fund (IMF) Kristalina Georgieva warned that COVID-19 will bring about the worst economic downturn since the Great Depression. In its annual flagship report World Economic Outlook (WEO) released in April 2020, the IMF forecast that global income will

---

[1]   *The Guardian, "Top economist: US coronavirus response is like 'third world' country," April 22, 2020.*

[2]   *N. Roubini, "The reasons why a 'Greater Depression' for the 2020s is inevitable," The Guardian, April 29, 2020.*

shrink by 3% in 2020. The IMF's WEO forecast contractions of 5.9% for the US, 7.5% for the eurozone, and 5.2% for Japan. The advanced economies as a whole are set to shrink by 6.1%. The IMF sharply downgraded its growth forecast for China from 6% to 1.2%. For the emerging markets and developing countries of Asia, which includes China, India, and Southeast Asian countries, the IMF forecast growth of 1.0%, an exceptionally slow growth rate for the world's fastest growing region. Emerging markets and developing countries as a whole are set to contract by 1.0%.

And the global economic outlook is worsening. In its June 2020 update of the WEO, the IMF further downgraded its global growth forecast to a contraction of 4.9%. The IMF downgraded its growth for advanced economies to a contraction of 8% and its growth forecast for emerging markets and developing countries to a contraction of 3%.

The world economy is already in its worst shape since the end of the Second World War. On a year-on-year basis, America's GDP grew by 0.3% in the first quarter of 2020, and then by 9.5% in the second quarter. The European Union (EU)'s GDP declined by 2.5% in the first quarter and then by 14.2% in the second quarter. Among the EU members, the Spanish economy was the hardest hit, with −4.1% and −22.1% growth rates in the first and second quarters, respectively. The French economy also shrank by 5.7% and then 19.0% in the first two quarters of 2020, respectively. The German economy, which is the biggest European economy and the main engine of growth for Europe, fell by 2.2% in the first quarter and then by 11.7% in the second quarter. The UK, which is no longer an EU member, saw its growth rate fall by 1.7% and 21.7% in the first and second quarters, respectively.

The Chinese economy, which is the world's second largest economy, fell by 6.8% in the first quarter year-on-year and then grew by 3.2% in the second quarter of 2020, which was the worst-ever performance of the Chinese economy since the 1980s. The Japanese economy, the world's third largest economy, fell by 2.0% in the first quarter and then by 10.0% in the second quarter. South Korea's GDP fell by 1.4% and then by 2.9% in the first two quarters of 2020, respectively. Other Asian economies are also recording historic negative growth rates. In the second quarter of 2020, Malaysia's GDP plummeted by 17.1% on a year-on-year basis. The Philippines' economy recorded a 16.5% decline, while that of Singapore declined by 12.6% and Indonesia by 5.3%. India recorded –4.5% GDP growth in the second quarter after declining by 5.0% in the first quarter.

Just as they did during the global financial crisis of 2008, the governments of advanced economies and emerging markets are ramping up public spending by astronomic amounts to support anemic demand and stave off economic collapse. For their part, the central banks are cutting interest rates and providing massive liquidity support. Global financial crisis seemed like an unprecedented crisis at that time, but in retrospect it was a textbook crisis requiring a textbook solution. All that governments and central banks needed to do to resuscitate the economy was to embark on massive fiscal and monetary expansion to offset the reduction in demand due to the financial crisis. By the same token, the US government tried to tackle the Great Depression of the 1930s through massive public spending, especially under an infrastructure investment program called the New Deal. What truly put an end to the Great Depression was an even bigger public spending program, namely the military expenditures of the Second World War.

However, the current economic downturn triggered by COVID-19 is a much more complicated and intractable proposition. Consumer confidence has been shattered by the reluctance of people to come into social contact with others lest they get infected with the coronavirus. There is clearly a limit to the capacity of conventional fiscal and monetary policy to improve consumer confidence in the current situation. No amount of government spending or interest rate cuts can lift consumer confidence in the face of a highly contagious disease which make people see others as viral vectors — i.e. potential threats to their health and life. Until COVID-19 peters out on its own or a safe and effective vaccine is developed, widespread fear of the pandemic will remain. And, as long as such popular fear remains, we cannot expect consumers to carry on as before. Depressed consumer confidence translates into depressed consumption, which is bad news for the economy.

But COVID-19 is not just a negative demand shock to the demand, it is also a negative supply shock. Not only does the pandemic affect the willingness and ability of consumers to spend, it also affects the ability of factories to produce products. Workers cannot go to work so factories cannot operate normally or operate well below capacity. Export and import procedures have become much more stringent. Since the countries of the world are tightly interwoven with each other in a global value chain, production disruptions in a single country disrupt the entire production process. In particular, given the central role of China in the global value chain, production disruptions in China can severely disrupt global production. When the Workshop of the World stops assembling the final product, the factories of other countries that produce parts and components for the Workshop also stop. And when the Workshop of the World stops producing parts and components, the factories of other countries cannot assemble the final products. China is as important in assembling final products as it is in producing parts and components. China is at the very heart of the global value chain. Production disruptions in other countries, including Italy and Vietnam, similarly disrupted the global value chain.

Furthermore, well before the advent of COVID-19, the global economy had already entered a period of secular stagnation due to several structural factors. Indeed, global growth has visibly slowed down since the global financial crisis of 2008–2009. Foremost among the structural headwinds against growth is population aging. The demographic transition toward older populations is well underway in advanced economies but it is also affecting emerging markets, especially in Asia. In China, the scale and speed of population aging is giving rise to fears that the country may grow old before it becomes rich. In short, the COVID-19 came on top of and exacerbated secular stagnation which was already under way. As such, it is unlikely that fiscal and monetary expansion will be enough to pull the world economy out of its current malaise. To the contrary, the buildup of public debt may herald something like Japan's lost decades since the early 1990s.

The Spanish Flu which broke out in 1918 infected 500 million people around the world and killed between 25 million and 100 million people. The Spanish Flu, which was the worst pandemic visited upon mankind in the 20th century, infected 5 times more people in the fall than it did in the spring of 1918. There is a substantial risk that this pattern of a much worse second wave may be repeated for COVID-19. Southern Hemisphere countries, most notably Brazil and other South American countries, have already been hit hard by the virus, which may migrate to the Northern Hemisphere and trigger a big second wave in the fall. This is what happened during the Spanish Flu. More worryingly, as of August 2020, the pandemic was far from contained even in the Northern Hemisphere. America's failure to contain the virus is especially worrisome. Shockingly, the world's richest, most powerful, and most technologically advanced country has become *the* global hotspot of the pandemic, accounting for 25% of global infections and deaths.

Despite lack of any clear evidence that the pandemic can be contained any time soon, the IMF and other international organizations, governments, and private-sector players such as investment banks are optimistically assuming at least partial containment by the second half of 2020. Such optimistic assumption is clearly evident in the optimistic growth forecasts. But the virulence of the virus in both Northern Hemisphere (e.g. US) and Southern Hemisphere (e.g. Brazil) raises the specter that the pandemic may not be stabilized or contained even by the fourth quarter of 2020.

Box 1.1. Economic forecasts are biased upward

In truth, the economic growth forecasts of IMF and other international organizations and governments tend to be based on overly optimistic assumptions. As an example, let us take a look at forecast versus actual economic growth during the global financial crisis of 2008–2009. In the early 2000s, the US Federal Reserve pursued a low interest rate policy to prevent economic stagnation following the bursting of the dot-com bubble. The combination of a prolonged period of low interest rates and Wall Street's reckless, greed-fueled pursuit of profit with no regard whatsoever for risk inflated a housing price bubble. The Fed's interest rate hikes since 2004 began to deflate the bubble. In the end, low-income, low credit rating, subprime home buyers defaulted on their mortgages, inflicting heavy damage on financial institutions that bought mortgage-backed securities. By 2007, many large subprime mortgage loan companies went bankrupt. The US subprime mortgage crisis quickly morphed into the global financial crisis of 2008, dragging in many large US and European financial institutions and threatening global financial stability.

In April 2008, when the effects of the US subprime mortgage crisis were already felt in global financial markets, the IMF predicted a global growth of 3.7% in its bi-annual flagship report WEO. Relative to IMF's 4.2% forecast of January, this was a downgrade of only 0.5%. On top of this, the IMF projected global growth to rebound to 3.8%. For America, the original epicenter of the crisis, rooted in a toxic combination of Wall Street greed abetted by lax financial regulation, the IMF forecast growth of 0.5% in 2008 and 0.6% in 2009.

But the IMF's forecasts turned out to be wildly optimistic and the global economy performed far worse than projected. In 2008, actual global growth was 1.9%, much lower than the IMF's forecast of 3.7%, and in 2009, the world economy shrank by 1.7%, a far cry from the robust recovery that the IMF had projected. America's actual growth performance was also significantly worse than the IMF's forecasts, shrinking by 0.1% in 2008 and by 2.5% in 2009.

Another example of excessively optimist growth forecasts comes from the growth of South Korea during the Asian financial crisis of 1997–1998. The crisis started in Thailand in the summer of 1997 and spread like a wildfire to other East Asian countries, including Malaysia and Thailand, before spreading to South Korea. The crisis was triggered by abrupt flight of foreign capital in response to deteriorating quality of investment. Prior to the crisis, East Asian countries had grown rapidly on the back of export-oriented industrialization. The World Bank produced a widely read research report which chronicled their economic success — **The East Asian Miracle** — and they became a model for other developing countries. East Asian countries quickly became the darlings of global investors who began investing massively in them, triggering capital inflows of billions of US dollars.

However, as more and money flowed in from abroad, the money financed progressively more unproductive investments. A classic example is speculative property and real estate construction financed by the capital inflows. In addition, capital inflows financed increasingly unproductive investments by companies, which sometimes used the money to finance investments in industries outside their core areas of competence. When global investors cottoned on to the deterioration of investment quality, they panicked and took their money out of the region. Foreign investors' sudden loss of confidence and the resulting flight of capital out of the region sent regional currencies into a tailspin. The Korean won, Thai baht, Malaysian ringgit, and Indonesian rupiah all depreciated sharply. Since many East Asian companies borrowed US dollars to finance projects that generated domestic-currency revenues, the depreciation made it even more difficult for them to repay their loans, further eroding investor confidence.

East Asian central banks sold billions of US dollars from their foreign exchange reserves in the foreign exchange market but to no avail. The resulting depletion of foreign exchange reserves only served to further alarm foreign investors, resulting in further downgrades of East Asian countries' external credit rating. They were facing the prospect of bankruptcy and they had no choice but to turn to the IMF for a bailout package. Indonesia, South Korea, and Thailand all turned to the IMF for financial assistance. In the case of South Korea, the government requested IMF's help on November 21, 1997, handing over economic sovereignty to the IMF. On December 3, South Korea's Finance Minister and the IMF's Managing Director agreed upon a loan package worth US$55 billion in exchange for structural reforms. Indonesia and Thailand also agreed to bailout packages in exchange for reforms. Malaysia, for its part, went its own separate way and imposed capital controls. But it too suffered a sharp economic downturn, as did the three other countries. The pre-conditions imposed by the IMF on the three countries were widely viewed as unnecessarily harsh, which is why to this day the IMF is viewed with a great deal of suspicion and even hostility in the region.

The IMF's forecasts for East Asian countries in the wake of the Asian financial crisis were too much optimistic. For example, when the IMF announced its bailout package for South Korea in December 1997, it forecast GDP growth rate of 3% for 1998. It downgraded its forecast to 1% in February 1998 and further to –1% in May. South Korea's actual growth performance in 1998 was a contraction of 5.1%. Similarly, the IMF also overestimated the growth of other East Asian countries hit by the Asian financial crisis. In general, the IMF and other forecasters tend to overstate economic growth during crisis. Optimism is also evident in their general failure to predict crisis.

If the COVID-19 pandemic is not contained in the second half of 2020 and persists into 2021, there is a sizable likelihood that many individuals and companies will go bankrupt and the amount of bad loans will rise sharply. In this scenario, the opposite of what happened during the global financial crisis will occur. That is, the economic crisis will spill over into the financial system due to a spike in bad loans and morph into a financial crisis as well. The financial crisis, in turn, will exacerbate the economic crisis by disrupting the flow of credit to individuals and companies. This kind of vicious cycle may very well transform the Great Pandemic into a second Great Depression.

The negative economic impact of COVID-19 is especially evident in industries and activities for which it is impossible to work from home. In particular, the lockdown and community quarantine are having a devastating impact on restaurants, retail stores, leisure, travel and tourism, accommodation, and other service industries. The services sector account for a much larger share of jobs than manufacturing or agricultural sectors, and the sector consists largely of small businesses — e.g. restaurants, auto repair shops, and barbershops. Therefore, the economic damage from the coronavirus is concentrated in small services businesses and the largely low-wage workers they employ. Furthermore, the elderly and the poor are especially vulnerable to the coronavirus and suffer disproportionately high death rates. Furthermore, many of the poor are not covered by health insurance and do not receive any unemployment benefits or other benefits from the government.

More generally, COVID-19 has hit the poor and vulnerable disproportionately harder. Poor and disadvantaged groups suffer the most during any disasters or crises, and this pandemic is no different. In fact, low-income populations are carrying the bulk of the health and economic burden of the pandemic. For example, in the US, blacks account for a disproportionately high share of infections and deaths. They also account for a disproportionate share of Americans who lost their jobs since the outbreak. And in Singapore, COVID-19 has been concentrated among migrant workers from poor Asian countries who lived in densely packed dormitories.

According to an April 2020 report from the International Labour Organization (ILO), around 76% of informal economy workers, some 1.6 billion people, are experiencing serious economic hardship due to the pandemic.[3] Informal economy workers included self-employed street vendors, construction site workers, and millions of other workers who are not captured by official statistics. Furthermore, the income of those workers are projected to drop by an average of 34%, further exacerbating the gaping income inequality which was already the world's most pressing economic and social problem even before the advent of COVID-19.

According to one of America's top newspapers, *The New York Times*, people without access to controllable personal space — e.g. prison inmates, farm laborers, native Americans, homeless, tenants of crowded inner-city housing units — are particularly vulnerable to the coronavirus infection. COVID-19 is thus exacerbating class divide, or the divide among middle-class and working-class Americans. The disturbing trend of the pandemic fueling already record-high levels of inequality is hardly confined to America. All across the world, blue-collar factory and store workers who have to work at a physical workplace face a much higher risk of catching the virus than white-collar office workers. They are also much likely to lose their jobs and livelihoods. Small wonder that blue-collar workers are increasingly resentful of their white-collar colleagues.

Bloomberg reports that America and Europe have seen a spate of ugly racist incidents targeting another minority, namely Asians.

---

[3] *International Labour Organization, ILO Monitor: COVID-19 and the World of Work, Third Edition, April 29, 2020.*

President Donald Trump's liberal use of racist words like the "Chinese virus" and "kung flu" are further fanning the flames of bigotry and racism. To make matters worse, the death of a black man at the hands of white police officers in Minneapolis, Minnesota, US, on May 25, 2020, lit up the powder keg of social discontent at systemic racism in America. While George Floyd, the victim, was no hero — he was an ex-convict and ex-criminal — the brutal manner of his death — a cop knelt on his neck for close to nine minutes — resulted in an explosion of protests which raged on for weeks and spread over to the rest of the world. The protests, which turned violent in many cities and resulted in large-scale destruction of property, were directed toward not only systemic racism but also the massive inequalities between the haves and the have-nots in America and the world.

America's class and racial divide is intensifying ahead of the US presidential elections scheduled for November 2020. One of the most harmful consequences of COVID-19 is that it is exacerbating inequality of income and wealth, which is already unacceptably wide. The widening of inequality is likely to intensify populism, which was already a major global force, as evident in the election of Donald Trump and Brexit, or the exit of the UK from the EU. Politicians are not only searching for domestic scapegoats but also foreign scapegoats, strengthening trade protectionism in the process. Rising trade protectionism, in turn, will deepen the global economic downturn. Worsening recession, in turn, will lead to even more trade protectionism. This was exactly what happened during the Great Depression of the 1930s. As the economy fell into recessions, countries competed with each other to erect more and higher tariffs and other trade barriers to protect their markets from foreign competition. The predictable end result was a lose-lose situation in which all economies suffered from the collapse of global trade. There is a risk that countries may be tempted toward the same kind of self-defeating protectionism in the post-COVID world.

While advanced economies such as America and Western Europe have suffered heavily from COVID-19, the health and economic toll on emerging markets and developing countries is expected to be even worse. The United Nations and Oxfam has warned that the coronavirus may push as many as 500 million people into poverty. The pandemic thus threatens a lot of the progress that the world has made in recent decades in reducing poverty. The developing countries of Asia, in particular, have reduced poverty on a massive scale in a remarkably short time period. Asia's poverty reduction miracle was a byproduct of Asia's economic miracle which lifted the continent from a largely low-income region to an overwhelmingly middle-income region within a generation. However, COVID-19 poses a serious risk to the unprecedented reduction in global poverty in recent decades. The fact that more than 100 countries have requested emergency financial assistance from the IMF reveals the severity of the economic downturn that the developing countries currently face.

Moreover, advanced countries are unlikely to be generous in extending financial assistance to developing countries. They will be too busy repairing their own shattered economies, which leaves them with little resources to help other countries. An even bigger concern for developing countries is the specter of growing protectionism in advanced countries, which are a big market for them. The amount of investment flowing from advanced countries to developing countries will also likely decline. All in all, the economic weakening of advanced countries due to COVID-19 will reverberate loudly on developing countries.

1.2. Global Value Chain is Halted

The acceleration of globalization in the 1990s not only witnessed rapid growth of international trade of goods and services but also cross-border movements of capital and labor. Furthermore, along with greater sharing of knowledge and culture across countries, English became the commonly spoken lingua franca of the world. The collapse of the Soviet Union further spread the popularity of the English language, which replaced Russian as the preferred second language in communist and former communist countries. The emergence of English as the de facto universal language marked a momentous shift from the Babel Tower. According to the biblical myth of Babel, God was enraged by the arrogant efforts of mankind to build up a sky-high tower that would reach the heavens. As a punishment, God divided mankind into a multitude of languages and scattered them across the world. Economic, intellectual, and cultural globalization undid God's punishment after centuries of a bewildering variety of different tongues.

The star players of the globalization process are huge global firms called multinational enterprises — i.e. MNEs — or transnational enterprises — i.e. TNEs. According to Tim Cook, the CEO of Apple, a highly successful and innovative high-tech MNE which operates across the entire world, MNEs assume inventories to be fundamentally evil. Common sense tells us that carrying large stocks of inventory is costly for firms and from their viewpoint, the smaller the inventory stock, the better. To enable inventory-minimizing just-in-time production, these global companies have set up global supply chains. Just-in-time production was first pioneered by Japanese carmaker Toyota which minimized costs and maximized efficiency by not leaving parts and components as idle inventories but using them immediately in production.

Global value chains, which typically operate in many countries across the world, are based on a similar underlying logic. Research and development, design, manufacturing, retail and distribution, marketing, and after-sale service are highly specialized stages in which various countries take part in the stages where they have comparative advantage. The value added of different stages typically follows a U pattern, as Figure 1.2 shows. The U-shaped value chain is also known as the smiling curve in business management theory. The concept of the smiling curve was first proposed by Stanley Shih, the founder of the Taiwanese IT company Acer. The early stages are typically high value-added services such as research and development, branding, and design while the latter stages are also typically high value-added services such as retail and distribution, marketing, and after-sales service. Manufacturing, right in the middle of the global value chain, is usually the lowest value-added stage of the chain. Not surprisingly, high value-added services in the

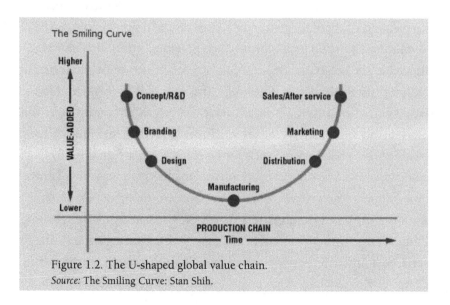

Figure 1.2. The U-shaped global value chain.
Source: The Smiling Curve: Stan Shih.

early and latter stages are typically done in advanced countries while low value-added manufacturing is typically done in developing countries.

Interestingly, before technological progress enabled the global value chain, advanced countries specialized in high value-added manufactured products such as automobiles while developing countries specialized in low value-added products such as agricultural and mining products. For example, cacao produced in Ghana, Cote d'Ivoire, and other West African countries would be exported to Europe to be processed and transformed into expensive Belgian or Swiss chocolates. Of course, the European chocolate will be more expensive than the African cacao by many times over. Due to drastic lowering of transportation and logistics cost — e.g. containerization — it has become possible to engage in different stages of production in different countries. And the global value chain has thus emerged as the dominant form of production for huge multinational companies which operate across the world.

Nor is the global value chain limited to manufactured products. The advent of the information and communication technology (ICT) revolution has made it possible to trade previously untradable services. Indeed in the pre-ICT days, economics textbooks routinely referred to manufactured goods as tradables and services as non-tradables. However, the growing tradability of services is rendering such distinction increasingly obsolete. India and the Philippines have emerged as global leaders in offshoring of back-office functions by large companies from advanced economies. This has given rise to an entire new industry known as business process outsourcing (BPO). A classic example of BPO is call centers in which thousands of Indians and Filipinos undergo American, British, and Australian accent training to serve customers in those rich countries. As in the manufacturing value chain, in the services value chain too, low value-added activities are dominated by developing countries while high value-added activities are dominated by advanced economies.

It is no exaggeration to say that the whole world is now linked closely together through global value chains, which consist of complex and tightly interwoven global production networks and global sales networks. Global value chains are no longer an interesting side story of the world economy. To the contrary, they have become a dominant feature of the world economy, at its front and center. In 2017, trade related to global value chains — e.g. high-tech Korean and Japanese parts and components and low-tech Malaysian and Thai parts and components shipped to China for final assembly and export to America and Western Europe — accounted for a staggering 74% of global trade and 20% of global GDP.

Whether high value-added or not, the ability to take part in the global value chain is now widely viewed as a prerequisite for economic prosperity. For example, Asian countries, especially East Asian countries, were able to grow so rapidly for decades because they were able to actively contribute to and benefit from global value chains. In particular, some Asian countries, most notably China but also newly industrialized economies such as South Korea and Singapore before them as well as ASEAN economies such as Malaysia and Thailand, leveraged the global value chain to power their world-topping growth. More specifically, the export-oriented East Asian economies collectively became the Factory of the World, with China at its center. While the Indian economy is much less dependent on exports, nevertheless it too benefited greatly from its active participation in the BPO industry. The Philippines too owes a lot of its economic dynamism to its world-class BPO industry.

In stark contrast to Asia, other developing countries were much less successful in latching on to the global value chain to power their growth. There were, of course, some isolated success stories, such as the maquiladora factories of northern Mexico. Foreign investors flocked into northern Mexico, which borders the American states of California, Texas, Arizona, and New Mexico, to build factories and hire Mexican workers, who command much lower wages than American workers. Those workers assemble manufacturing products and ship them to the US. However, while the maquiladora factories brought a measure of prosperity to some parts of northern Mexico, Mexico was never able to leverage them to build an export-oriented national manufacturing sector like East Asian countries. By and large, Latin American countries, African countries, Middle East and North African countries, and the former Soviet Union countries all failed to actively take part in the global value chain. That is, they failed to ride the wave of economic globalization, which is why they failed to grow and develop. Instead what they got was popular discontent at economic stagnation, resulting in social and political explosions like the Arab Spring.

From the viewpoint of multinational companies, the most important characteristic of the global value chain is that it minimized costs and maximized productive efficiency. Each stage of the global value chain can be performed at its optimal location. For high value-added services in the early and latter stages, advanced countries are the best location since they have a comparative advantage in producing such services. Indeed, in contrast to developing countries which tend to have inefficient services sectors, — e.g. street vendors, advanced countries have efficient services industries — e.g. financial services, ICT software, and industrial design. On the other hand, for manufacturing, the lowest value-added activity, the best locations are countries with abundance of low-wage, industrious, and technically competent workers — e.g. China. The final product produced by the global value chain is made in the world rather than made in a specific country. Made in America or made in China or made in Germany is obsolete in a world of global value chains.

However, global value chain will be hit hard by COVID-19 crisis. According to the World Trade Organization (WTO), the electronics and automobiles industries, which are interlinked in a tightly woven global value chain, will be especially affected by the pandemic. Both industries are technologically complex industries with thousands of parts and components. There is no reason why the same country will be the best location to produce so many parts and components. To the contrary, we can expect them to be produced in many countries across the world.

In fact, when China, the original epicenter of the pandemic, started to lock down the economy and close production facilities, the global value chains of large global companies which used China as a production base for producing intermediate goods — i.e. parts and components which are used in producing final goods — began to crumble. Indeed Wuhan, the city whose wet markets were the birthplace of the pandemic, was a major cog in the global supply chain and home to the factories of many multinational companies. The spread of COVID-19 exposed the extreme fragility of the global value chain. If there are production disruptions in even just one country, perhaps because it is experiencing a major outbreak, the entire global value chain was at risk of falling apart.

In fact, in February 2020, when the pandemic was gripping China, Apple's Chinese factory was closed and Apple's production fell by 60% compared to one year earlier. This disruption caused Apple to delay its launch of a new model, while its main rival Samsung was able to launch its new model earlier. Therefore, in the era of COVID-19, production resilience against pandemics is a big source of competitive advantage in companies. But having contingency plans or a Plan B — e.g. a second factory in another country — is costly and the higher costs will be eventually passed on to consumers.

Also in February, the Korean factories of Hyundai, one of the world's largest carmakers, were forced to halt production. The reason is that the Chinese factory producing Hyundai's wiring harness, which serves as the blood artery of cars, was forced to stop production. These kinds of incidents took place all over the world. All European carmakers experienced production disruptions due to production disruptions at the Italian factories of auto parts supplier MTA Advanced Automotive Solution, which produced key electronic components for cars.

While global value chains improved efficiency by enabling just-in-time production, the pandemic exposed their extreme vulnerability to big external shocks such as COVID-19. Such vulnerability was already evident before. For example, in 2011, massive floods in Thailand affected the global production of everything from cars to computer disk drives because Thailand had become a major manufacturing base for Japanese and American carmakers and global technology companies. That was just one country. The risks of global production are multiplied many times over when a global disaster like COVID-19 strikes and affects virtually the whole world. As a result of COVID-19, global companies will now place greater weight on risk of production disruption and lesser weight on productive efficiency.

To minimize and diversify the risk of disruptions, many global companies will be tempted to reduce their reliance on production in China and other developing countries. Of course, much lower production costs in developing countries and other considerations — for example, the huge Chinese market — limits the extent to which they can reduce their dependence on factories in developing countries. Nevertheless, for a more stable and secure production, they may turn to local suppliers for a substantial part of the parts and components produced by the global supply chain. Reshoring, or the opposite of offshoring, will gather momentum as companies from advanced countries shift a substantial part of their production back home.

In fact, COVID-19 has inflicted a severe blow to global trade and cross-border investment. At a press conference, the WTO chief Roberto Azevedo warned that global trade may shrink by as much as 32% due to the pandemic.[4] This scale of trade contraction is similar in magnitude to what the world suffered during the Great Depression. In the worst case, global trade volume may return to the levels of 2009, in the immediate aftermath of the global financial crisis. That is, COVID-19 may wipe out a decade of global trade expansion. Azevedo also warned that the rampant trade protectionism of the 1930s may rear its ugly head again, and this will further exacerbate the dire state of global trade and economy.

At the same time, the United Nations Conference on Trade and Development (UNCTAD) predicted that COVID-19 will reduce global foreign direct investment (FDI) by 30%–40% during 2020–2021.[5] This is bad news for developing countries since FDI, or investment in factories, power plants, and other production facilities, has been a major driver of economic growth in those countries, along with trade. Indeed China and other Asian countries have been able to grow faster than other developing countries thanks to rapid expansion of trade as well as massive inflows of FDI. If managed properly, FDI not only brings

---

[4] World Trade Organization, "Trade set to plunge as COVID-19 pandemic upends global economy," Press release, April 8, 2020.
[5] UNCTAD, "Investment Trends Monitor Special Issue," March 2020.

jobs but can also help improve the technology level, managerial capacity, and marketing and other skills of local firms. Singapore is a classic case of a county that leveraged FDI from global multinational companies to upgrade its economy to become one of the richest countries in the world. The UNCTAD report predicts that the 5,000 biggest global multinational companies will see their profits fall by 30%.

As noted earlier, the economic forecasts of the IMF and other organizations are predicated on the hopeful assumption that the COVID-19 health crisis will be stabilized by the second half of 2020. By the same token, the global trade and FDI forecasts of WTO and UNCTAD, as dire as they seem, are also based on optimistic assumptions about the trajectory of the pandemic. However, medical experts warn that a safe and effective vaccine will be developed by first quarter of 2021 at the earliest, and mass producing the vaccine for distribution to the broader population will take even more time. Taking all these factors into account, it is reasonable to expect the health crisis to persist into at least early 2021.

But even these assumptions are somewhat optimistic. If new mutations of COVID-19 keep appearing and the development of vaccines and treatments encounters delays, the global economy, trade, and investment may weaken as much as they did during the Great Depression of the 1930s. While there is a great deal of uncertainty about how COVID-19 will play out, and the health and economic outcomes may turn out to be much better than widely feared, there are strong grounds for pessimism on both the health and economic fronts.

1.3. Exit from China and Reshoring

One of the mainstays of Donald Trump's presidential election campaign in 2016 was China bashing. Shouting "America First" and pledging to "Make America Great Again," he vowed to raise tariffs against imports from China by as much as 45%. And, in July 2018, the US kicked off the US–China trade conflict in full force by imposing a 25% tariff on 818 Chinese import items worth US$34 billion. Thus began the trade war between the world's two largest economies. The conflict is bad for China, bad for America, and bad for the world. Above all, East Asian economies such as Japan, South Korea, and ASEAN economies trade heavily with both America and China so they stand to suffer a significant fallout from the Sino–American feud. The conflict has cast a dark cloud on the entire General Agreement on Tariffs and Trade (GATT)–WTO trade regime that advocated free trade and propelled the dramatic expansion of international trade after the second world.

In August 2018, when the US–China trade war was already in full swing, President Trump announced that he will order American companies to pull out of China. But in truth, even before the election of Trump, America made concerted efforts to reshore American companies and induce them to move production back to America. For example, under the slogan of "Remaking America," the Obama Administration explored corporate income tax reductions as a way to lure American companies home. Reshoring is widely seen by American politicians of both Democratic and Republican parties as a viable option to reduce imports, boost growth, and create jobs.

In fact, President Trump has pursued a robust reshoring policy after he took office. Most significantly, the Trump Administration reduced the US corporate income tax rate from 35% to 21%. Although the tax cut was offset to some extent by the reduction or elimination of some deductions and credits, this was a sizable tax cut by any measure. The primary objective of the tax was to boost investment and growth but one of its biggest consequences was to make it more attractive for American companies to make things in America than abroad. In addition, the Trump Administration toyed with the idea of imposing a border adjustment tax (BAT) on goods produced outside America even though it was eventually dropped. In short, well before COVID-19, there was a systematic effort by the American government to shift production from abroad to America.

The pandemic has given a strong additional impetus to such reshoring efforts, especially efforts to induce American firms to relocate their production from China to America. It has also given the Trump Administration an excuse to redouble its reshoring efforts. The American economy has been paralyzed and the number of unemployed American workers has skyrocketed due to the coronavirus. Regardless of the exact origins of COVID-19, there is almost universal consensus that the coronavirus first originated in China. As such, China is an easy and convenient scapegoat for the Trump Administration's catastrophic mishandling of the disease, which has resulted in the US becoming *the* global hotspot of the pandemic. On the surface, the Trump Administration is just trying to blame China for the pandemic. But more fundamentally, it is trying to exploit popular resentment that has been building up against China, whose massive exports make it a powerful symbol of globalization in America and elsewhere. That is, populist politicians can better leverage widespread anti-globalization sentiment — e.g. among blue-collar workers who lost their jobs to imports — by bashing China.

In April 2020, Larry Kudlow, a top White House economic advisor who is the Director of United States National Economic Council, announced in an interview with Fox Business News that the US government is 100% committed to supporting the moving costs of American firms coming home from China. While it is unclear what 100% commitment exactly means in terms of financial assistance, what is beyond doubt is that the current US government is strongly committed to reshoring. It is reasonable to view reshoring as official or semi-official American policy, and that the US government is serious about reshoring as a strategic objective.

It is not only the US that is committed to reshoring. Although reshoring does not enjoy nearly as much systematic support as in the US, major Western European countries such as Germany, UK, France, as well as Japan are also exploring the possibility of moving production back home from China. More specifically, the governments of those countries are encouraging their companies to reshore. However, those countries do not have America's economic weight and their economies depend much more on China than America's huge, domestic-demand–driven economy. As such, they are much more careful about antagonizing China, let alone engaging China in a direct economic confrontation. Furthermore, they face tighter constraints to the feasibility of reshoring than America. For example, Japan, one of the world's most rapidly aging societies, does not have the workers to take back manufacturing from China.

Nevertheless, from the perspective of the advanced countries, the COVID-19 crisis has exposed the dangers of over-reliance on China. All the more so since the companies of these countries suffered significant production disruptions due to factory closures in Wuhan and other parts of China. To some Western observers, the crisis reconfirmed the widely held view that China is a tightly controlled authoritarian society which lacks transparency and credibility. On the other hand, of course, it is precisely China's tightly controlled authoritarian system which allowed the country to impose draconian lockdowns that effectively contained the pandemic. Such draconian lockdowns would not be remotely possible in more open, liberal societies. Nevertheless, the big takeaway from COVID-19 for many foreign observers and investors is that China is not only highly efficient but also highly risky.

In addition to foreign factors, there are also powerful domestic Chinese factors that are promoting reshoring away from China. Under Made in China 2025, an industrial policy that began in 2015, under the government's leadership, China is making concerted efforts to move up the global value chain. The goal of Made in China 2025 is to turn China into a global powerhouse in state-of-the-art technologies and high-tech manufacturing. The stereotype of China as poor country with an inexhaustible supply of low-wage workers is badly outdated. According to World Bank classification, China has already been an upper middle-income country for some years. In addition, China is rapidly aging and its working-age population has already begun to decline. In light of all these realities, China is shifting from labor-intensive, low value-added industries and activities to skill- and technology-intensive, high value-added industries and activities. Therefore, many multinational companies, especially those in labor-intensive industries, were already shifting out of China well before COVID-19. Many multinationals that remain are drawn to China's huge domestic market and its non-labor cost advantages, such as high-quality infrastructure.

Perhaps the strongest driver of multinational companies relocating their production out of China back home or to third countries is the negative economic impact of COVID-19 on China. As noted earlier, the Chinese economy shrank for the first time in decades during the first quarter of 2020. A staggering number of Chinese workers, as many as 80 million, may be out of work. Anemic domestic demand and exports will harm the revenues and thus the balance sheets of Chinese state-owned enterprises (SOEs), many of which are leveraged to the hilt. A large number of SOEs may go bankrupt. In the long term, that would be a good thing since SOEs tend to be inefficient and act as a drag on growth, which was mostly driven by China's dynamic and entrepreneurial private sector notwithstanding the erroneous foreign misperception of China as a model of state-led capitalism. But in the short-term, the real economy, especially employment, will be hit hard.

On top of this, the real estate bubble is likely to burst. In this scenario, with distressed SOEs and households unable to repay their loans to banks, we cannot rule out a financial crisis triggered by a chain of bank failures. These dangers lurked just beneath the surface and were masked to some extent by China's healthy growth but COVID-19 has exposed and heightened the risk of such an economic and financial crisis.

1.4. Deglobalization Gains Momentum

The world economy is suffering a deep downturn due to COVID-19. The downturn has decimated global trade and international investment, dealing a severe blow to global value chains. But the slowdown of global trade and cross-border investment did not begin with COVID-19. They were clearly discernible trends well before the pandemic outbreak. Global trade collapsed during the global financial crisis of 2008 and did not return to pre-crisis levels (Figure 1.3). The figure shows that the ratio of global exports to global GDP peaked at 30.8% in 2008, when the global financial crisis broke out, before collapsing to 26.7% in 2009, the year of the Great Recession. The figure also shows that while there were some ups and downs, by and large the ratio rose continuously on a secular basis from 1970, when it was below 15%, until 2008. The recent stagnation of global trade likely reflects the tangible slowdown of global growth momentum since the global financial crisis. Initially, the world economy experienced a two-speed recovery, with advanced countries stagnating while developing countries grew at a relatively healthy pace. However, the growth of developing countries also slowed down, resulting in slowdown of global growth and trade. In more recent years, rising global trade protectionism in general and the US–China trade conflict in particular also put the brakes on the growth of global trade.

The retreat of globalization is even more clearly evident in global FDI trends (Figure 1.4). The figure shows that the ratio of global FDI to global GDP rose to 5.3% in 2007 but fell sharply to 2.3% in 2009 as a result of the global financial crisis. The ratio subsequently fluctuated between 2% and 3% before dipping to 1% in 2018. Given that global multinational companies account for a large share of global FDI and

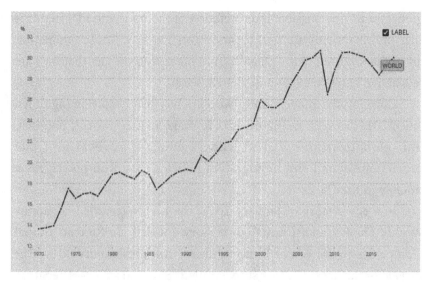

Figure 1.3. World's exports of goods and services (% of GDP), 1970–2018.
Source: World Bank's DataBank (accessed August 11, 2020).

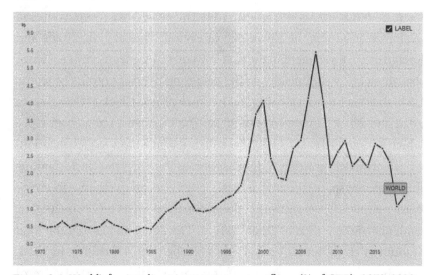

Figure 1.4. World's foreign direct investment, net outflows (% of GDP), 1970–2019.
Source: World Bank's DataBank (accessed August 11, 2020).

global trade, one possible interpretation of the trade and FDI trends is that multinationals are trading and investing less. Those companies are at the forefront of the globalization process so the fact that they are less active helps to explain deglobalization.

Cross-border movement of workers has also been slowing down since 2011, as seen in Figure 1.5. To make matters worse, populist, anti-globalization political leaders who are advocating trade protectionism and anti-immigration policies have won power, most notably in the US.

In a cover story of January 2017, the highly regarded economic weekly *The Economist* ran a cover story entitled "In Retreat: Global Companies in the Era of Protectionism." And, in January 2019, *The Economist* ran another cover story entitled "Slowbalisation – The Steam Has Gone Out of Globalisation". "Slowbalisation" is the combination of "slow" and "globalisation". The primary evidence that *The Economist* used to back up its argument that the world was experiencing deglobalization was the slowdown or even decline of global trade and foreign direct investment in the past few years. Another piece of evidence that the weekly produced was the declining overseas profits of iconic US brands such as McDonald's and Kentucky Fried Chicken (KFC) since 2012 and 2013. Finally, in May 2020, *The Economist* ran a cover story which announced that COVID-19 will deal a fatal blow to globalization.

In an article entitled "Globalisation in Retreat," the world-famous financial newspaper *Financial Times* cited the sharp decline in cross-border capital flows since the global financial crisis of 2008–2009 as evidence of the retreat of globalization. The figure shows that the total amount of cross-border capital flows reached US$4.3 trillion in 2016. This is only about one-third of the corresponding 2007 figure of US$12.4 trillion. Cross-border capital flows consist of not only FDI but

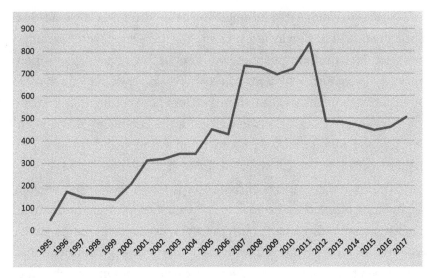

Figure 1.5. Work migrant flows in the world (Thousand), 1995–2017.
Source: Migration Data Portal (accessed August 15, 2020).

also portfolio flows such as stocks and bonds as well as cross-border lending by banks and other financial institutions. The key driver of the decline in cross-border capital flows seems to be the sharp reduction of cross-border lending.

There are several reasons behind the visible stagnation and decline of global trade and international investment in recent years. Above all, income inequality between the rich and the poor due to globalization in the advanced countries has exceeded tolerable or manageable levels. In addition, the biggest driver of the income polarization is the advanced-country companies' extension of the value chain from the home country to the world, which shifted large numbers of jobs to developing countries. From the viewpoint of rich-country workers, to add insult to injury, large numbers of migrant workers from poorer foreign countries entered rich countries, threatening to take away the locals' jobs.

Besides reducing jobs and employment opportunities, globalization put a great deal of downward pressure on the wages of rich-country workers. Globalization put those workers in the unenviable position of having to compete with poor-country workers. The competition took many forms. Sometimes cheap imports from poor countries restrained the wage increase of workers in rich countries producing the same or similar good. Other times, the competition was more direct — e.g. call center workers in the US versus call center workers in India. In any case, the low-wage workers of rich countries lost. As a result, income inequality worsened in the advanced economies, evoking resentment against globalization among both the working class and middle class. Only the rich elite benefited from their shares in large multinational companies that produced all over the world to minimize costs and maximize profits. The increasingly popular view was: "Globalization of the elite, by the elite, for the elite."Of course, there was an array of other complex factors behind the growing deglobalization momentum. These factors will be elaborated upon in Chapter 2. One significant effect of COVID-19 is that it will turn slowbalisation — or a slowdown in the pace of globalization — to downright deglobalization — or a reversal of globalization. That is, the pandemic will intensify and accelerate the retreat from globalization.

Western Europe, along with the US, were the pioneers of globalization. Among themselves, Western European countries formed the EU, which freed up movement of goods, capital, and labor within the union. The EU expanded to encompass many Central and Eastern European countries since the fall of the Iron Curtain. As if free movement of goods, capital, and labor were not enough, most EU members formed a monetary union around the euro, maximizing efficiency of trade within the union. Furthermore, EU members agreed upon a Stability and Growth Pact which limited annual fiscal deficits to 3% of GDP and government debt to 60% of GDP. And, they also cooperated to form an EU budget every year.

However, despite such close linkages, EU members failed to agree on a common EU response to COVID-19. Italy first unilaterally closed its borders, followed by France. Germany and France banned exports of medical face masks, including exports to other EU countries. The principle of a common market was thus shattered. When Italy, which suffered the first major COVID-19 outbreak in Europe in early March, appealed to other EU countries for help when it experienced shortages of emergency medical equipment, none of them responded. Furthermore, the production value chain which closely binds together EU countries was disrupted in many instances.

All EU countries are facing an economic crisis. In particular, southern European countries like Italy and Spain are hit especially hard. Suffering under the burden of a huge public debt and with their real economies facing paralysis, these economies are hoping for stronger northern EU economies such as Germany and the Netherlands to help. If no help is forthcoming, southern European countries will be unhappy. On the other hand, if the help turns out to be too generous and thus too burdensome for their taxpayers, northern European countries will balk at helping their southern neighbors. There is a risk that the intra-EU tension over intra-EU financial assistance will weaken the sense of common purpose and unity among EU countries at a time when the EU is already badly weakened by Brexit. In the worst-case scenario, there is a risk that the EU or the eurozone will break up.

Like Europe, East Asian countries are interwoven together in a tight regional production value chain. The US and Japan led the way in transforming China, Vietnam, and other East Asian countries into a manufacturing base for parts and components and final goods. But the lockdown of China due to the coronavirus halted the regional value chain. The subsequent lockdown of other Asian countries such as the Philippines and Vietnam is giving an impression to outside investors that the region is not a stable, secure production base. When COVID-19 broke out, it was difficult to assess the true public health situation, and multinational companies could not send their managers to manage the emergency production. As such, those companies realized that they could not manage their own assets in a severe crisis.

Such a profound realization can potentially lead to the breakdown of the physical global supply chain, which is the currently dominant form of the global supply chain. Some firms will reshore their production back home while others will shift their production to more stable locations. We can thus expect the global pattern of manufacturing production to change significantly in the aftermath of the pandemic.

Many countries unilaterally imposed export restrictions on face mask and diagnostic medical equipment as well as rice and other staple grains. The restrictions served as a powerful reminder that free trade is limited by national health security and national food security. For example, Vietnam, the world's third largest exporter, temporarily banned rice exports in March 2020, citing national food security concerns. The ban was partly lifted in April and fully lifted in May. The ban raised serious concerns in the Philippines, which depends on Vietnam for much of its rice imports. Ironically, for Philippines, one of the world's biggest rice importers, rice imports are truly vital for national food security. Rightly or wrongly, the key takeaway for many countries is the need to seek self-sufficiency, at least for vital medical supplies, food, and other basic necessities.

COVID-19 spread like a wildfire because the world is closely interlinked thanks to globalization. At the same time, precisely because the pandemic is a common global enemy, it requires a common global response. However, instead of forging a common response, countries are liberally exchanging recriminations and blaming each other for the pandemic. President Trump has called the disease "the Chinese virus," while Chinese officials claimed that the virus was brought into China by US military personnel. The World Health Organization (WHO) has been accused of being partial to China by the US, which has threatened to withdraw from the international body, which would seriously weaken its capacity to lead a global effort. The United Nations, G20, UNCTAD, and other international organizations have similarly failed to lead. But the fundamental problem is that the international community, especially its two giants, are busy fighting each other rather than joining forces to fight the common enemy.

But in order to cushion the supply shock, the countries of the world must reduce trade barriers rather than erect them. But the reality is flowing in the opposite direction. Countries are competing with each other to blame foreign countries and imposing restrictions on exports and imports in self-defeating efforts to support their economies. Yet the WTO stands powerless to slow down the rapid descent into trade protectionism. As a result, the postwar GATT-WTO trade regime, which spearheaded the multilateralism that drove dramatic trade expansion and globalization, is under serious threat. Due to COVID-19, the world is moving beyond slowbalisation into deglobalization, an issue we explore in greater detail in Chapter 2.

Chapter 2

Root Causes of Deglobalization

2.1. A Brief History of Deglobalization

I t is worth emphasizing that while COVID-19 will intensify and accelerate deglobalization, the process of deglobalization was already well under way. In this chapter, we will explain the root causes of deglobalization. The postwar wave is by no means the only historical episode of globalization. It is useful to briefly review the history of globalization in order to better understand why it is inevitable that the postwar wave of globalization will retreat.

The period between the First Industrial Revolution of early 19th century and today marks the fastest improvement in mankind's living standards and quality of life. According to economic historian R.W. Nielsen, the per capita income of the world virtually stood still until around the year 1500 AD (Figure 2.1). For thousands of years, mankind did not experience any revolutionary, game-changing technological progress which improved living standards by leaps and bounds.

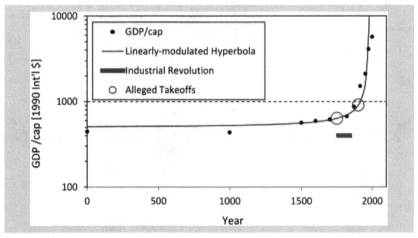

Figure 2.1. World's GDP per capita trajectory.
Source: R. W. Nielsen (2016). "Puzzling properties of the historical growth rate of income per capita explained," *Journal of Economics Library*, Vol. 3, No. 2, Figure 3.

Instead, while there was steady technological progress, the progress was limited and marginal and thus insufficient to fundamentally alter the global economic landscape. However, the Industrial Revolution spearheaded by Britain spread to the rest of Europe and North America, enabling economic growth to takeoff, and mankind has not looked back since.

The Industrial Revolution transformed Western economies from primarily agricultural economies in which manufacturing played a much larger role. The transition from agriculture to manufacturing included shifting from hand production to machine production, emergence of new chemical manufacturing and iron production processes, the growing use of water power and steam power, the rise of the mechanized factory, and the development of machine tools. By consistently improving living standards, the Industrial Revolution unleashed a sharp increase in population growth rate. The main industry of the Industrial Revolution, which gave rise to modern manufacturing, was textiles, which accounted for a large share of output, employment, and investment of the manufacturing sector. Great Britain, the pioneer of the Industrial Revolution, leveraged its economic prowess to become the dominant power in the global stage.

The catalyst of the rapid economic growth was the dramatic technological progress under the First Industrial Revolution, which later gave rise to the Second and Third Industrial Revolutions. In addition, the globalization that accompanied the industrial revolutions also contributed significantly to rapid economic growth. The First Industrial Revolution sharply increased the demand for raw materials and the supply of industrial output. The invention of steam ships and steam locomotives drastically reduced transportation costs, which made it possible to transport raw materials and finished products cheaply and quickly. The transportation revolution caused a dramatic expansion of global trade and foreign investment.

This marked the first wave of globalization, which was brought about by the First Industrial Revolution and fueled further technological progress. For example, the economic opportunities opened by the expanded access to foreign markets served as an incentive for innovative activity. The combination of the First Industrial Revolution and the first wave of globalization became the engines of growth which lifted mankind's living standards, which had stagnated for thousands of years. Between the years 1870 and 1913, global trade expanded by around seven times while global output increased by around five times. Great Britain, the undisputed leader of the Industrial Revolution, naturally also led the first wave of globalization. Britain established colonies all over the world, from Asia to Africa to Middle East to the Americas, giving rise to the famous dictum: "The sun never sets on the great British empire."

In fact, one major long-lasting consequence of the Industrial Revolution was that it led to the Western dominance of the world which, many observers would argue, continues to this day, notwithstanding the rise of China and other non-Western countries. Other European countries besides Britain, most notably France but also Germany, Belgium, Italy, the Netherlands, and others, competed furiously with each other to colonize other parts of the world. For example, in Africa, the official language changes from English to French to English as you cross borders. The official language of Cote d'Ivoire is French, that of neighboring Ghana is English, that of neighboring Togo and Benin is French, and that of Nigeria is English. Nor was the European dominance limited to just Africa. For example, in Southeast Asia, Malaysia and Myanmar were ruled by the British, Indochina was ruled by France, and Indonesia was ruled by the Netherlands. The Industrial Revolution gave Britain and other European countries the economic and military capacity to dominate the world, and they used that capacity to mold the first wave of globalization in their image and to their benefit.

The first wave of globalization was brought to an end by the 1914 outbreak of the First World War which pitted Britain and France and their allies against Germany and its allies. But another wave of globalization immediately followed. More precisely, the end of the war in November 1918, when Germany surrendered, kicked off the second wave of globalization. The second wave was made possible by the robust V-shaped recovery of the world economy right after the war. Global trade and production recovered rapidly so that by 1928, just before the outbreak of the Great Depression, they had reached 1.3 times their levels in 1913. The central engine of the game-changing technological progress was the Second Industrial Revolution. This period between the two world wars witnessed the invention of electricity and the automobile. Both are tectonic, game-changing technologies. Electricity provides large amounts of stable energy to power factories and homes while automobiles reduced the cost of transportation. Electricity enabled the production of much larger amounts of goods and automotive vehicles, which enabled the transportation of the much larger output.

Another revolutionary supply-side change was the introduction of mass production. Henry Ford, the founder of Ford Motor Company, was an innovator who played a major role in the development of mass production. More specifically, he installed the first moving assembly line for mass producing entire automobiles. He got the idea from the assembly line of a slaughterhouse in Chicago, which he decided to adopt to his automobile factory in Detroit. Ford's innovation cut down the time it took to produce an automobile from more than 12 hours to less than 3 hours. By making it possible to produce automobiles in a cheaper, faster way, the assembly greatly reduced the price of automobiles, putting it within the reach of ordinary citizens. Mass production thus resulted in mass demand and a mass market. Replicated in other industries and across the entire economy, mass production contributed to a quantum leap in productivity and a quantum increase in output.

The interwar period of mass production, globalization, and general economic prosperity was led by America. Henry Ford and his company's mass-produced Model T became symbols of American entrepreneurial energy and economic dynamism. In addition to Ford and other automobile makers, this period witnessed the robust growth of large innovative American manufacturing companies such as General Electric. America's geopolitical influence grew in tandem with its rising economic power. In fact, it was during the interwar period that America replaced Britain as the world's most powerful country and the dominant superpower. Reflecting this shift of economic and geopolitical power across the Atlantic Ocean, the US dollar steadily replaced the sterling pound as the preferred currency for international transactions and foreign exchange reserves held by central banks. The US dollar maintains its position as the dominant global currency to this day and seems unlikely to be displaced in the foreseeable future.

However, this golden era of economic boom and trade expansion came crashing down to earth with the onset of the Great Depression. The immediate catalyst of the Great Depression was the US stock market of 1929, when stock prices fell by 33%. Prior to the Wall Street crash, US stocks went up in a seemingly unstoppable upward trajectory. The postwar mood of optimism, combined with millions of rural Americans moving to the cities, fueled an economic boom which, in turn, fueled the inexorable rise of the stock market. Irrational exuberance, evident in the fact that even ordinary Americans borrowed money to invest in stocks, was fed by the erroneous belief that stock prices would go up forever. When the stock market began to decline, as it inevitably must, panic set in and investors rushed to sell their shares, driving the stock market further down. The Wall Street crash subsequently led to bank runs — i.e. depositors flocking to their banks to withdraw their deposits — and bank failures. The resulting financial crisis spilled over quickly into the real economy, causing widespread business bankruptcies and massive unemployment. The Great Depression remains the longest and deepest economic downturn in modern history.

The Great Depression sparked a surge of protectionism and deglobalization around the world as countries adopted beggar-thy-neighbor trade policies of keeping out imports by erecting high tariffs and other trade barriers while trying to promote their own exports. Of course, such protectionist policies, which were initiated by America's Smoot–Hawley tariffs, were doomed to fail since foreign countries face the same incentives to protect their own firms and industries from foreign competition. As a result of the global trade war, global trade and production initially declined sharply. Global trade recovered after 1931 to eventually 1.5 times the level of 1913. On the other hand, global production failed to fully recover and only returned to the levels of 1913. The second wave of globalization came to an end with the outbreak of the Second World War in 1939.

The current, third wave of globalization arose from the ashes of the Second World War, which ended in 1945. Right before imminent victory, the Western Allied powers led by the US set up the International Monetary Fund (IMF) in 1944. The IMF became the centerpiece of the postwar international monetary system — the Bretton Woods system — based on the primacy of the US dollar and fixed exchange rates. At the same time, the US and its Western Allies agreed upon the General Agreement on Tariffs and Trade (GATT), which provided the institutional framework for rapid expansion of global trade. One central objective of the multilateral Bretton Woods economic system was to bind the advanced countries closer together and thus prevent another global war. Another was to promote economic openness, market-based economic systems, and economic growth so as to prevent the spread of socialism in developing countries.

The third wave of globalization accelerated and intensified since the 1990s. The collapse of communism in the Soviet Union and Eastern Europe, along with China's strong embrace of the market and integration into the world economy, greatly expanded the domain of globalization. Previously, these economies were largely cut off from the world economy. In particular, the integration of China into the global trade and investment network since 1978 had colossal ramifications for both China and the rest of the world. After the successful conclusion of the 8th multilateral trade negotiations — i.e. Uruguay Rounds — the GATT was re-born as the World Trade Organization (WTO) in 1995. The WTO targeted not only manufactured goods as subjects of multilateral trade negotiations, as did the GATT, but also targeted agricultural products and services. Furthermore, China's accession to the WTO in 2001 gave even more impetus to its growing globalization.

Meanwhile, in Western Europe, the European Community was reborn as the European Union as a result of the Maastricht Treaty of 1991. Economic cooperation was deepened under the EU, which created a common market with free movement of goods, people, and capital. European integration gained even more momentum with the 1991 introduction of the euro, a common currency used by 19 of the 27 EU countries, including big economies such as Germany, France, Italy, and Spain. The EU was not only deepened but also broadened. Many formerly Soviet satellite countries of Eastern Europe, such as Poland and Hungary, eventually joined the EU. At a broader level, the transition of the formerly socialist economies of the Soviet Union and Eastern Europe to market-oriented economies contributed to the strong expansion of global trade and investment during this period. In North America, the North American Free Trade Agreement (NAFTA) eliminated most tariffs between the US, Canada, and Mexico when it came into effect at the beginning of 1994. Although some economic integration took place at the global level — e.g. WTO — and some took place at the regional level — e.g. EU and NAFTA — the momentum toward more trade and foreign direct investment (FDI) seemed unstoppable. This period might be viewed as the golden period of globalization within the third wave of globalization.

As if all the global and regional momentum toward freer trade was not enough, the golden period was also home to the Third Industrial Revolution, also known as the information and communication technology (ICT) revolution. By drastically reducing the cost of information and communication, the ICT brought the world closer together and thus contributed to the expansion of global trade and FDI. As noted earlier, the sharp fall in transportation costs due to the development of containerization technology played a key role as well. Another big contributor was the general economic prosperity of the advanced economies. The US hosts what is the most dynamic, entrepreneurial, and innovative economy in the world, epitomized by the Silicon Valley. For their part, Western European economies managed to recover quickly and thrived in the postwar period. Japan too rapidly reconstructed its shattered economy and served as an engine of growth for other East Asian economies.

However, globalization has been showing clear signs of a retreat in recent years. The retreat is the consequence of a wide range of factors. Those factors will gain even more traction due to COVID-19, which may kick off deglobalization with full force.

Box 2.1. The World Economic Forum's classification of globalization waves

The World Economic Forum (WEF), which is held annually in Davos, Switzerland, classifies the time periods of the different globalization waves differently than we do here. They define the first wave as from the 19th century to the outbreak of the First World

War in 1914, as we do. However, they do not view the interwar period as a globalization wave. In addition, they divide our third wave further into three periods. The 1945–1989 period marks Globalization 2.0, the 1989–2008 period marks Globalization 3.0, and the post-2008 period marks Globalization 4.0. Although the definition differs from ours, both definitions make it clear that the current wave of globalization is not the only wave. Furthermore, globalization continues to evolve and reinvent itself in new forms.[1]

1 P. Vanham (2019). "A brief history of globalization," World Economic Forum, (accessed August 15, 2020), https://www.weforum.org/agenda/2019/01/how-globalization-4-0-fits-into-the-history-of-globalization/.

2.2. Widening Income Inequality Triggers Resentment Toward Globalization

In the current, third wave of globalization which began with the end of the Second World War, international trade of goods and services expanded greatly, as did cross-border flows of capital and labor. As noted earlier, this wave of globalization was made possible by technological progress — e.g. containerization and ICT revolution — as well as concerted multilateral policy efforts to expand trade, epitomized by the GATT-WTO global trade regime. The liberalization of international movement of both outputs — goods and services — and inputs — capital and labor — contributed to large improvements in productivity due to greater specialization — countries engaging in industries and activities which they did more efficiently than other countries — and realization of economies of scale — average cost falling as firms produced for larger global markets rather than small domestic markets. The productivity-enhancing potential of trade was recognized back in the 18th century by Adam Smith, the father of modern economics. While global trade has grown and changed beyond all recognition, Smith's key insight about why trade is beneficial — i.e. gains from specialization and division of labor — remains the fundamental economic argument in favor of trade to this day.

Productivity growth, in turn, fueled economic growth, and the postwar period has seen a significant rise in general living standards. In fact, the sustained improvement of mankind's quality of life in the postwar period is historically unprecedented. Never before have so many people seen their living standards rise on a sustained basis. Some regions and countries benefited more than others. Interestingly and significantly, how well a country's economy performed in the postwar era was shaped largely by its success in integrating itself into global trade and investment landscape. This explains why Asian countries, indisputably the star performers and increasingly the leading growth engines of the global economy, fared so well. The defining feature of their sustained rapid growth was an outward-looking growth model which relied heavily on international trade and cross-border investment. Most strikingly, global trade and foreign investment transformed China from a struggling poor country into an economic superpower within a generation.

However, economic globalization is turning out to be a double-edged sword. While boosting economic growth and living standards, globalization has intensified inequality of income and wealth between the rich and the poor. The widening of inequality is occurring not only in the advanced economies that spearheaded the golden age of globalization since the 1990s but also in the developing countries that actively participated in and benefited from the post-1990 surge of globalization.

Economic theory tells us that while international trade is a win-win proposition that benefits both countries, there will be winners and losers within each country. Overall the economy gains from trade, but some industries, firms, and workers gain while others lose. For example, steelworkers in rust belt American states like Pennsylvania lose their jobs when American steel industry and steel mills are wiped out by imports of cheaper steel. On the other hand, American farmers in the Midwest reap big gains when China opens up its huge market to soya bean imports. Again, just like the rationale for why trade is beneficial has not changed for centuries, the rationale for why some win but others lose from trade remains the same. Firms and industries that can outcompete their foreign rivals will thrive. Those which cannot compete will suffer.

The essence of trade and globalization is that markets become more competitive due to competition from imported foreign goods. By the same token, exporters must compete with domestic firms as well as firms from other countries. The benefit from trade is ultimately the benefit from greater competition. As more companies from more countries compete with each other, price falls and quality improves. This is the simple logic for why trade is good for the economy. The logic is not only simple but unassailable, which is why a large majority of economists support free trade, a rare semi-consensus in a profession which is marked by fierce arguments and intellectual disagreements. But the same logic — namely, that the essence of trade is greater competition — makes it inevitable that trade will benefit some but hurt others. In short, the overall gains from trade and its asymmetric effects are nothing new. They existed ever since mankind began to trade. What is different about the current wave of globalization is its sheer scale and speed. As a result, the overall gains are magnified many times over. So are the losses of the losers and the gains of the winners. This is what underlies the growing anti-globalization mood.

As Figures 2.2 and 2.3 show, in the major Western economies of America, Britain, and France, both income and wealth inequalities have widened since the 1990s, during the golden age of globalization. Furthermore, inequality has widened greatly in China, a transition economy that opened up its markets to foreign goods and capital and shifted from a socialist economic system to a market-oriented economy. The worsening of inequality in China is exactly what one would expect. The transition to the market frees up entrepreneurial energy and economic dynamism but inequality inevitably rises since more productive individuals move ahead while less productive individuals are left behind.

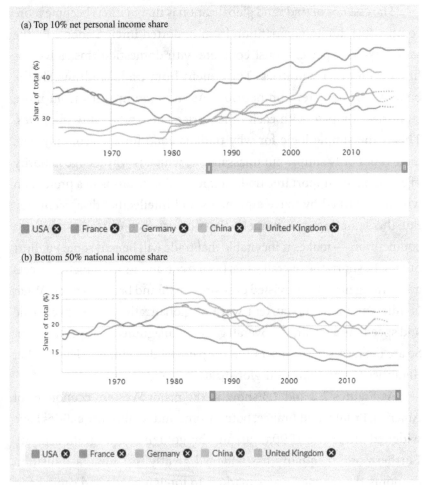

(a) Top 10% net personal income share

■ USA ⊗ ■ France ⊗ ■ Germany ⊗ ■ China ⊗ ■ United Kingdom ⊗

(b) Bottom 50% national income share

■ USA ⊗ ■ France ⊗ ■ Germany ⊗ ■ China ⊗ ■ United Kingdom ⊗

Figure 2.2.   Widening income inequality in the world.
Source: World Inequality Database (accessed August 11, 2020).

In America, which spearheaded the post-1990 golden age of globalization, widening of income and wealth inequalities was already evident in the 1980s, as seen in Figures 2.4 and 2.5. Rapid widening

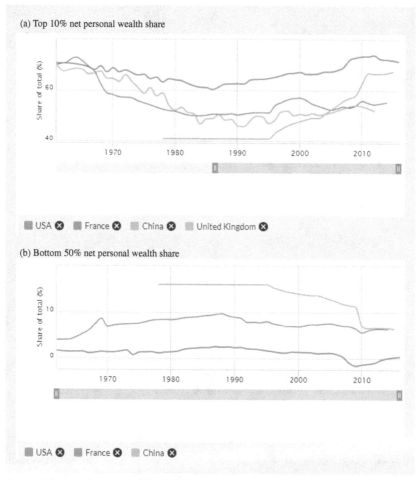

(a) Top 10% net personal wealth share

Figure 2.3.   Widening wealth inequality in the world.
Source: World Inequality Database (accessed August 11, 2020).

of income inequality was accompanied by the rapid widening of wealth.
As Figure 2.4 shows, up to the early 1990s, the share of income going to
the bottom 50% of the population still exceeded the share of the top 1%.

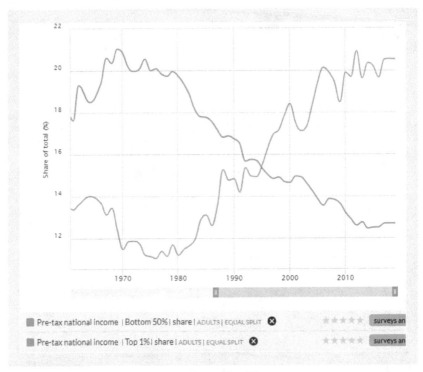

Figure 2.4.　Widening income inequality in the US.
Source: World Inequality Database (accessed August 11, 2020).

However, the situation was reversed and the income share of the top 1% overtook the income share of the bottom 50% in the second half of the 1990s, when the golden age of globalization was in full swing. The gap between the two continued to widen until 2016, when more than 20% of income went to the richest 1% while only 13% went to the bottom 50%.

It is more accurate to describe these recent income and wealth inequality trends as inequality between a tiny super-rich elite and the vast majority of the population rather than inequality between the rich

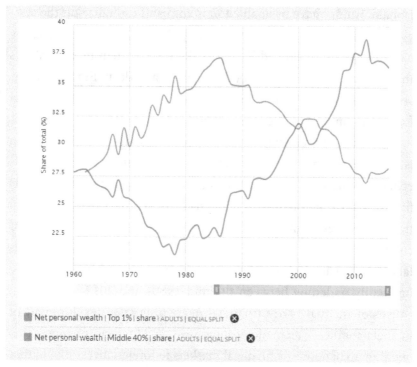

Figure 2.5. Widening wealth inequality in the US.
Source: World Inequality Database (accessed August 11, 2020).

and the poor. A natural consequence of the extreme concentration of wealth and income in a tiny elite is that a large majority of the population, encompassing both the middle and working classes, is becoming increasingly hostile to globalization. There is a close link between popular discontent on inequality and popular discontent on globalization. More precisely, a large majority is unhappy at income polarization that benefits only a tiny few and they believe that the root cause of this unhealthy trend is globalization, and hence the rising tide of popular anger at globalization. Populist politicians, most notably

Donald Trump, have been able to tap into and capitalize on the anti-globalization public mood to capture political power. The shocking election victory of Donald Trump as the US President in 2016 shows that the anti-globalization mood runs wide and deep. Europe too has seen a rise of powerful nationalist, anti-globalist, populist political forces, epitomized by Brexit or Britain's exit from the EU.

The link between widening inequality and growing globalization is not a mere coincidence or speculation but confirmed by rigorous economic analysis. For example, a 2017 research report from OECD finds a positive and significant relationship between expansion of global trade and investment and domestic income inequality in each major country.[2] Another example is a 2015 IMF research report, which finds labor market flexibility to be the most important cause of income inequality widening between the mid-1980s and 2012.[3] Additional causes of inequality are financial deepening (i.e. development of financial markets), technological progress, and financial openness (i.e. opening up of domestic financial markets to foreign investors), in that order.

Labor market flexibility is a direct consequence of globalization. More precisely, it is the direct consequence of the intense competition which resulted from the indiscriminate opening up of goods, services, and capital markets. Surviving such intense competition requires flexible labor markets, which is why countries have been trying to make their labor markets more flexible. Although labor-market flexibility lowers labor costs, makes firms more competitive, and improves

---

2 A. Bergh, A. Kolev, and C. Tassot (2017). "Economic globalisation, inequality and the role of social protection," Working Paper No. 341, OECD.

3 E. Dabla-Norris, K. Kochhar, N. Suphaphiphat, F. Ricka, and E. Tsounta (2015). "Causes and consequences of income inequality: A global perspective," IMF Staff Discussion Note, SDN/15/13.

economic efficiency, it also has the side effect of exacerbating income inequality.

For instance, as a pre-condition for financial assistance from the IMF during the Asian financial crisis of 1997–1998, the South Korean government implemented extensive structural reforms in the corporate, financial, public, and labor sectors. Until the Asian crisis, the dominant employment model of South Korea, and its neighbor Japan, was lifetime permanent employment. The IMF-mandated reforms to enhance labor market flexibility made it easy for firms to fire workers and hire part-time workers. As a result, the number of non-regular and part-time workers rose sharply, intensifying income inequality. The factor that the IMF study found to be the second most important factor, financial deepening, is part of financial globalization. In South Korea's case, it opened up its financial markets to foreign competition in the wake of the Asian crisis, as part of its IMF-mandated structural reforms.

The IMF report found that in the case of the advanced economies, skill premium (i.e. difference in education level) was the single most significant driver of income inequality. The reason why education and skills have become such a powerful driver of inequality is the huge increase in global demand for globally competitive talent with professional and language skills. Indeed the global competition for such global talent has become fierce during the golden wave of globalization. Professionals such as investment bankers, computer scientists, and airline pilots can work anywhere in the world. In contrast to vast majority of workers, who face stringent immigration restrictions, world-class professionals move unfettered from country to country. In fact, countries compete furiously with each other for such talent. Some countries such as Singapore actively court foreign talent as a way to enhance their international competitiveness. Globalization, epitomized by trade liberalization and opening up of financial markets, is driving the widening income and wealth inequality to unacceptable levels. Adding fuel to the fire, the global competition for global talent is pushing up the skill premium even further.

As discussed earlier, the essence of globalization is greater competition. The intensification of competition under globalization is magnifying the losses of the losers and the gains of the winners. Globalization forces companies that were used to competing only with domestic rivals to compete with more efficient foreign rivals. Many of them will be unable to compete and will go out of business. Many minor-league football, baseball, or basketball players will not make it after they move up to the major league. On the other hand, globalization offers more efficient domestic companies the opportunity to outcompete foreign companies and expand, and even become global companies. In fact, one novelty of recent decades is that many companies from the South — i.e. developing countries — have become global multinational companies. Just a few examples include Huawei from China, Infosys from India, Vale from Brazil, Anglo American from South Africa, and Turkish Airlines. Prior to the 1990s, there were very few globally active multinational companies from the South, and the North — i.e. advanced economies — dominated the list of such companies. The picture has changed a lot in the past 30 years or so.

It is inevitable that the intense, relentless competition unleashed by the golden age of globalization widens the income gap between those in the "winner" industries and those in the "loser" industries. Furthermore, the regulations of the international organizations which set the rules of the game — e.g. WTO and its regulations regulate global trade — prevent countries from mitigating the social conflict stemming from worsening inequality. For instance, WTO regulations prohibit

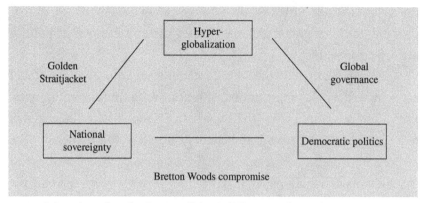

Figure 2.6.   The political trilemma of the world economy.
Source: D. Rodrik (2007). "The inescapable trilemma of the world economy," [blog]. Available at: https://rodrik.typepad.com/dani_rodriks_weblog/2007/06/the-inescapable.html.

countries from subsidizing industries and firms which are not internationally competitive. Of course, such regulations promote fair competition among firms of different countries and thus fair trade. They are essential to the fundamental role of the WTO. But at the same time, such regulations stand in the way of government's ability to help the "losers" of globalization. This has given rise to the globalization paradox, which refers to the political trilemma intrinsic to the global economy.

According to Professor Dani Rodrik of the Kennedy School of Harvard University, each country can at any time have only two of the following three — democratic politics, national sovereignty, and hyper-globalization.[4] Figure 2.6 shows that the Bretton Woods multilateral system combined national sovereignty and democratic politics but gave up on hyper-globalization. That is, Bretton Woods permitted

---

4   D. Rodrik (2007). "The inescapable trilemma of the world economy," [blog] (accessed May 20, 2020). Available at: https://rodrik.typepad.com/dani_rodriks_weblog/2007/06/the-inescapable. html.

international trade and cross-border investment only to the extent that they did not infringe the national sovereignty and democratic politics of each country.

The integration of the world's economies into a single global economy is the polar opposite of the Bretton Woods multilateral system. Put differently, replicating the European Union, where there is free movement of goods, capital, and labor, on a global scale is the opposite of Bretton Woods. In a single global economy, each country has to surrender its national sovereignty. Perhaps a better analogy than the EU is the 50 states of the US which jointly form a single economy and country. There is unrestricted movement of goods, capital, and people across the US, and democratic politics prevail in each state, as evident in free state-level elections for US senators, US congressmen, state governor, and other state officials. On the other hand, while each state has a certain level of autonomy — e.g. during the COVID-19 pandemic, state governors had the ultimate authority over whether and how each state would lock down its economy — there is a clear limit to a state's sovereignty.

It is reasonable to characterize the current global economic and financial architecture, anchored around the GATT-WTO trade framework, as an intermediate position between the multilateral Bretton Woods system and a single world economy. Under the current global architecture, which seems to be coming to an end, each country retains its sovereignty but there is relatively free movement of goods, capital, and labor across borders. This architecture maximizes global income and wealth but impedes the capacity of democratic politics to mitigate the undesirable side effects of globalization, in particular inequality and social polarization. Domestic democratic politics is subordinate to the global rules of the game set by the WTO and other multilateral institutions.

Therefore, hyper-globalization offers all countries the golden jacket of unprecedented economic and trade opportunities but simultaneously constrains them in the straight-jacket of binding multilateral rules of the game. That is, hyper-globalization is, in effect, a golden straight-jacket. However, the worsening of inequality to unacceptable levels is altering the cost-benefit calculus of globalization to a growing segment of the population in many countries, resulting in increasingly vocal opposition to globalization and evoking increasingly louder calls to throw off the golden straight-jacket. Deglobalization directly stems from the globalization paradox. They are one and the same. The sheer force of the anti-globalization sentiment was underscored by Brexit. The European Union is an incomparably tighter economic union than the global WTO system and represents a much higher level of economic integration. The fact that the voters of the UK chose to leave such a tight union attests to the virulence of the anti-globalization mood. Given the strength of the anti-EU sentiment in Italy and other member countries, we cannot rule out other countries following the UK to the exits. There is even a risk that the EU will eventually disintegrate in the face of the growing anti-globalization mood.

Upon closer thought, it was a foregone conclusion that the losers of globalization will oppose globalization. That opposition to globalization has grown more vocal in recent years and for an obvious reason. As noted earlier, the sheer speed and scale of the golden wave of globalization magnifies the size of the winners' gains and losers' losses. Furthermore, there was a growing perception that globalization is by the elite, of the elite, and for the elite. The notion that a small global elite captured the lion's share of the gains from globalization while the vast majority of the global population gained little or none further galvanized the anti-globalization popular sentiment. In other words, globalization was viewed by many as a tool for enriching the privileged elite at the expense of the population. According to American journalist John Judis, populism is the natural byproduct of a wide gap between actual governance structure and the governance preferred by the population.[5] The increasingly virulent popular hostility toward globalization enabled populist political leaders and parties to gain strength in America and Europe and take power in some cases.

Box 2.2. Anti-globalization and anti-capitalism

Anti-globalization popular mood was reinforced and buttressed by another equally powerful popular mood, namely anti-capitalism. Anti-globalization and anti-capitalism are related but distinct, and both fuel the rise of populist forces. The election of Donald Trump, Brexit, and the emergence of powerful populist, nationalist parties across Europe are intimately connected to the anti-globalization, anti-capitalism strain of public sentiment. While globalization was widely seen as the cause of high and rising income and wealth inequality, such unacceptable inequality was one of the main causes of the growing popular opposition to capitalism. Even in America, the bastion of entrepreneurial and dynamic capitalism (e.g. Silicon Valley), the population is losing faith in capitalism and the market. The fundamental reason is that a growing number of Americans believe that capitalism is rigged and it favors the rich. The extreme concentration of wealth is eroding the American public's confidence in the American dream — i.e. anyone with talent, drive, and determination can make it big in America. Yet the American dream

---

5 J. B. Judis (2016). *"The Populist Explosion: How the Great Recession Transformed American and European Politics (Columbia Global Reports), New York.*

was the moral basis of capitalism and the reason why capitalism enjoyed genuine widespread popular support in America.

The global financial crisis of 2008–2009 served as another major catalyst of anti-capitalism. The crisis was triggered by so-called financial innovations of greedy Wall Street bankers who sought to sell mortgage loans to poor people with poor credit ratings, an inherently risky proposition. They were, in effect, selling homes to people who should not be buying homes. No amount of financial engineering, not even by some of the world's most brilliant minds, can reduce the inevitable risk of such a business model. When the crisis inevitably broke out, the US government spent billions of dollars of taxpayers' money to bail out those same greed-crazed Wall Street bankers whose reckless greed paralyzed the global financial system and almost brought the world economy to its knees. Main Street bailing out Wall Street! Plundering the poor to pay the rich — Robin Hood in reverse!

The taxes paid by millions of ordinary middle-class and working-class Americans were rescuing the tiny privileged Wall Street elite from their reckless disregard for risk in their blind pursuit of profit. When Wall Street bankers made profits from the subprime mortgages, the profits were theirs and theirs alone. And yet when their fraudulent financial engineering blew up in a massive crisis, taxpayers had to pick up the bill. The displacement of entrepreneurial capitalism — which adds plenty of social value with new products and technologies that are useful to societies — by financial capitalism — which has little social value and can be downright harmful — is further fueling anti-capitalism, which, in turn, is fueling political populism and nationalism. Popular disillusionment

with capitalism also owes to the rise of hereditary capitalism —
"I am rich because my family is rich" — and corresponding decline
of self-made, entrepreneurial, merit capitalism — "I am rich because
I make a better product than others." Anti-globalization and anti-
capitalism are the twin engines of the rise of political populism.

As noted earlier, COVID-19 is hitting the poor disproportionately
harder, both on the health and economic fronts. White-collar workers
can continue to work from home, unlike restaurant workers and store
clerks who are furloughed when the economy is locked down.
Furthermore, due to unhealthy diets and other factors, the poor are
more likely to have pre-existing medical conditions such as obesity,
which make them more vulnerable to infection and death. For instance,
in America, blacks account for a disproportionately high share of
coronavirus cases and deaths, as well as lost jobs. Furthermore, small
businesses are being hit much harder than larger corporations with
deeper pockets. As a result, in every country, COVID-19 is likely to
exacerbate inequality and polarization between different income groups.
At the end of the day, the pandemic will broaden and deepen populism
and anti-globalization sentiment.

2.3. Playing Catch-up Causes Tension Between Advanced Economies and Emerging Markets

Economic theory tells us that poorer countries will catch up with richer countries over time. Economists call this phenomenon economic convergence, or the convergence of the income level of poorer countries toward the income level of richer countries. That is, GDP will grow at a faster pace in, say China, than in, say America, which would narrow the gap in average income and living standards between the two countries. Intuitively, there are a number of reasons why economic convergence is plausible. For one, returns to investment or capital will be higher in poor countries than in rich countries. This is due to what economists call the law of diminishing marginal returns to capital. For example, when a poor country builds its first international airport, it will yield huge benefits by connecting it to the world. On the other hand, for a rich country which already has 10 international airports, the benefits of building an additional (i.e. marginal) airport will be much smaller. Another reason is that poor countries can adopt and use superior technologies already developed by rich countries. Rich countries, on the other hand, have to continuously invent and develop new technologies, which is inherently much more difficult than adopting technology that has already been developed.

Of course, the above is a highly simplified and simplistic description. If all poor countries grow mechanically and automatically over time, then there would be no poor countries in the world. In reality, poor countries grow, or fail to grow, for a large number of reasons. For example, many developing countries suffer perennially from incompetent, corrupt, and predatory governments which view the countries they rule as a piggy bank to plunder for personal enrichment.

The health and education of their citizens is the last thing on the mind of those governments. For instance, many economists argue that a big reason that sub-Saharan Africa has been and remains by far the world's poorest region is that the region is riddled with incompetent, corrupt governments which care little for economic development or the welfare of their citizens. Nor is bad government limited to Africa. Incompetent, populist governments have reduced the citizens of Venezuela, which has the world's largest oil reserves, to rubbish-scrounging poverty. Similarly, many countries in the Middle East are saddled with weak, ineffective governments which failed to create an environment conducive for economic growth. The predictable result was the social explosion known as the Arab Spring of 2011, when millions rose up against lousy governments and lack of economic opportunities.

At the same time, some developing countries have indeed managed to grow rapidly and greatly narrow the income gap with advanced economies in the postwar period. The most prominent example of such success was the East Asian Miracle of eight Northeast and Southeast Asian economies, made famous cited by an influential 1993 World Bank report.[6] These countries succeeded in growing rapidly on a sustained basis by doing the right things — investing a lot in physical and human capital, maintaining macroeconomic stability, and opening up to foreign trade. In particular, the newly industrialized economies or the NIEs — South Korea, Taipei,China, Hong Kong, and Singapore — grew rapidly for so long that they were able to make the jump all the way to advanced economies. The student had caught up with the teacher. South Korea in particular has become a benchmark or model for developing economies because the three other economies are much

---

6   World Bank (1993). *The East Asian Miracle (Oxford University Press), Oxford.*

smaller — indeed Hong Kong and Singapore are cities — and hence less relevant for developing economies with larger populations. South Korea has become one of the most innovative countries in the world and a high-tech manufacturing powerhouse.

The stunning catchup of the four NIES was followed by a much more significant catchup, that of China, the world's most populous country. China followed in the footsteps of South Korea and Singapore and grew very rapidly — in fact by double digits for many years — to become the world's second biggest economy. The immediate catalyst of China's remarkable economic surge was Deng Xiaoping's market reforms of 1978. The reforms unshackled the inherently entrepreneurial Chinese people from the numbing shackles of socialism and unleashed their colossal pool of entrepreneurial energy. As the share of the economy controlled by the state fell and the share controlled by private sector entrepreneurs correspondingly rose, the productivity and efficiency of firms, industries, and the entire economy improved by leaps and bounds. Nicholas Lardy of Peterson Institute for International Economics makes a powerful case that, notwithstanding the popular nonsensical myth that China is the epitome of state capitalism, China's growth was driven predominantly by the private sector.[7]

The resulting improvement in general living standards and the sharp reduction in poverty in the world's biggest country is undoubtedly one of the greatest achievements in economic history. In addition to the shift from the inefficient state to the efficient market, the other indispensable ingredient of China's success was international trade and foreign investment into China. In fact, successful globalization was the

---

7 N. R. Lardy (2014). *Markets over Mao: The Rise of Private Business in China* (Peterson Institute for International Economics), Washington D. C.

common denominator of China, South Korea, Singapore, and other Asian countries that grew rapidly during the third wave of globalization.

Not only did China benefit hugely from globalization, which powered its world-topping growth, but it was at the forefront of globalization, along with the US. In fact, it would be accurate to say that globalization was possible due to the leading roles of America and China. America actively supported China's entry into the WTO in 2001. China's membership in the WTO cemented its participation in global trade and investment and added even more momentum to its globalization. America's strong support was predicated on the belief that China's full integration into the world economy would help to bring about changes to China's economic and political system. Until the advent of the Trump Administration, American governments actively supported the entry of American firms into China. As a result of massive investment by American firms, along with firms from Western Europe, Japan, South Korea, Taipei,China, and other advanced economies, China became the Factory of the World. China became a key player in the production of intermediate goods — i.e. parts and components — as well as the assembly of intermediate goods into final goods for exports to the rest of the world. China stood at the front and center of the global supply chain, which meant that the rest of the world came to depend on China for the smooth production of manufacturing products.

However, changes to China's economic and political system were slow to come and fell far short of American hopes. Like South Korea and Singapore before it, China relied on an economic model that combined political stability with economic freedom. More specifically, ever since Beijing crushed student-led, pro-democracy Tiananmen Square protests in 1989, it tolerated very little political dissent while allowing entrepreneurs and the private sector to drive economic growth.

As noted earlier, contrary to popular myth, the basic essence of the Chinese model is most definitely not state capitalism. Instead, it is the paradoxical mix of tight political control by the Communist Party of China and one of the most capitalistic economies in the world. Whatever one's view of the model, it has delivered world-topping economic growth, dramatic improvement in living standards, and sharp reduction in poverty rates. From Beijing's viewpoint, there was precious little incentive for change. As Americans say, "if it ain't broke, why fix it?"

Decades of sustained rapid growth catapulted China from the periphery of the global economic stage to the front and center. China has risen to the extent that the G7 (the Group of 7), the rich countries' club of America, Britain, Canada, France, Germany, Italy, and Japan, is giving way to the G2, consisting of the two economic superpowers — America and China. The leaders of the G7, the international intergovernmental economic organization consisting of the seven advanced economies which was founded in 1975, meet regularly to discuss global issues. But due to the steady decline in the advanced economies' share in global output and the corresponding increase in the share of the emerging markets, the G7 has become badly outdated. G7 used to be the head table of global economic dialogue, but no longer.

Instead China has replaced the non-American members of the G7 at the head table. The G2 implies that America and China are the two most globally influential economies. America has been the world's top economic power since it replaced Britain as the world's leading economy and the dollar replaced the sterling pound as the world's dominant currency after the First World War. Despite its relative decline in recent decades, the US still remains the world's pre-eminent power, economically, geopolitically, and militarily. But China is catching up fast and has emerged as a credible rival that can challenge America's hegemony. Economically, China is without any doubt a heavyweight with a tangible and significant global reach and impact. For example, China's global economic influence was felt during the global financial crisis. While the output of advanced economies shrank by more than 3%, the Chinese economy grew by almost 9%, providing much needed demand for both rich and poor countries. Germany and Japan export high-tech machines and automobiles to China while Brazil and African countries export farm products and commodities to China. Both groups of countries benefited greatly from Chinese demand during the global financial crisis.

More worryingly for America, not only is China catching up rapidly with America, it is trying to surpass it. Its current leader President Xi Jinping makes no attempt to hide China's global leadership ambitions. President Xi's grand vision of the Chinese Dream can be viewed as a sign of greater Chinese nationalism and assertiveness on the global stage. While the Chinese Dream is a vague, ill-defined concept — Xi defined it simply as the great rejuvenation of the Chinese nation with many different dimensions — the emergence of a strong China, economically, politically, militarily, diplomatically, scientifically, technologically, and culturally is its defining feature. From America's perspective, a possible interpretation of China's newfound assertiveness, epitomized by the Chinese Dream, is that China is trying to unseat America as the world's pre-eminent power. But just as President Donald Trump has every right to make America great again — whether he actually succeeded is an altogether different matter — President Xi has every right to make China strong.

Americans point to "Made in China 2025," the Chinese government's strategic blueprint for making China a dominant force in new advanced technologies and high-tech manufacturing, as yet another proof of

China's hegemonistic ambitions. But from China's perspective, it has every right to move from labor-intensive, low-wage economy to a skill- and technology-intensive economy. Much more than that, it is in China's self-interest and the self-interest of its people to do so. Nevertheless, it is possible for Americans to interpret the Chinese Dream and Made in China 2025 as direct challenges to American leadership. Rapidly changing on-the-ground economic realities lend further weight to American fears. In 1995, the Chinese economy amounted to just one-tenth of the American economy. Within less than two decades, by 2011, China's output was already one-half of America's. And by then, China had surpassed Japan to become the world's second biggest economy (Figure 2.7). Economic experts believe that China will surpass America by 2030 or even by the late 2020s. While China's growth has been

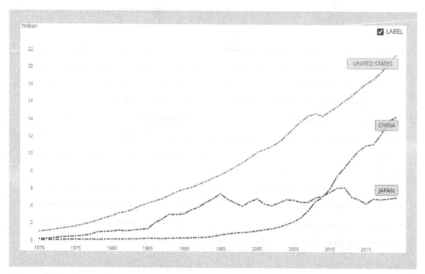

Figure 2.7. Gross domestic product (GDP) of China, Japan, and the U.S. (Current US$), 1970–2019.
Source: World Bank's DataBank (accessed August 13, 2020).

exceptional, other emerging markets too have grown rapidly. As a result of the rapid catch-up, the privileged position of the advanced economies in the world economic order is under threat.

Furthermore, the catchup of the emerging markets shows no signs of slowing down any time soon. It is unclear how COVID-19 will affect the speed and scale of income convergence between emerging markets and advanced economies. Both groups of countries have been hit hard by the pandemic, and it is uncertain which group has greater economic resilience. Based on purchasing power parity, which takes into account the fact that local services such as haircuts are cheaper in poorer countries, the E7 or group of seven major emerging markets — China, India, Brazil, Russia, Indonesia, Mexico, and Turkey — already have a bigger collective economy than the G7. According to estimates by leading global consulting firm PwC, the E7 still lags behind the G7 in terms of collective output calculated by converting GDP into dollars based on market exchange rates, but even by this measure, the E7 will surpass the G7 by around 2030.[8]

The advanced economies are thus hearing the footsteps of the rapidly advancing emerging markets. As the emerging markets, especially economies such as China which invest heavily in R&D and produces many innovations, improve their technological capacity and their overall productivity, the international competitiveness of the industries of advanced economies is eroded, leading to firm closures and higher unemployment. In this scenario, trade protectionism becomes an increasingly attractive option for advanced economies, especially in the wake of COVID-19, which has weakened demand and growth. Furthermore, from the viewpoint of multinational companies

---

8 *PcW (2015). The world in 2050 — Will the shift in global economic power continue?, (PricewaterhouseCoopers: London).*

from rich countries, the cost of investment in emerging markets is increasingly outweighing its benefit. The competitiveness of domestic firms in emerging markets is improving, and the wages of domestic workers are rising very rapidly, especially in fast-growing countries such as China. Emerging markets are losing their appeal as investment destinations for advanced-economy multinational companies. Indeed for many multinational companies in both manufacturing and financial sectors, foreign investment is becoming a burden rather than a source of competitive advantage.

In the middle of such seismic changes, the COVID-19 pandemic, which originated in China, is giving the advanced economies, in particular America, the perfect excuse or justification to contain China. The Trump Administration has already criticized Beijing for what it sees as Beijing's covering up or downplaying the severity of the health crisis during the early stages. It has also denounced what it calls China's neglect in allowing the virus to spread outside China to the rest of the world. The Trump Administration has also dabbled in conspiracy theories, such as China intentionally spreading COVID-19 abroad. Of course, the assertive Chinese government does not take such attacks lying down. It has gone on to propose equally far-fetched conspiracy theories of its own, like the one about US soldiers planting the virus in China. Neither giant shows any signs of backing off and it feels like the beginning of a long Cold War, a critical issue that we will examine in more detail later. America is likely to use the pandemic to decouple itself from China.

The same option is not available to the other advanced economies. European economies and Japan are export-dependent economies, unlike America, which depends on domestic demand for the bulk of its growth. Interestingly, contrary to another popular misperception about China,

China too is an economy which is largely based on domestic demand. This explains why China was able to grow by almost 9% during the global financial crisis in 2009 when global output and trade shrank. But Japan as well as Germany and other major European economies are not large enough to base their growth on domestic demand. Globalization is not a choice for them, it is a necessity for their very economic survival. This explains why they have been much more subdued in their criticism of China's early-stage handling of the pandemic.

2.4. Fourth Industrial Revolution Will Reshape the Global Supply Chain

The postwar period marked the third wave of globalization and the Third Industrial Revolution. Beginning in the 1950s, the Third Industrial Revolution introduced a number of revolutionary technological innovations to the world — semiconductors, mainframe computing, personal computing, and the internet — which jointly gave birth to the digital revolution. If one thinks about it, the digital revolution is one of the most profound and momentous technological breakthroughs in human history. The digital revolution has reduced the cost of information and communication, which is used to produce everything. In every industry, managers have to inform and communicate with each other and with staff, and the staff has to inform and communicate with each other. Before the advent of the internet, we had to go to the library and manually search through library colleagues to dig out whatever information we need. Now anybody with a mobile phone that is connected to the internet has a world of information at his fingertips. Just Google any subject and you will get what you need. Furthermore, COVID-19 has underscored the vital role of the internet in economic resilience. Working from home, online shopping, and video conferencing are all possible due to the internet.

Given the game-changing nature of the digital revolution, also known as the ICT revolution, one might be tempted to think the scope for further technological progress is limited. But anybody who thought this way would be seriously underestimating human ingenuity and creativity. In fact, the next wave of technological progress, the Fourth Industrial Revolution, was already well under way before the COVID-19 outbreak. The pandemic will now give it a strong impetus which will accelerate and strengthen its momentum. The Fourth Industrial Revolution includes technologies in emerging fields such as robotics, artificial intelligence, nanotechnology, quantum computing, biotechnology, the internet of things, the industrial internet of things, decentralized consensus, fifth generation wireless technologies (5G), 3D printing, self-driving automobiles, big data, and machine learning. The collective impact of the exciting new technologies shapes up to be every bit as profound as that of the digital revolution.

It is possible to trace the origins of the Fourth Industrial Revolution to Industrie 4.0, which was a national strategic initiative from the German government which aimed to promote digital manufacturing. The initiative sought to achieve the digitalization of manufacturing by making production more efficient and flexible by digitalizing data. Factory smartization, as some choose to call it, denotes the digitalization and networking of all processes, products, and resources. According to this definition, workers, machines, and parts share all information relevant to production and have the capacity to utilize the information in the production process. For example, Nobilia, a German kitchen equipment maker, applies information and communication technology to automatically order, process, and assemble parts. Factories then digitalize all relevant information and use it in decision-making. Smart production is widely credited with turning Nobilia, which has just two factories, into Europe's biggest kitchen equipment manufacturer. South Korea, which has a large manufacturing sector like Germany, is also investing heavily in smart factories. The South Korean government has set a target of 30,000 smart factories by 2022, and 2,000 new AI-based smart factories by 2030.[9]

---

9   Yonhap News Agency (2019). "Moon declares renaissance vision for S. Korea's manufacturing industry," 19 June.

The ultimate goal of German and South Korean initiatives to digitalize their manufacturing industries was to make them more efficient and productive via smart factories. The quest for greater efficiency, in turn, was driven by growing competition from China and other emerging markets which are rapidly catching up technologically. Since German and South Korean manufacturing cannot compete with emerging markets which have significantly lower wages, the only avenue left for them to compete was by efficiently leveraging technology. More precisely, by digitalizing all data relevant to manufacturing production, German and South Korean factories sought to enhance their efficiency and add more value. At a broader level, the two countries are seeking to revitalize their manufacturing sectors to boost economic growth, which had fallen sharply since the global financial crisis. The initiatives of the two countries seek to automate production by connecting machines to the internet. However, there is no reason why the smart (i.e. digital) technological revolution, which can mobilize artificial intelligence and big data, should be confined to manufacturing production. Indeed the Fourth Industrial Revolution also encompasses new product development, services industries, and indeed the entire economy.

The term "Fourth Industrial Revolution" was first coined by its pioneering prophet Klaus Schwab, the executive chairman of the WEF, in an article in *Foreign Affairs* in 2015. The Forum opened a Center for the Fourth Industrial Revolution in San Francisco in 2016. At the WEF Annual Meeting in 2016, which was themed "Mastering the Fourth Industrial Revolution," Schwab proclaimed that "mankind is at the crossroads of an industrial revolution which will fundamentally change the way we live, work, and interact with each other." Furthermore, he pointed out that "the size, scope and complexity of this revolution will be unlikely mankind has ever experienced before." Quite clearly, what the prophet had in mind was something big enough to alter the future course of human history.

The first three industrial revolutions replaced human physical labor with machines. At the same time, they created entire new industries and millions of new jobs. The Fourth Industrial Revolution, on the other hand, not only replaces physical work but also mental work. Artificial intelligence, big data, machine learning, robots, 3D printing, internet of things, and the other emerging technologies can do things that human minds can do, not just simple mental tasks but sophisticated mental tasks. For example, in March 2016, AlphaGo became the first computer program to beat a professional player in Go, a very complex board game that is played mainly in China, Japan, and South Korea. Not just any professional but Sedol Lee, one of the world's top players. Just like the earlier industrial revolutions, the Fourth Industrial Revolution will lift the productivity of all industries and the entire economy. However, one difference, and it is a big difference, is that the Fourth Industrial Revolution will create jobs only for highly skilled workers whereas the first three revolutions created jobs for all workers.

As a result, unskilled workers and workers who are unwilling or unable to acquire the skills required by the Fourth Industrial Revolution will be unable to find jobs. On the other hand, workers who have or acquired the necessary skills will do well. The income gap between skilled and unskilled workers will thus grow due to the Fourth Industrial Revolution. The inequality of wealth and income, which is already unacceptably wide, will widen even further. Although inequality is being driven by technological progress, historically politicians have a habit of blaming foreigners — i.e. globalization — for inequality, polarization, and other economic and social problems. Foreigners are always the easiest and most convenient scapegoats. It will be no different this time. The Fourth Industrial Revolution will add fuel to the fires of nationalism and populism, which are already burning bright and strong.

At the same time, the relative importance of human physical labor in the production process is set to decline sharply. This means that the lower wages of emerging markets, which has traditionally been one of their main attractions for foreign investors, will lose much of its appeal. More specifically, robotics technology has been making dramatic progress in recent years, and COVID-19 will speed up the development and use of robots at the workplace. The desire to reduce human-to-human interaction and thus limit the risk of infection means that robots will perform many of the tasks that are now performed by humans. For instance, in South Korea, robots have been re-tooled since the outbreak to measure body temperatures and distribute hand sanitizers, and Walmart, America's biggest retailer, is using robots to scrub the floors of its gigantic stores.

In this environment, it makes more sense for the advanced countries which are at the forefront of the Fourth Industrial Revolution to bring production back home. Deploying the exciting new technologies for production in home-country factories and thus improving productivity and efficiency is a more profitable strategy than continuing to produce in emerging markets. To repeat, the relative importance of human physical labor and thus the wages of unskilled workers will decline sharply in deciding where to produce. According to a report published by America's Reshoring Institute in 2015, internet of things, robots, and automation of machines will be the key factors in the speed and scale of reshoring by American manufacturing firms. Similarly, a

2019 research report in the *LSE Business Review* finds that automation will speed up reshoring.[10]

We will explain in more detail later but COVID-19 is a big catalyst of the Fourth Industrial Revolution. We already outlined the government-led efforts of Germany and South Korea to smartize their factories and manufacturing industries to improve efficiency and productivity. But the digital manufacturing revolution will not be confined to Germany and South Korea but spread rapidly to all advanced economies. The efforts of companies to leverage robotics, big data, artificial intelligence, machine learning, 3D printing, and other state of the art technologies to smartize their factories will receive a big push from COVID-19, which mandates the minimization of human-to-human contact. The Fourth Industrial Revolution thus challenges the central logic of the global supply chain — the location of activities requiring unskilled, low-wage workers in emerging markets. This will weaken global supply chains and give further impetus to reshoring. To sum up, the Fourth Industrial Revolution will exacerbate the anti-globalization popular mood by exacerbating income inequality and, at the same time, accelerate deglobalization by reducing the importance of unskilled labor.

10 Krenz, K. Prettner, and H. Strulik (2018). "Robots, reshoring, and the lot of low-skilled workers", Discussion Paper No. 351, (Center for European, Governance and Economic Development Research: Göttinggen).

2.5. Population Aging Leads to Secular Stagnation

As seen in Figures 2.8 and 2.9, the world's population is aging rapidly. In particular, population aging is advanced in the advanced economies of Europe, North America, and East Asia. According to United Nations statistics, in 2019 the share of population aged 65 years and above is as follows — Japan (28%), Italy (23%), Portugal (22.4%), Finland (22.1%), Greece (21.9%), Germany (21.6%), France (20.4%), Sweden (20.2%), and Denmark (20.0%). These countries have already reached the status of super-aged societies, where one-fifth of the population is 65 or older. A number of other Western European countries are rapidly approaching that status — Spain (19.6%), the Netherlands (19.6%),

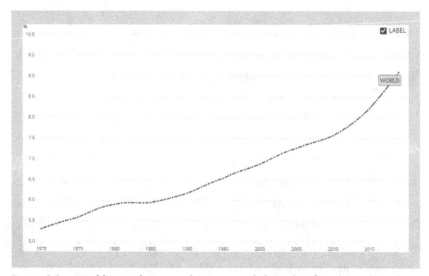

Figure 2.8.   World's population aged 65 years and above (% of total population).
Source: World Bank's DataBank (accessed August 13, 2020).

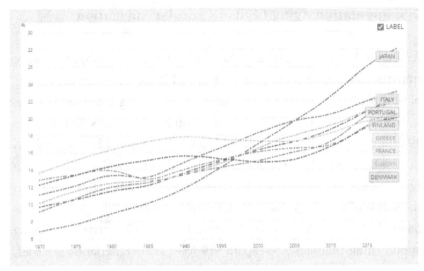

Figure 2.9.   Population aged 65 years and above (% of total population) for most aged countries.

Source: World Bank's DataBank (accessed August 13, 2020).

Austria (19.1%), Belgium (19%), Switzerland (18.8%), and UK (18.5%). The share of the 65+ population is 16.2% in the US, 17.6% in Canada, and 15.1% in South Korea.

There is a significant correlation between a country's income level and population aging. Richer countries tend to be older. This explains why the world's oldest countries are the rich countries of Europe, North America, and East Asia. On the other hand, the world's poorest region — sub-Saharan Africa — is also the world's youngest region. There are several reasons for this robust correlation between income and demographic structure. For one, due to higher quality of life — e.g. nutrition — and better health care systems, life expectancy is higher in richer countries. That is, there are relatively more elderly people because people live longer. Women tend to better educated and are more likely to have jobs in richer countries and, as a result, they tend to have fewer children. Rich-country parents tend to have fewer children but invest more in each child — i.e. quality over quantity. Besides income, religion and culture seems to influence a country's demographic structure. In particular, Islamic countries tend to be younger.

A natural solution to the world's asymmetric population problem — i.e. greying rich countries and young poor countries — is to promote immigration from poor to rich countries. However, due to political factors, cross-border movement of workers remains much more restricted than cross-border trade and investment. Of course, as noted earlier, highly skilled global talent is an exception. Every country wants highly skilled world-class professionals, and countries compete fiercely with each other to attract them. Most workers are not so fortunate. Thousands of desperate economic refugees from the Middle East and Africa trying to cross the Mediterranean to reach far richer European countries are most definitely not welcome. Nor are the thousands of Central American economic refugees trying to cross the US–Mexico border. Allowing immigration to mitigate the growing demographic crisis makes perfect economic sense. However, hard political realities stand in the way, especially in this age of populist, anti-globalization nationalism.

Population aging is harmful for economic growth. Indeed aging has been put forth by most economists as the biggest reason why economic growth has stagnated in recent years. They point to Japan as a prime example of the heavy toll that population aging takes on the economy. Japan, the world's oldest country, has been economically stagnant ever since an asset price bubble burst in early 1990s. Since then the economy never managed to regain any sense of dynamism or vibrancy. Japan, which once boasted a powerful, dynamic, technologically advanced economy with world-class manufacturing firms, has become a synonym for long-term economic stagnation and deflation. Deflation means that the demand is so weak that prices are falling; it is the opposite of inflation. The popular term is Japanization. While there are a number of explanations for Japan's economic decline, economists invariably point to rapid population aging as the primary suspect.

Intuitively, when a country's population becomes older, a smaller share of the population works. Even when seniors keep their jobs or take new jobs, they are not as productive nor do they save as much as younger workers. As people age, their physical and mental capabilities typically deteriorate. Of course, how well people age depends on how well they take care of their bodies and minds, but overall those in their 30s are physically stronger and mentally sharper than those in their 60s. Therefore, when a country has relatively more people in their 60s and relatively fewer in their 30s, the average labor productivity — i.e. the amount of goods and services produced by a worker, on average — is bound to suffer. Furthermore, each worker must support more seniors on average, and the burden may eventually become unsustainable. Governments will have to spend more on health care, pensions, and other elderly-related areas as the elderly population grows. The economy's potential growth rate, or its long-run average growth, thus inevitably slows down as the population ages.

There is yet another powerful reason why population aging is bad for economic growth — entrepreneurship. Entrepreneurs are the central players of a market economy, the people who take risks, create new businesses, and create jobs. Think of Steve Jobs and his friends creating Apple in a suburban California garage. Innovative entrepreneurs who drive economic, social, and technological progress tend to be young because younger people tend to be more comfortable with new technologies and less afraid to experiment with new ways of doing things. This is why Silicon Valley and other hubs of innovative entrepreneurship are dominated by young people eager to experiment with new ideas, technologies, and business models. Therefore, as the population grows older, and there are relatively fewer and fewer younger people, the potential pool of the next Steve Jobs or Jack Ma shrinks. In addition, the loss of young people deprives communities of their general dynamism. For example, many rural communities in Japan and South Korea, where only the elderly remain, feel like ghost towns, without any vitality. The danger is that as population aging proceeds further, even cities will become ghost towns inhabited only by the elderly.

In connection with the negative impact of population aging on economic growth, we would like to introduce two research papers. A 2017 paper by us and Professor Kwanho Shin of Korea University, South Korea, uses data from 142 countries between 1960 and 2014.[11] Our analysis confirms that the share of the working-age population (i.e. 15–64 years) in the total population is positively related with economic growth. In this connection, a key factor behind the sustained economic growth of China, Japan, South Korea, and other East Asian countries was favorable demographics. They had relatively young populations with relatively large numbers of workers who had to support relatively few seniors. However, a young population does not automatically guarantee rapid economic growth. One key ingredient of the East Asian miracle was that those countries were able to capitalize on their demographic window of opportunity by putting in place sound institutions and policies. For example, East Asian countries invested

---

11 H.-H. Lee, K. Shin, and D. Park (2017). "Population aging and its impact on economic growth," *Economic Analysis*, Vol. 196, pp. 159–179, Economic and Social Research Institute, Cabinet Office, Government of Japan.

heavily in education so that their young workers acquired the basic skills necessary to become productive workers. The report also found a negative relationship between the share of the population aged 65 years and above in the population and economic growth. More specifically, if the share rises by 10%, annual economic growth falls by 3.5 percentage points.

The second research paper, by Professors Hyun-Hoon Lee and Kwanho Shin, finds that the relationship between population aging and economic growth is not linear but nonlinear.[12] That is, as population aging intensifies, the negative effect of population aging on economic growth becomes greater. For example, the negative effect of aging on growth will be greater when the share of the elderly is 25% rather than 20%. For countries such as South Korea, which is aging very rapidly, the uncomfortable implication is that the negative economic impact of aging will be magnified in the coming years.

Indeed many advanced countries are already facing prolonged economic stagnation due to population aging. As noted earlier, Japan has become a byword for the negative impact of aging on growth. The Japanese asset price bubble burst in early 1990s, after real estate and stock market prices moved up relentlessly between 1986 and 1990, a period of irrational exuberance which was similar to America's Roaring Twenties just before the stock market crash of 1929. Since the bubble burst in early 1990s, when the share of the population aged 65 years and above already exceeded 15%, the Japanese government spent an enormous amount of money in a futile bid to resuscitate the economy. As a result of massive fiscal spending, the ratio of government debt to GDP stood at 238% in 2018, the highest in the world. But in the face

---

12 H.-H. Lee and K. Shin (2019). "Nonlinear effects of population aging on economic growth," Japan and the World Economy, Vol. 51. Article 100963.

of powerful demographic headwinds, even such fiscal mega-spending proved ineffective to inject any life into the moribund economy. Japan may not be alone in suffering an extended period of economic stagnation.

Many European countries find themselves in economic stagnation since the global financial crisis. In 2013, former US treasury secretary Larry Summers proposed in a seminal speech that the global economy had entered a long-term economic slump, which he termed secular stagnation, invoking a 1930s theory which was used to explain the Great Depression. Summers argued that just like during the Great Depression, it will be difficult to boost growth by lowering interest rates to encourage more investment and consumer spending. The answer, he argued, was for governments to spend more instead. But the Japanese experience shows that even concerted government spending may be impotent in the face of irresistible demographic forces. Since the global financial crisis, the advanced economies are clearly experiencing slower growth and loss of economic dynamism. The one common denominator among the advanced economies is their rapidly aging populations. This explains why there is almost universal consensus among economists that aging goes a long way toward explaining the post-global financial crisis slowdown. It is too early to tell whether America and Europe will suffer secular stagnation and the widely feared Japanization. But for sure, population aging lurks as a big risk.

To make matters even worse, COVID-19 came at a time when the advanced economies are facing a serious risk of secular stagnation due to population aging. The pandemic has been an unprecedented shock for all the countries of the world but for the advanced economies in particular, it could not have come at a worse time. As it is, the advanced economies were struggling to gain any growth momentum since the global financial crisis. Even before the COVID-19 outbreak, the advanced economies were facing some formidable challenges to growth. For example, the US–China trade conflict added a great deal of uncertainty to the global trade and economic environment. And, they are feeling intense pressure from rapid catch-up by emerging markets. In this scenario, COVID-19 may deal a fatal blow to their hopes for economic revival. As a result, nationalist, anti-globalist populism will become even stronger and spread to even more countries.

Chapter 3

The World After Coronavirus

3.1. History Repeats Itself

T here have been countless epidemics throughout human history. A classic example was the Black Death, a devastating global epidemic of bubonic plague that devastated Asia and Europe in the mid-1300s. The plague arrived in Europe in October 1347, when 12 ships from the Black Sea docked at the port of Messina in the Italian island of Sicily. The authorities quickly ordered the dozen infected ships out of the port but it was too late. Over the next 5 years, the Black Death killed around 25 million Europeans, almost one-third of the continent's population. The disease was not only highly contagious but also frighteningly deadly and could kill perfectly healthy people within hours of infection. The bacillus that spread the plague traveled from person to person through the air, as well as through fleas and rats. The Black Death epidemic had run its course by 1351 but it had wrought extensive changes in medieval Europe.

The epidemic not only took away the lives of millions of ordinary European citizens but also thousands of clergymen. As a result, the church began to lose its authority and privileged position in society. The church-centered society gave way to the human-centric Renaissance period in which science and the arts took center stage. The Renaissance was a fervent period of European cultural, artistic, political, social, and economic rebirth and marked the transition from the Middle Ages to modernity. Famous Renaissance artists included Leonardo da Vinci, Michelangelo, and Raphael. As populations declined in the aftermath of the Black Death, the nobility competed with each other to secure farm workers, driving up the wages and social position of farm workers. Higher wages increased the purchasing power of the farm workers and thus boosting demand and consumption. The First Industrial Revolution stemmed from the efforts of employers to cope with scarcity of labor and higher wages and was closely associated with the birth of modern capitalism.

As the First World War came to an end, the Spanish Flu (1918–1920) erupted in the US. The epidemic spread easily among trench soldiers who were physically and mentally exhausted from long battles of attrition. When the soldiers returned home after the war, they spread the epidemic to the broader society and it spread like a wildfire across the world. The Spanish Flu was perhaps the closest to the ongoing COVID-19 in terms of its global spread and impact although its death toll is likely to be far higher. More specifically, the epidemic claimed between 25 million and 100 million human lives, which amount to 2%–6% of the global population of 1.6 billion at that time. These numbers far exceed the number of military deaths during the First World War. The Spanish Flu came in 4 successive waves and infected about 500 million people, almost one-third of the global population.

International cooperation on tackling the Spanish Flu was out of the question during the First World War. The combatant countries even banned releasing data related to the epidemic lest their enemies detect any sign of national weakness. Only Spain, which was not a combatant in the conflict, reported publicly on the epidemic, which was why the epidemic came to be known as the Spanish Flu. Just like the earlier Black Death, a key consequence of the Spanish Flu was a significant reduction of population, especially working-age people like the World War soldiers who succumbed to the disease. The reduction of population, in turn, served as a catalyst of the Second Industrial Revolution via the rapid development of capital-intensive industries which relied more on capital and less on labor. More specifically, massive investment in factories and machines promoted and accelerated technological progress in steel, automobiles, electricity, and other new technologies. While the economic expansion brought about economic prosperity, capital-intensive mass production which took root sowed the seeds of the Great Depression of the 1930s.

It remains to be seen whether COVID-19 will trigger such far-reaching economic, social, and technological changes as the Black Death or the Spanish Flu. For one, there is a great deal of uncertainty about the coronavirus and its future trajectory. There is still a lot which remains unknown about the pandemic and how it will play out. For example, it is still not clear whether developing antibodies — i.e. having been infected earlier and recovered — gives you immunity from future infections. Of course, a definite game-changer in the war against COVID-19 would be the development of a safe and effective vaccine. A safe and effective treatment would also change the picture for the better. Medical experts agree that a safe and effective vaccine is likely to be available to the public only after 2020. In the case of the Spanish

Flu, the number of infections during the second wave in the fall of 1918 was five times larger than during the first wave in the spring of 1918.

There is a risk that coronavirus too may migrate to the southern hemisphere during the summer and return to the northern hemisphere and explode during winter. Alarmingly, as of August 2020, large developing countries like Brazil, India, Russia, South Africa, and Mexico were suffering large numbers of outbreaks. Of particular concern is the pandemic situation in the US, where the government's incompetent and ineffective response gave rise to a public health catastrophe. Astonishingly, as of August 2020, the world's richest, most powerful, and most technologically advanced country was home to around 25% of global cases and deaths.

The seemingly invincible nature of COVID-19 is adding to the gloom and pessimism about the world economy's prospects. As noted earlier, the world economy was already slowing down visibly since the global financial crisis, partly as a result of deglobalization, most evident in the declining relative importance of international trade. Well before the outbreak, there were also growing concerns that the advanced economies, many of which were or about to become super-aged societies, were entering a period of secular stagnation or long-term economic decline. On top of this, the social distancing restrictions and lockdowns imposed by many countries further dented global growth. Therefore, we cannot rule out the possibility that the world economy will underperform the growth forecasts of the International Monetary Fund (IMF) and other organizations, as dismal as they are.

Even under optimistic scenarios — for instance, the pandemic dies down or a safe and effective vaccine comes to the market much sooner than expected — economic dynamism is unlikely to recover to pre-COVID levels any time soon. Even if social distancing restrictions and lockdowns are eased, many people will instinctively avoid going to airports and markets out of fear. They will think twice about taking airline flights or having meals in crowded restaurants. The highly contagious nature of COVID-19 has destroyed the social fabric of human trust because we now tend to view other people as viral vectors who can potentially infect us. Until the social fabric is rebuilt, and its rebuilding will be a lengthy and difficult process, consumer confidence will remain depressed. When consumers are reluctant to spend, production remains depressed, and the economy may be stuck in first gear for years to come.

History often repeats itself. Historical experience tells us that countries pursue free trade when the world economy is booming. Expansion of global trade, in turn, further reinforces the global economic boom. But historical experience also tells us that countries turn their backs on free trade and turn to protectionism when their economies are down. Although America championed and led the third wave of globalization after the Second World War, as a latecomer to industrialization it often resorted to protectionist trade policies in an effort to protect and nurture the growth of its nascent industries. Such protectionist policies gain even more momentum when the economy heads south.

Let us take an example. The US was not a combatant in the First World War, which devastated the other advanced economies, which were in Europe. As a result, American agriculture enjoyed an unprecedented boom. However, European agriculture came back to life in the 1920s after the war's end. Due to increased production, the global prices of agricultural products fell due to intense competition and excess supply. In response, special interest groups representing

American farmers lobbied their government to impose restrictions against imports. Herbert Hoover, the 31st American president, promised to raise tariffs on agricultural imports during his presidential election campaign. After he was elected, Republican President Hoover came under pressure for higher tariffs on non-agricultural products as well. However, the opposition of centrist Republican congressmen defused such protectionist pressures.

However, protectionist pressures gained a strong dose of impetus when the Wall Street stock market crash of October 1929 set off a severe economic downturn and popular demands to protect American industries and firms from foreign competition. The result of the pressures was the Smoot–Hawley Tariff Act which raised tariffs against imports by around 20%. The protectionist legislation passed the US Senate by 44 to 42 votes and also secured a majority in the House of Representatives. Despite the petition of 1,000 prominent American economists expressing their opposition to the Act, President Hoover signed it on June 17, 1930. The act increased America's average tariff rate to a staggering 59.1% by 1932.

The Smoot–Hawley Tariff Act precipitated retaliatory tariffs from America's key trading partners — i.e. Western European countries. Like America, European countries imposed tit-for-tat beggar-thy-neighbor tariffs. As a result, America's foreign trade fell by two thirds during 1929–1932 while global trade dropped by one-third. The world economy, which was already in very bad shape due to the Wall Street crash of October 1929 and the subsequent weakening of consumption and investment, was dealt an almost fatal blow by the transatlantic tariff war. There is a strong consensus among economists that while the Great Depression was due to a wide range of factors, trade protectionism made the economic downturn much worse. Indeed only massive government spending, epitomized by the public work projects of the New Deal program implemented by the government of President Franklin D. Roosevelt during the 1930s, staved off complete economic collapse. In fact, many economic historians believe that the world economy was unable to regain its pre-Depression growth momentum until the outbreak of the Second World War, which entailed massive government spending in the combatant countries.

Upon closer examination, the current COVID-19 situation is not all that different from the 1930s. As explained earlier, the Western countries led by America find themselves facing the risk of losing their privileged position at the head of the table of the world economic order. The Western countries had dominated global economy and politics for centuries, ever since the UK spearheaded the First Industrial Revolution. The rapid catch-up of emerging markets, in particular China, must be a rude shock to the group of countries that enjoyed unchallenged authority and leadership for so long. The friction and hostility between the advanced economies and emerging markets manifests itself in many global issues. For instance, the governance structure of the IMF, which oversees the world economy and global financial system, is badly outdated. Major Western European countries such as the UK, Germany, and France continue to play a dominant role in the IMF despite the fact that their share of the world output is significantly reduced due to the rapid expansion of emerging markets, in particular China. To make matters even worse for the advanced economies, COVID-19 threatens to paralyze their economies at a time when population aging is already pushing them toward secular stagnation.

In the current scenario of global health and economic crisis, each country will look out for its own self-interest rather than pursue cooperation with other countries. President Donald Trump has repeatedly blamed China for his own catastrophic mishandling of COVID-19, even calling coronavirus the China virus. He has also hinted at economic retaliation against China, including re-escalation of tariffs against Chinese imports. The Trump Administration may even rescind the US–China Phase One trade deal that was reached in January 2020, re-igniting the US–China trade war that began in 2018 with US tariffs against Chinese goods and China's retaliatory tariffs against US goods. The US–China trade war bears an uncanny resemblance to the US–Europe trade war of the 1930s. History repeats itself.

3.2. Cold War Between America and China

Professor Graham Allison, who served as Assistant Secretary of Defense during the Clinton Administration, wrote in his book *Destined for War* that the US and China are predestined for war.[1] According to Professor Allison, during the last 5 centuries, there were 16 instances when the incumbent superpower came into a sharp conflict with an aspiring superpower; 12 out of the 16 conflicts resulted in a war. The inevitability of conflict between the incumbent hegemon and the rising challenger is known as the Thucydides Trap. The term was coined by Greek historian Thucydides to analyze the origins of the Peloponnesian War between the incumbent hegemon Sparta and rising challenger Athens. The tension between the incumbent and the challenger is often intense, which is why it often ends up in military conflict. One of the rare instances in which the tension was managed peacefully was the transfer of global leadership from Britain to America between the two world wars. But Britain and America have strong historical and cultural ties and have long had a special traditional relationship. Therefore, their peaceful rivalry and transfer of hegemony is the exception to the rule.

The Sparta and Athens of today's world is undoubtedly America and China. The two countries do not enjoy any special relationship and in contrast to America and Britain, they do not share many common values. For example, the two countries have fundamentally different political systems — multiparty democracy versus authoritarian one-party rule. America has, in effect, dominated the world ever since the end of the Second World War in 1945. Between the end of the Second World War and the fall of the Iron Curtain in early 1990s, America was

---

1   G. Allison (2017). *Destined for War: Can American and China Escape Thucydides's Trap?* *(Houghton Mifflin Harcourt), Boston, MA.*

engaged in a superpower rivalry with the Soviet Union. However, since the breakup of the Soviet Union, America had emerged as the world's only superpower. Pax Americana, which refers to global peace and prosperity under the relatively benign hegemony of the US, seemed destined to last for a long time. However, the dramatic rise of China as an economic juggernaut fundamentally challenged this scenario. From China's perspective, its spectacular economic resurgence merely presaged its return to its rightful place in the world, which was at the head of the table. The Chinese name for their own country is the Middle Kingdom, meaning that it is the center of the world, surrounded by less civilized barbarians.

To add insult to injury, China has been invaded and humiliated by Western countries and Japan during the 19th and 20th centuries. China's humiliation was epitomized by the two Opium Wars which pitted the Qing Dynasty against Western powers in 1839–1842 and in 1856–1860. The First Opium War fought between the Qing and Great Britain was triggered by the dynasty's campaign against opium trade, which was controlled by Britain. This is like Mexican drug lords invading California because Washington is clamping down on cocaine use! An outrageous infringement of Chinese sovereignty, by any measure. As a result of the wars, in which European forces used advanced military technology to defeat Chinese forces, the Chinese government was forced to grant favorable tariffs, trade concessions, and even territory. The loss of Hong Kong to Britain in particular compromised China's territorial integrity. This explains why Western lecturing of China about democracy and human rights in Hong Kong is likely to fall on deaf ears. China suffered greatly as a result of Japan's invasion of its territory between 1931 and 1945. Between 10 and 25 million Chinese civilians lost their lives due to the Japanese invasion.

As a result of COVID-19, the incumbent superpower America and the fast-rising challenger China find themselves being sucked deeper into a Thucydides Trap. America has rebuked the Communist Party of China for failing to inform the World Health Organization (WHO) of the novel coronavirus soon enough. Furthermore, America, which has now become the world's biggest COVID-19 hotspot, is actively spreading conspiracy theories to the effect that China intentionally spread the disease around the world. At the same time, Washington has hinted that it may raise tariffs against China and seek financial compensation for the damages that it suffered because of what it sees as China's negligence. In fact, the US state of Missouri filed a lawsuit against the Chinese government for causing the COVID-19 outbreak. The Chinese government is vehemently opposing such efforts to blame it for the coronavirus.

Not surprisingly, COVID-19 has worsened the perception of China among the American general public. The pandemic has inflicted unprecedented suffering, pain, and hardship on Americans, on both health and economic fronts. It is thus only natural to be angry at the country where the pandemic first originated. According to a public opinion survey carried out by Pew Research in mid-April 2020, around 66% of Americans had an "unfavorable" perception of China. This is the highest share of unfavorable perception since the survey began in 2005. Furthermore, 61% of respondents viewed China's growing power and influence as a threat to America.

The bad vibes between America and China cut both ways. According to a public opinion survey carried out at the end of 2019, 28% of Chinese had an unfavorable perception of America. The proportion of Chinese who had a favorable perception of America dropped sharply, from 58% to 39%. Note that this survey was carried out before the COVID-19. Anecdotal evidence suggests that the hostility of Chinese toward America has grown further since the outbreak. This is hardly surprising since President Trump explicitly and blatantly blames China for America's massive outbreak, even calling COVID-19 the Chinese virus. The US government's catastrophic mishandling of the pandemic, which has resulted in the country becoming the leading global COVID-19 hotspot, has also reduced its stature among the Chinese public. All the more so since the US government is trying to blame China for its own incompetence and ineptitude.

As explained earlier, the current wave of globalization is the third wave of globalization in modern history. The previous two waves of globalization brought about a disruptive shift in the balance of power between first-mover industrializers and latecomer industrializers, which then resulted in two world wars. Worryingly, the current third wave of globalization is disrupting the existing global economic order. More accurately, the current order is being shaken to its foundations. The rapid rise of emerging markets, spearheaded by China, is threatening the privileged position of the advanced Western countries. In addition, globalization is precipitating far-reaching changes to the social and economic structure of each country. More precisely, the widening of income and wealth inequality and the resulting compression of the middle class has fueled implacable hostility against globalization.

As the economic downturn deepened and income inequality further widened as a result of COVID-19, antipathy toward the other side was not limited to the American and Chinese governments. The American and Chinese general public have an increasingly negative perception of each other. Americans' anger at China for being the original epicenter of the coronavirus is counterbalanced by Chinese disrespect for America for its incompetent mishandling of the pandemic and for blaming China for its own shortcomings. The two giants are escalating their rivalry for global leadership to another level. The frightening question is, will the current wave of globalization end like the earlier two waves of globalization? In a catastrophic world war?

Fortunately, the likelihood of such a disastrous outcome is limited. As noted earlier, during the last 5 centuries, in only 4 out of 16 instances, tension between incumbent superpower and rising challenger did not lead to a war. One of the four exceptions was the US–Soviet Cold War. The US and Soviet Union were able to avoid a military conflict because both countries were armed with nuclear weapons. Both countries knew perfectly well that a direct military conflict could escalate into a nuclear war, which would annihilate both of them. To avoid highly risky direct confrontation, the US and Soviet Union chose instead to engage in a large number of proxy wars — i.e. wars by their proxies — around the world. For example, America supported South Korea while the Soviet Union supported North Korea during the Korean War (1950–1953). During the Vietnam War (1955–1975), America supported South Vietnam while the Soviet Union supported the Viet Cong rebels and North Vietnam. Yet another example is the Afghanistan war (1979–1989). In that conflict, the Soviet Union supported a communist government while America supported anti-communist, Islamist rebels. America and the Soviet Union often backed different countries or different factions within a country.

Two nuclear superpowers — America and China — are revving up to fight a new Cold War with each other. The previous Cold War was a contest between capitalism and democracy, led by America, and socialism and authoritarianism, led by the Soviet Union. In the end, America and its allies won not because they won decisive victories on the battlefield but because millions of people living behind the Iron

Curtain eventually became aware how much richer and more fulfilling life is on the other side of the Curtain. Western countries are far from perfect but their way of life is incomparably superior to the materially deprived, politically oppressive, inhumane lives suffered by the millions chafing under communism. The new Cold War will be a contest between advanced economies, led by America, and emerging markets, led by China. Although the two antagonists are America and China, they are the champions and leaders of two groups of countries with fundamentally different world views.

China understands the historical grievances of the emerging markets, which have not had a seat at the head of the table or often a seat anywhere in the table, for a long time. Simply put, emerging markets are sick and tired of being bossed around by advanced economies. All the more so since they now command a much larger share of the world economy due to their rapid growth. China in particular has grown by double digits for decades to become an economic superpower within a generation and is spearheading the emerging markets' efforts to reshape the international economic order. The current international order is badly in need of a fundamental reset to better reflect the shift in the global balance of economic power.

While emerging markets are united in their desire to change the international economic architecture or the rules of the game of the world economy, only China has the economic muscle to bring about change. One prime example of China's new leadership role is its establishment in 2016 of the Asian Infrastructure Investment Bank (AIIB), a multilateral development bank (MDB) that aims to support the building of infrastructure in the Asia-Pacific region. Asia already had a well-established MDB with exactly the same mandate of infrastructure investment — i.e. the Asian Development Bank (ADB), which was set up in 1966. The ADB was initiated by Japan, with strong American support, and its president has always been Japanese. As such, ADB reflected American geopolitical dominance and Japan's economic leadership of Asia back in 1966. China's establishment of AIIB was motivated by China's desire for greater leadership, commensurate with its newfound status as the biggest, most influential economy in Asia. Interestingly, America was vehemently opposed to the establishment of the AIIB, and it has still not joined it, along with Japan. One cannot but suspect that a geopolitical desire to "contain" the rise of China is a major motivation behind its vehement opposition to the AIIB.

America's strong opposition to the establishment of the AIIB is, in many ways, puzzling and inexplicable. After all, America wants China to use its rising economic and geopolitical power responsibly and benignly — i.e. to become a peaceful soft power rather than an aggressive hard power. However, what can be more responsible and benign than improving the infrastructure — e.g. roads, ports, power plants, water and sewage, and communications networks — of developing countries, where poor infrastructure is a serious impediment to economic growth and development? Moreover, China has a clear competitive advantage in infrastructure building. China's bullet trains and expressways are as good as any in advanced countries, if not better. America's baffling opposition to AIIB forebodes the shape of the coming US–China Cold War. The two giants will pick fights with each other over all kinds of issues, large and small, just as America and the Soviet Union did during the earlier Cold War. The other countries of the world will be forced to choose sides, just as in the first Cold War. They will often find themselves stuck between a rock and a hard place.

One example of the superpowers forcing smaller countries into a difficult, almost impossible, dilemma is the Economic Prosperity

Network (EPN). The purported objective of EPN, reportedly being conceived by Washington, is to reduce China's role in the global supply chain. As stated earlier, due to its seemingly inexhaustible supply of disciplined, hardworking, low-wage workers, China had become the central hub of the global supply chain and it still remains the hub despite the contraction of workforce and rapid rise in wages in recent years due to population aging. Washington is asking Australia, India, Japan, Korea, New Zealand, and Vietnam to join the EPN. All six countries depend heavily on China for their prosperity. For example, exports to China account for a quarter of Korea's total exports and are twice as much as its exports to America. All other five countries are in a similar situation. For example, Australia benefited enormously from China's insatiable appetite for its iron ore, gas, coal, and other raw materials; farm products; education; and tourism. The six countries are in no position to join an American-led economic coalition that explicitly excludes and targets China.

Astonishingly, due to the monstrous incompetence of the Trump Administration, the US is now in the unenviable position of being *the* global hotspot of COVID-19, with by far the highest number of confirmed cases and deaths. The world's richest, most powerful, most technologically advanced country has 4% of the world's population but 25% of the world's coronavirus cases and deaths. America's inept response to COVID-19 has made it a global laughing stock as well as an object of global pity and greatly diminished international respect for America and America's stature on the global stage. In addition to its complete lack of leadership in fighting the pandemic at home, the Trump Administration has refused to participate in, let alone lead, international cooperation against the virus. Shockingly, in the midst of a worsening outbreak in the US, on July 7, 2020, President Trump formally notified the United Nations of America's withdrawal from WHO. Whatever one's view of the WHO, and the organization has received plenty of criticism for its alleged pro-China bias and mishandling of the pandemic early on, it is the foremost organization that coordinates global response to a global health crisis. America is thus not only abdicating its global leadership, it is in effect abdicating its global responsibility.

In stark contrast to America's impotence, China, the original epicenter of COVID-19, managed to contain the pandemic quickly, largely through draconian lockdowns which turned Wuhan and other Chinese cities into urban prisons. Such draconian restrictions are unimaginable in liberal Western democracies, but they seem to have been highly effective. Draconian or not, most neutral observers would view those lockdowns much more favorably than the coronavirus parties allegedly held by some American youths, with the first to be infected getting a prize. At the same time, China dispatched ventilators, face masks, protective clothing, and other vital medical supplies around the world, and sent 300 medical personnel to Italy when that country was suffering a big outbreak. Those actions will help China recoup some of the international goodwill that it lost by being the original epicenter of the virus.

In a fundamental sense, China's active assistance of other countries in the global war against COVID-19 is a continuation and extension of its assuming a much stronger and more visible leadership role in the global stage in recent years. China's growing global leadership is epitomized by its Belt and Road Initiative (BRI), formerly known as One Belt One Road, a global development strategy that Beijing adopted in 2013. BRI, which is centered on infrastructure development, has made infrastructure investments in more than 70 countries and international organizations so far. The ultimate objective of BRI is to create a New Silk Road that connects China with Asia, Europe, and Africa through more and better infrastructure across three continents. BRI showcased the effectiveness of the "Chinese model" by leveraging China's infrastructure planning and building prowess. China's effectiveness in containing the pandemic is doing the same for the Chinese model, especially since it stands in sharp contrast to the disastrous US mishandling of the virus.

However, it will be difficult for China to be recognized as a global leader that can supplant America, especially among Western countries. For example, *Bild*, Germany's biggest daily newspaper, wrote an open letter to President Xi Jinping in which it said "Before Corona, China was known as a surveillance state. Now, China is known as a surveillance state that infected the world with a deadly disease."[2] In addition, *Bild* strongly criticized China's massive provision of face masks and medical supplies to the world as imperialism hidden behind a smile — a Trojan Horse. But Western opposition to and criticism of China's global aspirations was in full swing well before COVID-19. For example, Western media like to portray the BRI as an attempt by Beijing to force developing countries to over-borrow until they are in hock to Beijing. But it is not logically clear at all how developing countries can be forced to borrow or over-borrow. Similarly, the American government and media have rounded on AIIB as lacking transparency and good governance. Furthermore, China's imposition of the National Security Law in Hong Kong and its mass detention of its Uighur Muslim minority is giving plenty of anti-China fodder for Western media.

---

2   Reichelt, J. (2020), "You are endangering the world", *Bild*, April 17. *https://www.bild.de/politik/ international/bild-international/bild-chief-editor-responds-to-the-chinese-president-70098436. bild.html.*

On the other hand, many developing countries in Africa and Latin America are likely to support China in the new Cold War, just as some of them backed the Soviet Union during the old Cold War. Some developing countries backed Soviet Union out of antipathy toward Western imperialism, which colonized and exploited them for centuries. In truth, China is a much more attractive partner than the old Soviet Union, which did not have much to offer except arms and military advisors for leftist governments or leftist rebels seeking to overthrow pro-Western governments. Above all, China is the world's second biggest economy with huge amounts of resources. Furthermore, China offers a viable model that is highly appealing to many developing countries — a mix of political stability, often abetted by political authoritarianism, and economic growth and development, powered by more and better infrastructure. Indeed many developing economies see the Beijing model as something to emulate.

In fact, Beijing is not just talking the talk, but walking the walk. The Chinese government is putting its money where its mouth is. Many developing countries are receiving substantial amounts of financial and material assistance from Beijing via the BRI. Chinese firms invested massively in Africa at a time when Western companies shied away from the continent. The investments were a much-needed vote of confidence for a region that had been increasingly marginalized in the world economy. In fact, some African economies such as Ethiopia and Rwanda have grown rapidly on the back of the Chinese model and financial support. Not only does China offer much more than the former Soviet Union. From the viewpoint of developing countries, China's no-strings-attached financial support is a much more attractive proposition than high-handed lectures about democracy and good government from

Western countries. Since many of these countries have authoritarian political systems that are broadly similar to China's, they do not hesitate at all about siding with China. Finally, further enhancing China's stature, the country actively supports the effort of the developing countries to fight COVID-19, with medical supplies and technical advice, while the US is knee-deep in the world's biggest outbreak and is cutting itself off from the world.

Although inept mishandling of the COVID-19 crisis has dealt a heavy blow to America's global leadership authority and role, at the end of the day, the Western world will side with a democratic America against an authoritarian China. A major caveat is that a genuine rapprochement between America and its traditional Western European allies is more likely if Trump is not re-elected in November 2020. But even if Trump, whose erratic, unpredictable, and incompetent leadership caused a deep rift in the transatlantic partnership, is re-elected, it is difficult to see Western countries choosing China over America. In the final analysis, the US–China Cold War will be part of a broader conflict that pits the North — i.e. US and other advanced Western economies plus Japan — against the South — i.e. China and its emerging-market allies. The looming North–South conflict is a natural consequence of the growing economic power of the South and the unwillingness of the North to fully recognize and adapt to this uncomfortable reality.

Some scholars instead predict an East–West conflict in the post-COVID world. This conflict would pit Western countries led by America against Eastern countries led by China. According to this school of thought, the US–China Cold War may morph into a clash of civilizations between Western values versus Asian values. This kind of thinking is in line with the predictions of Professor Samuel P. Huntington. In a seminal 1996 book *Clash of Civilizations*, Professor Huntington predicted that cultural and religious differences will be the primary source of conflict in the post–Cold-War world.[3] He argued that future wars would be fought between cultures, not countries. However, some Asian countries, most notably Japan, have close political and security links with America and thus they will hesitate to side with China. At the same time, Asian countries are geographically close, and in some cases culturally close to China. More importantly, most Asian economies depend heavily on the Chinese juggernaut for their growth. For instance, during the global financial crisis, China's remarkable growth contributed greatly to Asia's economic resilience. Therefore, it will be difficult for Asian economies to turn their backs on China and side with America. Asian economies will find themselves in an impossible dilemma.

Japan, Korea, Taipei,China, Hong Kong, Singapore, Malaysia, Thailand, and other East Asian economies were able to grow rapidly on a sustained basis due to their outward-looking, export-oriented growth strategy. China followed in their footsteps to leverage its huge, hardworking, low-wage workforce to power its export-oriented industrialization. India, which followed a different growth strategy geared more toward domestic demand, also benefited substantially from its exports of IT-enabled services — e.g. back office support. Asia benefited more from economic globalization than any other region of the world. In addition, in more recent decades, the emergence of global supply chains benefited Asia far more than any other region. The entry of large multinational companies from America, Japan, and Western Europe into Asia enabled specialization and division of work among Asian countries.

---

3   S. Huntington (1996). *The Clash of Civilizations and the Remaking of World Order (Simon & Schuster)*, New York.

But the US–China Cold War will disrupt the global supply chain, which will depress international trade and foreign investment. The depression of global trade and investment, in turn, seriously dampens global growth momentum. Asia, the biggest beneficiary of globalization, will suffer disproportionately from deglobalization.

Tensions between America and China may give rise to many proxy wars. During the old Cold War, there were a number of proxy conflicts in Central and Eastern European countries that bordered the former Soviet Union. The geographical focus of the new Cold War is likely to be East Asian countries that are China's neighbors. In particular, as Tim Marshall pointed out in *Prisoners of Geography*, the Korean Peninsula may become a dangerous flashpoint due to its strategic geographic location between China, Japan, and Russia.[4] The Korean Peninsula is divided between capitalist South, which hosts some 28,500 US troops, and communist North, which remains close to China. The border between the two countries is the most militarized border in the world. The Peninsula is by no means the only potential location for a proxy war between China and the US but it is probably the most dangerous location.

---

4   T. Marshall (2016). *Prisoners of Geography: Ten Maps that Explain Everything about the World* (Elliot and Thompson).

3.3. The Fourth Industrial Revolution Gathers Momentum

While information and communication technology (ICT) and the internet have been around for more than a generation, COVID-19 has seen a dramatic acceleration, amplification, and intensification in the use of ICT. Indeed it is hard to imagine life without the internet in the Age of COVID-19. The pandemic has fundamentally reshaped the way we work, play, and live. More specifically, after the outbreak, while we are forced to stay at home during lockdowns and community quarantines, we do most things virtually — i.e. via the internet — rather than physically. Work from home is perhaps the most prominent example. Since we cannot go to office, which is closed, we have to stay home and do our work at home. But working from home would be impossible without the internet. We cannot communicate with our colleagues without the internet. Skype for Business, Microsoft Teams, and other apps allow us to chat, meet (online), and call our colleagues. Zoom, a video conferencing app which has become hugely popular since the outbreak of the pandemic, facilitates holding meetings, workshops, and conferences. In fact, for white-collar office workers, working from home is not all that different from working at the office.

Work from home is nothing new. The option of working from home has been around ever since the internet was popularized. Work from home is a social innovation that was made possible by technological innovations. Yet this game-changing social innovation was vastly underutilized. Most office workers continued to drag themselves out of their beds every morning, changed into office-appropriate attire, and took jam-packed subway trains to their little cubicles in tall concrete office towers. Social habit and inertia, like the physical office, are a powerful force. You commute to your physical office today because you did so yesterday. However, in the digital age, you can do anything anywhere; you certainly do not need to be holed up in your little cubicle to do your work in the digital age. COVID-19 re-awakened us to the huge potential of ICT in transforming our work environment. We were barely scratching the surface of ICT's potential, not only in work but also in all spheres of life. COVID will change that!

Indeed, the post-COVID world will see the advent of the Super Digital Age, an age which will see the comprehensive incorporation of ICT into our everyday life. One of the defining features of the post-COVID world will be a transition from the Digital Age, when ICT made life convenient, to the Super Digital Age, when ICT is an indispensable part of life — i.e. from luxury to necessity. The untapped potential of ICT will be fully realized in a world where social distancing is the new normal. Furthermore, COVID-19 will give a big impetus to the further development of ICT and its applications. While virtual meetings will never be as good as face-to-face meetings, the gap has narrowed tremendously thanks to apps like Zoom. The gap will shrink even more with the enhancement of ICT and video-conferencing apps. Working from home will become the new normal, the default option, and the physical office will be relegated to a secondary option, at least for office workers.

The second digital revolution — i.e. fully realizing the potential of ICT — will not only affect work. For instance, online shopping has replaced physical shopping as the dominant form of shopping. Under lockdowns and quarantines, when you cannot venture outside, you have no choice but to order online. But even when there is no lockdown or quarantine, why risk COVID-19 infection by going to crowded restaurants, stores, or shopping malls? Online shopping was always more convenient than offline shopping. Now it is more convenient and safer. This explains why even consumers who were reluctant to shop online, such as ICT-challenged older consumers, are now flocking to e-malls like Alibaba and Amazon. The online shopping boom also explains why Amazon's market value reached a staggering US$1.4 trillion and the personal fortune of Jeff Bezos, its founder and CEO, surpassed US$171 billion on July 2, 2020. Bezos is now the world's richest man.

All other facets of everyday life are also going digital. Students are no longer taking classes in physical classrooms but in front of their laptops. Millions of consumers watch movies online on Netflix, the movie streaming company, to fight the boredom of being locked up at home. Netflix saw its market capitalization reach a record US$226.5 billion on July 10, 2020. Even some medical services are moving online via remote health care as the governments of many countries are lifting restrictions against remote health care. Internet-connected monitoring devices allow doctors to see and treat far more patients ever before, while lowering costs across the board.

In short, the second digital revolution due to COVID-19 will drastically transform companies, schools, government (e.g. e-government or the online provision of government services), work, play, learning, medical care, entertainment, and every sphere of life. The demand for all kinds of online services is increasing sharply. More intensive use of the internet since the outbreak has led to an explosive growth in data and information traffic across the world. Despite widespread concerns about disruptions due to the demand surge, the world's ICT infrastructure held up remarkably well so far.

In addition to the second digital revolution, the Fourth Industrial Revolution will also receive a big boost from COVID-19. Equally significantly, the exciting new technologies of the Fourth Industrial Revolution are being deployed to fight the pandemic, including the development of treatments and vaccines. For instance, big data and artificial intelligence (AI) are used to trace the contacts of people who have been infected with COVID-19. China is being credited with containing COVID-19 quickly and effectively. By deploying artificial intelligence, smartphones, CCTV, and face recognition technology to track personal movement, China was able to stop the spread of the virus in a short time. In addition, for people using smartphones and WeChat app, Chinese authorities were able to track their movement in real time. Ordinary citizens could track the movement of people in their neighborhoods via mobile apps. In addition, by tracking the movement of infected people, they could find out whether they had any contact with them.

Interestingly and significantly, China's quick and effective containment of COVID-19 is a testament to its technological prowess as well as its technological ambitions, especially in frontier technologies which are part of the Fourth Industrial Revolution. China deployed drones to provide supplies to isolated areas and make public announcement warnings to people outside their homes and people who did not wear face masks. In apartments, supermarkets, airports, and other public places, robots were able to identify people with high temperatures through infrared thermal measurement. Chinese authorities gave away COVID-19 relief subsidies via mobile payment systems like Alipay or WeChat Pay. In addition, the authorities could track how their subsidies are being used, by geographical location, activity, and time. Such technology — i.e. financial technology or FinTech — allows governments to find out how they can maximize the impact of their fiscal stimulus spending.

At a broader level, all across the world, COVID-19 has alerted us to the enormous potential economic contribution of artificial intelligence, big data, cloud computing, digital platforms, e-commerce, FinTech, internet of things, robots, and 3D printings. All these exciting new technologies can lift productive efficiency greatly. While the Fourth Industrial Revolution has been given a big impetus by COVID-19, the pandemic is also forcing many low-tech firms out of business and depriving millions of workers of their jobs. This portends a fierce competition among industries and countries in the Fourth Industrial Revolution. Survival of the fittest looms.

As explained earlier, the Fourth Industrial Revolution began well before the COVID-19 outbreak. In their 2000 book *Robo Sapiens*, photographer Peter Manzel and TV news producer Faith D'Alusio announced the arrival of the age of the intelligent robot, a lifelike smart machine.[5] They asked whether *Robo Sapiens*, the union of robot and human, will evolve into even more sophisticated machines. The evidence suggests that the answer to their question is a loud and clear yes. In the 20 years since the publication of the book, smart robots have not only proliferated at workplaces but are also increasingly becoming part of our everyday life. Robots are now set to play a bigger role in the post-COVID world when they will help to ensure public health safety — e.g. taking temperatures and cleaning hospital floors — as well as do a lot of the work that used to be done by human workers — e.g. factory work.

In February 2015, *The Economist* coined the term *Phono Sapiens* to describe 21st century mankind, who could not live without their smartphones. In fact, around three billion people, or close to 40% of

---

5 P. Manzel and F. Faith D'Alusio (2000). *Robo Sapiens: Evolution of a New Species* (The MIT Press), Cambridge, MA.

the global population of 7.8 billion, own a smartphone. Humans no longer just own smartphones, which are becoming part of our mind and body. We use smartphones to watch movies, shop, watch news, make financial transactions, and venture into virtual reality. In January 2007, at the launch of iPhone, Steve Jobs boldly predicted "This will change everything." Indeed a decade after his bold prediction, the mobile revolution has fundamentally reshaped the world.

In his 2008 book *Digital Human*, British financial expert Chris Skinner argued that today's human beings are fourth-generation human beings.[6] First-generation humans became fully human, second-generation humans became civilized and built civilizations, and third-generation humans were commercial beings who industrialized the world and brought about the modern global economy. According to Skinner's diagnosis, fourth-generation humans became digital humans due to the advent of digital technology. It is as if the digital human of the virtual world became one with the *Homo sapiens* of the real world, like in a science fiction movie. *Homo digital* has become a reality.

The famous Israeli historian Yuval Noah Harari went so far as to say that *Homo sapiens*, after conquering Planet Earth over a period of 70,000 years, now harbored loftier ambitions. In his book *Homo Deus*, Harari argued that in the future, mankind will redouble its efforts to achieve happiness and even seek immortality and God-like powers.[7] The book speculates about how *Homo sapiens* might be able to realize its God-like ambitions. Among mankind's possible future strategies, Harari develops and emphasizes the concept of dataism, which refers to a philosophy or mindset of worshiping big data. Harari argues that

6 C. Skinner (2018). *Digital Human: The Fourth Revolution of Humanity Includes Everyone* (Wiley), Hoboken, NJ.
7 Y. N. Harari (2016). *Homo Deus: A Brief History of Tomorrow* (Harvill Secker), London.

a scientific revolution centered on algorithm and data will create a world which puts humans within touching distance of God's immortal powers, heralding the imminent birth of *Homo Deus*.

Professor Robert Shiller, a behavioral economist who is a Nobel laureate in economics, predicted that COVID-19 will fundamentally reshape the way that labor markets and companies operate. As emphasized earlier, thanks to the pandemic, mankind is discovering the underutilized potential of ICT. In particular, employers and office workers are discovering that work from home is almost as efficient as work at office. In general, the pandemic is making companies, people, and the government much more receptive to new technologies. The unprecedented health and economic crisis is, in effect, forcing the world to try and experiment with new ideas, new technologies, and new ways of doing things. People who did not believe in the Fourth Industrial Revolution found out that it is already here and here to stay. Their involuntary participation in the revolution — e.g. work from home, Zoom video-conferencing, and distance learning — is making believers out of them. Seeing is believing, and what is more, doing is believing.

In its April 2020 report on how global consumer trends are changing during COVID-19, McKinsey Consulting found that total consumption in 40 countries fell. On the other hand, the report found that the consumption of online products and services increased. Another report, on five questions facing CEOs in the digital post-COVID recovery, asserted that the digital age had arrived. It advised CEOs to take bold actions to speed up digitalization, which would revive their companies and the global economy.

As noted earlier, in 2016 AlphaGo became the first computer program to defeat a professional Go player, in fact one of the world's top Go players. While the Fourth Industrial Revolution and its many exciting new technologies were under way well before 2016, AlphaGo's shocking victory announced the arrival of the revolution with a big bang. Somewhat ironically, it took an unprecedented pandemic which is shaking the world to its very foundations to make true believers out of skeptics in the Fourth Industrial Revolution. Work from home, distance learning, online shopping, and remote health care is making believers out of all of us. When the revolution is part of your life, you have no choice but to believe in it. In the post-COVID world, the evolution of *Homo sapiens* toward *Robo Sapiens*, *Phono Sapiens*, *Homo Digital*, and *Homo Deus* will gather momentum.

3.4. The Fourth Wave of Globalization Will be Digital Globalization

As noted earlier, COVID-19 will give a strong impetus to retreat from globalization and even champion deglobalization. The third wave of globalization that began with the end of the Second World War was centered on international trade in manufactured goods and international investment in production of manufactured goods. Asia, in particular East Asia, played a central role in the global supply chain of manufactured goods. East Asian countries benefited hugely from their extensive participation in global supply chains. However, COVID-19 exposed the vulnerability of the global supply chain, which is basically a global production paradigm based on international division of labor (with different parts and components produced in different countries), to disruptions in any single country. For example, the lockdown of Wuhan, the original epicenter of the pandemic and a major hub in the global supply chain, disrupted the production of many manufactured goods. To minimize such risks, some global firms may consider reshoring.

Each wave of economic globalization was preceded by an industrial revolution. The first wave of globalization was preceded by the First Industrial Revolution, which witnessed the transition to new manufacturing processes — e.g. hand production to machines, new chemical manufacturing and iron production processes, and the growing use of steam power and waterpower. The second wave of globalization was preceded by the Second Industrial Revolution, which witnessed the expansion of telegraph and railroad networks, gas and water supply, and sewage systems as well as the introduction of new technological systems, especially electrical power and telephones. The third wave of globalization evolved in tandem with the Third Industrial Revolution, which was the digital revolution based on semiconductors, mainframe computing, personal computing, and the internet. The third wave of globalization was already in full retreat before COVID-19 and the pandemic will speed up the retreat. At the same time, COVID-19 will accelerate the Fourth Industrial Revolution, which will spawn its own fourth wave of globalization.

In fact, the fourth wave of globalization may have already started about a decade ago at about the same that the third wave of globalization began to beat a retreat. The global financial crisis slowed down the momentum of global growth. Slower economic growth led to slowdown of international trade and international investment which, in turn, led to further slowdown of global growth. The world economy is thus stuck in a vicious cycle or stagnation trap, which is killing off the third wave of globalization. The malaise of weaker growth initially affected primarily the advanced economies but it soon spread to emerging markets, resulting in a synchronized global slowdown. The slow growth of advanced economies, whose financial systems were paralyzed by the global financial crisis due to the heavy exposure of their banks to US subprime mortgage assets, was exacerbated by structural factors, in particular population aging. Even fast-growing China has visibly slowed down since the global financial crisis. For one, China too is aging rapidly, which is a drag on its economic growth. But above all, as a result of decades of world-topping growth, China has reached income levels at which growth typically slows down. There is no reason to expect China to defy the laws of economic gravity. China, like all other fast-growing economies, has thus begun to slow down, predictably and naturally.

The fourth wave of economic globalization will be centered on skill-intensive services, information and data, and the internet rather than labor-intensive manufacturing, goods, and physical trade. The last 10 years or so have seen a fundamental shift in the global economic landscape, away from manufacturing and toward services. Services have dominated the advanced economies for decades, accounting for the bulk of their national output. Globalization, especially the outsourcing of manufacturing activity to emerging markets with much lower wages, contributed to the hollowing out of the manufacturing sector. This process helps to explain the simmering anger of blue-collar factory workers in advanced economies, such as those in American states with large but declining manufacturing bases such as Michigan and Pennsylvania. Their anger carried Donald Trump to his stunning election victory in November 2016. But there is now a visible shift toward services even in emerging markets such as China. It will be far-fetched to say that China's manufacturing base is hollowing out like Michigan or Pennsylvania, but it is becoming smaller and more high-tech. The share of services in China's GDP is growing steadily as China begins to exit labor-intensive manufacturing industries.

Services are a highly diverse group of industries, ranging from street vendors and mom-and-pop stores to industrial design, marketing, and financial services. They can be low-tech and low-value-added or high-tech and high-value-added. Just as countries competed furiously with each other to capture the high end of the spectrum of the manufacturing, they are competing furiously to capture higher-end services. The most visible trend of the services sector in recent decades has been the dramatic expansion of the ICT services sector, driven by digital entrepreneurship. US tech giants such as Alphabet (the successor to Google), Amazon, and Facebook and Chinese tech giants such as Alibaba and Tencent barely existed a generation ago but have become the world's biggest companies in terms of market value. Jeff Bezos and

Jack Ma are among the world's best-known entrepreneurs. It is these companies and entrepreneurs that best capture the tectonic shift in the structure of the world economy, away from manufacturing toward services, more precisely, toward high-tech, high-value-added services and industries that are based on and driven by the latest technologies.

We noted earlier that the global value chain is U-shaped, with high-value-added services such as research and development and industrial design in the early stages of a production, flanked by high-value-added services such as branding, marketing, and after-sales services in the later stages. The middle was occupied by mass manufacturing, which was low-value-added. Therefore, the bulk of the value of a product lies in high-value-added services in the early and later stages which encircle low-value-added manufacturing in the middle stage. The technologies of the Fourth Industrial Revolution — e.g. robots and artificial intelligence — are reducing the relative importance of low-wage workers, thus eroding the economic rationale underlying the third wave of globalization. But this same technological revolution will give rise to the fourth wave of globalization.

At the same time, there has been a remarkable globalization of information since the advent of the internet. Globalization of information is one type of globalization that is clearly not in retreat. To the contrary, it is marching forward with full force. People all over the world, whether in Bangkok, Nairobi, New York, Paris, or Rio de Janeiro, now watch the same video or read the same news article on the internet all at the same time. Deglobalization may be lifting barriers to the cross-border movement of goods, capital, and labor in the physical world, but there are no such barriers in the virtual world. However, this is not entirely true. For instance, foreign visitors to China find out, to their annoyance and inconvenience, that they cannot access Youtube or Google, due to government-imposed restrictions, also known as the Great Firewall of China. Nevertheless, digital technology has largely demolished the barriers to the international movement of information and data. Thanks to the internet, a person in Shanghai can instantly communicate with and share a document or a picture or a data set with a colleague or friend in Buenos Aires, at the other end of the world for free.

KOF Swiss Economic Institute has been estimating and announcing a comprehensive globalization index, for the world as a whole and for each country. Furthermore, KOF also estimates and announces globalization indices for three key spheres of human activity — economy, society, and politics. According to KOF's estimates (Figure 3.1), for the entire world, the economic globalization index

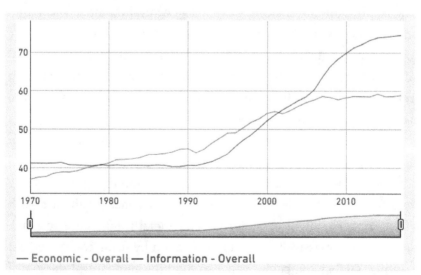

— Economic - Overall — Information - Overall

Figure 3.1. Population aged 65 years and above (% of total population) for most aged countries.
Source: KOF Globalisation Index, KOF Swiss Economic Institute (accessed April 15, 2020).

has stood still since 2008 when the global financial crisis broke out. In contrast, as the figure shows, the information globalization index surpassed the economic globalization index in the early 2000s and it continues to grow. In fact, the gap between the two indices has been widening. The advent of digital technology and its diffusion to developing countries is likely to play a big role in the globalization of information.

According to a 2019 McKinsey report, during the past decade, global value chains based on abundant labor and low wages are declining whereas global value chains based on knowledge-intensive services and highly skilled labor are on the rise.[8] Furthermore, the new emerging global value chain is taking new forms based on digital platforms, internet of things, robots, and artificial intelligence. As noted earlier, the World Economic Forum (WEF) argues that the fourth wave of globalization began around 2008. The central theme of the WEF's annual meeting in 2019 was Globalization 4.0. More specifically, the fourth wave of globalization refers to the transformation of the global supply chain on the basis of the Fourth Industrial Revolution. Each industrial revolution has spawned its own wave of globalization, and it will be no different this time.

In addition, COVID-19 will accelerate the Fourth Industrial Revolution and hence the fourth wave of globalization. Global companies will be able to conclude contracts without physical meeting by using blockchain technology, without any concerns about breach of security. They will be able to use artificial intelligence to make decisions and massively scale up production by using robots and 3D printing. Global companies can also monitor and control the global

---

8 McKinsey Global Institute (2019). "Globalization in transition: The future of trade and value chains," McKinsey&Company.

production and distribution of their products by connecting industrial internet of things to cloud computing. While these developments may sound like science fiction fantasies, in fact the Fourth Industrial Revolution will turn them into realities soon.

The efficiency of the new global value chain will be maximized when all the knowledge of the world is simultaneously deployed through the digital revolution — i.e. the internet and mobile phones. For example, ICT professionals living in Seoul, Tokyo, Mumbai, London, or Mexico City can work closely together with their colleagues at Facebook's headquarters in Silicon Valley. Unskilled factory workers in low-wage developing countries stood at the front and center of global value chains during the third wave of globalization but knowledge workers and professionals will take their place during the fourth wave. This new wave of economic globalization will be reinforced and supported by globalization of knowledge and culture.

The third wave of globalization was characterized by the dominance of American culture and the English language. As such, globalization was sometimes criticized as Americanization. However, during the fourth wave, the culture and knowledge of different countries will spread across the world via the internet. Although English will remain the universal common language, especially among the global elite, languages that were one considered exotic or peripheral are gaining a following in this era of cultural globalization. For instance, K-pop or Korean pop culture has become popular among the youth across the world and the Korean-language songs of BTS, one of Korea's top boy bands, is sung by adoring fans in Asia, the Middle East, Europe, North America, and Latin America. To sum up, while the trade-dominated third wave of globalization is beating a hasty retreat, the digital fourth wave of globalization is in full bloom.

Finally, we noted earlier that economic globalization was already in retreat well before the COVID-19 outbreak and the pandemic may push the world economy into outright deglobalization, or reversal of globalization. At the same time, the dramatic acceleration, amplification, and intensification in the use of ICT or digital technology is giving rise to virtual globalization. National borders become irrelevant as individuals and companies move online.[9] Above all, the rapid flow of ideas, the most significant dimension of globalization, will be facilitated by increased digital connectivity. For example, there has been unprecedented international cooperation on the quest for a COVID-19 vaccine. Therefore, the retreat of the world economy from physical globalization may herald a new golden era of virtual globalization.

---

9 I. Goldin (2020). *"Covid-19 proves globalization is not dead," Financial Times, August 26.*

PART II

Chapter 4

A Tough Road Ahead

4.1. Deglobalization Pushes Asian Economies to the Brink

Asia has benefited from economic globalization more than any other region in the world. Globalization has been hugely beneficial to Japan, South Korea, Taipei,China, Hong Kong, Singapore, Thailand, and Malaysia — all part of the World Bank's *East Asian Miracle* report.[1] These economies grew rapidly for decades on the back of international trade, international investment flows, knowledge exchanges, and global growth. Japan is a special case because it adopted Western technology and had become a high-income economy well before the other Asian economies. Indeed it was the dominant Asian economy from 1960s to 1980s and served as the region's engine of growth and a lead goose in a flying geese paradigm of the region's economic development. The newly industrialized economies or

---

1 World Bank (1993). *The East Asian Miracle (Oxford University Press)*.

NIEs — South Korea, Taipei,China, Hong Kong, and Singapore — are among the very few developing economies that made the leap from low income to middle income to high income within a generation. The vast majority of developing economies never make the jump from middle income to high income. This phenomenon is known to economists as the middle-income trap. Manufacturing exports were the silver bullet that enabled the NIEs to become high-income economies.

In more recent years, the region's middle-income economies have become more prominent.[2] This is largely due to the stunning rise of China, which is now the world's second largest economy. But to a lesser extent, it is also non-negligibly due to the emergence of the five large Association of Southeast Asian Nations (ASEAN) middle-income economies: Indonesia, Malaysia, the Philippines, Thailand, and Vietnam. The success of a developing East Asia can be attributed to a set of policies that include outward orientation, investment in human capital, and sound economic governance. In particular, policies to promote trade openness exposed the domestic industries of these economies to international competition while facilitating inflows of foreign investment and know-how. Indeed, globalization-powered rapid growth spread from Japan to the NIEs to the five ASEAN economies in what has been described as a flying geese paradigm.

Malaysia and Thailand grew rapidly on the back of manufacturing exports although they were not as successful as the NIEs. While Indonesia lags behind Malaysia and Thailand in export-oriented industrialization, it exports large amounts of commodities such as palm oil, coal briquettes, petroleum gas, copper ore, and gold. In fact, Indonesia is also continuously increasing exports of manufactured

---

2   *A. D. Mason and S. Shetty (2018). A Resurgent East Asia – Navigating a Changing World (World Bank).*

products. The Philippines has long been viewed as the laggard of East Asia and it was the only major market economy that was not part of the World Bank's East Asian Miracle economies. However, the Philippines is one of the world's largest exporter of workers, and the remittances from those workers, which exceeded US$35 billion (about 9.3% of GDP) in 2019, have long been a mainstay of the economy.

One country that was too big to be a flying goose following Japan's lead was China. In fact, China's economic transformation is probably the single most significant development in the global economic landscape since the second half of the 20th century. Never before had such a huge country grown so fast for so long in human history. Given China's prominent role in today's world economy, it is easy to forget that the country endured crushing poverty before it began to adopt market-oriented reforms under Deng Xiaoping, who was the country's paramount leader from 1978 to 1989. The centrally planned economy under socialism bottled up the Chinese people's huge reservoir of entrepreneurial energy, and China remained a typical poor, underdeveloped country. When Beijing finally threw off the numbing shackles of sclerotic socialism and allowed the market to allocate resources, the predictable outcome was an explosion of entrepreneurship and private enterprise which kept China growing at double-digit rates for a generation. Undoubtedly, the shift of economic system from a centrally planned economy dominated by government bureaucrats to a market economy dominated by entrepreneurs was the central catalyst of China's remarkable emergence as an economic superpower.

Another potent driver of China's stunning rise was globalization or, more precisely, China's ability to effectively leverage globalization for its economic benefit. As soon as Deng Xiaoping started to open up the economy to market forces, foreign investors started to flock to China from all over the world. The marriage of foreign capital and Chinese labor was a marriage made in heaven. Companies from America, Western Europe, Japan, South Korea, and the other NIEs poured in to build factories to take advantage of China's seemingly inexhaustible supply of low-wage workers. In addition to low wages, Chinese workers were hardworking and disciplined, which meant that they were ideal factory workers. In addition, labor laws and regulations were relatively weak, minimizing the risk of labor unrest. Therefore, the companies of the advanced countries that invested in China were able to drastically cut their production costs. Millions of Chinese workers found jobs at the foreign-owned factories, which contributed greatly to China's rapid export-oriented industrialization. The arrangement was win-win for both China and foreign investors. China has become the Factory of the World and the world's top exporter, selling almost US$2.5 trillion worth of goods abroad in 2019. China has also become the world's second biggest importer, buying US$2.13 trillion worth of goods from abroad in 2019.

Even India, which is widely viewed as having missed the globalization boat, is, in fact, benefiting tangibly from globalization. India, which is a large economy based mainly on domestic demand, has carved out a global niche for itself as a leading exporter of information and communication technology (ICT) services. In 2018–2019, India exported around US$137 billion worth of ICT services. The industry boasts globally competitive companies such as Infosys, Tata Consultancy Services, and Wipro, and has been a significant engine of growth for the economy.

According to a September 2019 McKinsey report,[3] not only has Asia benefited hugely from globalization but also its share of globalization

---

3 O. Tonby, J. Woetzel, W. Choi, K. Eloot, R. Dhawan, J. Seong, and P. Wang (2019). "The future of Asia — Asian flows and networks are defining the next phase of globalization," McKinsey Global Institute.

is rising rapidly. Asia's share of global trade has risen from 27% in 2005–2007 to 33% in 2015–2017 and its share of capital flows has similarly increased from 13% in 2005–2007 to 23% in 2015–2017. All other indicators of globalization point to a growing imprint of Asia. The corresponding figures are 52% and 65% for global patents filed, 58% and 64% of global cargo traffic, and 43% and 48% for international students. Asia's growing role in globalization goes hand in hand with its growing role in the global economic landscape. The center of gravity of the world economy is clearly shifting toward Asia from Europe and North America. In 2000, Asia accounted for 32% of world output in terms of purchasing power parity (PPP) — i.e. taking into account the cheaper prices of non-tradable goods such as haircuts in poorer countries. Asia's share of global output increased to 42% in 2017 and is expected to rise further to 52% by 2040. Even in non-PPP terms, Asia's share was 34% in 2017 and is projected to increase to 46% by 2040. Furthermore, Asia, especially China, has become the main engine of growth for the rest of the world. Asia is not only a huge exporter but also a huge market for other regions due to its rapidly rising living standards. In this connection, while Asia accounted for 23% of global consumption in 2000, its share rose to 28% in 2017 and is projected to rise further to 39% by 2040. In short, successful globalization transformed Asia's role from a supporting actor to a leading actor on the global stage. Globalization has brought on the onset of the Asian Century.

What is remarkable about the Asian experience with globalization is that in Asia, globalization contributed to more inclusive growth that has benefited large segments of the population rather than an elite few. Asian countries witnessed the emergence of a large middle class and a drastic reduction of poverty. Export-oriented industrialization enabled millions of poor rural workers to receive higher wages in the manufacturing sector. The expansion of trade and upgrading of technology gave rise to an overall sense of optimism and can-do spirit, which imbued Asia with a unique economic dynamism unparalleled in the rest of the world. The key to Asia's successful globalization was that the governments invested heavily in both human capital — i.e. health and education — and physical capital — e.g. roads and power plants — which enabled the region to take full advantage of the opportunities offered by globalization.[4] Just as significantly, the government created an environment that was conducive for private businesses to globalize — e.g. relatively low trade barriers and liberalized foreign exchange markets — which enabled Asian companies to import the inputs they need to produce manufactured products.

The defining feature of the Asian economic miracle is globalization. That is, for Asia as a whole, the single most important factor driving the region's remarkable economic success, which resulted in a dramatic improvement in general living standards and historically unprecedented reduction in poverty, is its active participation in international trade and investment. The contrast between Asia, especially East Asia, and Latin America, in terms of their approach toward globalization is striking. While Asian countries fully embraced globalization with an outward-looking, export-oriented growth strategy, many Latin American countries instead chose an inward-looking growth strategy that sought to replace imports with domestic production. The verdict is in and it is crystal clear. While Asia grew by leaps and bounds to become the

---

4 A. D. Mason and S. Shetty (2018). *A Resurgent East Asia — Navigating a Changing World* (World Bank: Washington D.C.); I. Nabi (2016). "Globalization: What the West can learn from Asia," Brookings blog. (https://www.brookings.edu/blog/future-development/2016/06/30/globalization-what-the-west-can-learn-from-asia/).

world's most dynamic region, Latin America has stagnated in a low-growth trap.

Given the central role of globalization in Asia's economic miracle and the huge economic benefits that Asia derived from globalization, it is no surprise that Asia has emerged as a champion and advocate of globalization. China, in particular, has become a leading spokesperson for globalization at various international forums. For instance, in May 2017, China hosted 27 leaders in a summit in which it touted a new Silk Road as a major avenue to new globalization. It is also possible to interpret the Belt and Road Initiative discussed in the previous chapter as an example of China's leadership in globalization. China's newfound status as a champion of globalization stands in sharp contrast to America's inward-looking, isolationist "America First" worldview under the Trump Administration. But "America First" is merely a symptom of a much broader trend in America and Europe. Although America and European countries also benefited greatly from globalization, there is much less popular support for globalization there than in Asian countries. The reason is that a large part of the American and European populations believe that globalization only benefits a tiny elite — e.g. investment bankers in London or New York. They associate globalization with blue-collar workers losing their jobs due to cheap imports and widening inequality. The erosion of popular support for globalization is turning to downright hostility toward globalization. Therefore, there is a big gulf in public attitudes toward globalization between Asia versus America and Europe.

As explained earlier, globalization was already in full retreat before COVID-19, and the pandemic will strengthen and accelerate the slowdown of globalization — i.e. slowbalisation — into downright reversal of globalization — i.e. deglobalization. Precisely because Asia benefited the most from globalization, in particular the third wave of globalization, Asia will suffer the most from deglobalization. A region that grew rapidly for decades on the back of international trade and investment is bound to be hit hard by slowdown and perhaps even contraction of trade and foreign direct investment (FDI). Asia's success in leveraging globalization to its advantage is epitomized by the region playing the leading role in global supply chain of manufactured products. However, COVID-19 brutally exposed the vulnerability of the global manufacturing supply chain to any single country along the chain. Furthermore, the pandemic will accelerate and reinforce the Fourth Industrial Revolution, including technologies that will enable the replacement of factory workers with machines — i.e. robotics and artificial intelligence. The global supply chain of manufacturing, which was anchored around Asian countries, is under serious threat.

Asia's outward-looking, export-oriented growth strategy was tailor-made for the free trade, free market world order spearheaded by America after the Second World War. However, retreat from globalization, which was already underway a few years ago, will morph into full-scale deglobalization due to COVID-19. Deglobalization, in turn, will make it more difficult for the world economy to recover from the economic downturn brought about by the pandemic. Just as globalization — more trade and more foreign investment — was a potent driver of growth, deglobalization — less trade and less foreign investment — will act as a drag on growth. In the worst-case scenario, if the pandemic is not contained and the confidence of businesses and consumers fails to recover, deglobalization may even push the world economy over the precipice into a second Great Depression. Globalized Asia, which depends heavily on trade and foreign investment, thus faces an existential crisis.

As explained earlier, global trade and foreign investment were already on the wane for a decade or so before the COVID-19 outbreak. Global trade, which collapsed after the global financial crisis of 2008, has not yet recovered to pre-crisis levels, in terms of global GDP. As seen in Figures 4.1 and 4.2, most Asian economies, except Vietnam and Japan, have seen a decline in exports as a share of GDP.

Global cross-border investment has not even recovered to 50% of its pre-crisis level. Furthermore, the international movement of labor has also slowed down since 2011. Globalization refers to the growing integration of international goods, capital, and labor markets. Yet we are now witnessing the growing disintegration of global goods, capital, and labor markets. The tangible deceleration of Asia' growth since the global financial crisis is partly due to the slowdown of globalization. China's maturing and consequent slowdown is another major factor

Figure 4.1. Share of exports in GDP for most outward Asian economies.
Source: World Bank's DataBank (accessed August 15, 2020).

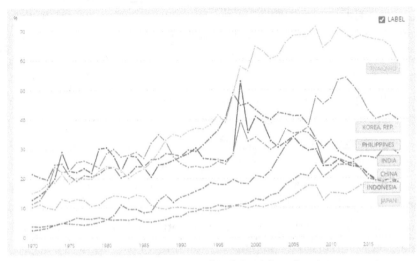

Figure 4.2. Exports of goods and services (% of GDP) for other Asian countries.
Source: World Bank's DataBank (accessed August 11, 2020).

but a region that grew rapidly on the back of globalization will inevitably suffer the fallout from slower globalization.

It is revealing to look at the recent trends of South Korea, a country widely admired and emulated by developing countries in Asia and beyond for its jump from a low-income to high-income economy within one generation. South Korea has become the global benchmark for leveraging globalization to power economic growth so it is worthwhile to focus on South Korea as we assess the economic impact of deglobalization on Asia. South Korea has attracted more attention than the other NIEs, which are much smaller economies. Indeed Hong Kong and Singapore are cities so their relevance for countries is somewhat limited. South Korean exports have been steadily declining in relative terms. In 2008, the year that global financial crisis erupted, the ratio of goods and services exports to GDP was 47.6%. The figure fell only slightly to 45.5% in 2009, the worst year of the crisis. The ratio subsequently rose to 54.1% by 2012 but it fell steadily to 39.8% in 2019. There has thus been a 14.3% drop between 2012 and 2019. This is a troubling development for a country that depends heavily on international trade for growth.

FDI has been falling for quite some time now. The decline began well before the global financial crisis. Immediately after the Asian financial crisis of 1997–1998, the South Korean government actively courted foreign investors as part of the structural reforms mandated by the International Monetary Fund (IMF) in an effort to shake up South Korea's corporate governance. As a result, the ratio of FDI to GDP shot up to 2.2% by 1999. However, as seen in Figure 4.3, the ratio

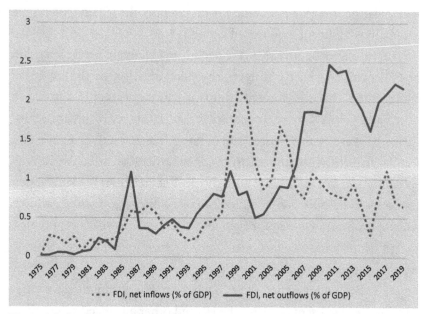

Figure 4.3. South Korea's foreign direct investment (% of GDP), 1975–2019.
Source: Authors' graphical representation using World Bank's World Development Indicators.

steadily declined afterward to reach 0.3% by 2015 and 0.6% in 2019. On the other hand, foreign investment by South Korean companies in other countries continued to rise until in 2006 it exceeded investment by foreign companies in South Korea. By 2010, FDI by South Korean companies reached 2.5% of GDP, almost three times the FDI by foreign companies in South Korea. In 2019, South Korean FDI was 2.2%, more than three times the foreign FDI. The rapid growth of South Korean FDI reflects the growing strength of South Korean companies.

By the way, South Korean companies are not alone in investing abroad. The three smaller NIEs have long been major sources of investment in other countries, especially China. China itself has become one of the world's biggest foreign investors, investing US$98 billion in 2019. Even Indian companies invested US$12 billion in 2019. In line with Asia's growing weight in the world economy, the region has become a globally significant exporter of capital.

In the case of South Korea, the decline in FDI inflows and expansion of FDI outflows partly reflects the deterioration of the business environment. That is, foreign companies are investing less in South Korea and South Korean companies are investing more outside South Korea because South Korea is becoming less attractive. Those FDI trends, in turn, contributed to the steady decline in South Korea's economic growth rate, along with the decline in exports. A small open economy like South Korea will inevitably suffer a growth slowdown when globalization retreats or even reverses. All major Asian economies, except China and India, are small open economies, which is why they are also experiencing a slowdown.

To make matters worse, COVID-19 wrought economic havoc first on China and subsequently on the US and other advanced economies. For South Korea and the rest of Asia, China, America, and Europe are core export markets. According to official statistics, South Korea's exports fell by 25.4% in April 2020 compared to April 2019 and then by 23.7%, 10.9%, and 7.0% year on year, respectively, in the following three months. The situation varies across Asia but clearly the pandemic has had a pronounced negative impact on the region's export. For instance, China saw its exports contract by 6.2% year on year in the first half of 2020. The contraction was smaller than expected due to strong exports of medical equipment and supplies used in the fight against COVID-19. On the other hand, the exports of other major Asian economies suffered a bigger blow to their exports. For instance, the exports of India, Indonesia, and Japan fell by 36.5%, 29%, and 28%, respectively, in May 2020 compared to a year earlier. Countries with large tourism industries, such as Thailand and Cambodia, have suffered sharp reductions in the number of foreign tourists due to flight bans and border closures. Deglobalization is dealing a heavy blow to Asian economies.

In contrast to the Asian financial crisis of 1997–1998, exports do not hold the key to Asia's economic recovery. During the Asian crisis, the IMF's bailout packages helped to stabilize the crisis-hit economies, but they did not bring growth. Instead what enabled South Korea and the other crisis-hit Asian economies to grow again after contracting sharply in 1998 was exports, especially to a booming America. The sharp depreciation of Asian currencies made Asian exports cheaper in global markets and contributed to the export surge. That is, Asia was able to export its way out of the Asian crisis. In fact, thanks to soaring exports, the region was able to mount a rapid and robust V-shaped recovery. For example, South Korea saw its economy shrink by 5.1% in 1998 but bounce back with a strong growth rate of 11.5% in 1999.

The global financial crisis of 2008–2009 originated in the US financial sector. More specifically, the US financial regulator's lax regulation allowed greed-crazed Wall Street to develop so-called financial innovations, most notably mortgage-backed securities, which artificially hid the risks inherent in mortgage loans to subprime borrowers — i.e. borrowers with poor credit ratings. The US subprime mortgage crisis spread like a wildfire across the Atlantic to paralyze the financial systems of Western European countries as well. European banks, like their American counterparts, were also heavily exposed to subprime mortgages. However, the financial systems of financially backward countries such as China and other Asian countries had only minimal exposure to the toxic US assets, which explains why they were able to continue to function more or less smoothly without any major disruptions.

China then embarked on massive government spending and monetary loosening that supported not only China's growth but also indirectly the growth of other Asian countries and the world. Astonishingly, in 2009, China grew by 9.1% when world trade volume fell by 11% and global output fell by 0.6%. Small, open, export-dependent Asian countries such as South Korea, the other NIEs, and ASEAN economies were again able to export their way out of crisis, albeit to China rather than US and other advanced economies. While Asia's financial underdevelopment contributed to the resilience of its financial systems, exports to the robust Chinese economy were the key to the resilience of its economies.

So far the economic damage from COVID-19 has been largely limited to the real economy rather than the financial systems. In America and Europe, decisive and forceful liquidity support by central banks helped to stabilize financial systems and keep credit flowing from banks to firms and households. Asian central banks too are loosening their monetary policies — i.e. lowering interest rates — to support their banks and financial markets. However, if the economic downturn persists, many companies and households will be unable to repay their loans. The growth of bad loans will jeopardize the stability of financial systems and may even lead to a financial crisis. In this worst-case scenario, the world economy and global financial systems will be paralyzed at the same time, potentially triggering another Great Depression.

To make matters worse, the trade and technological war between America and China shows no signs of abating and, to the contrary, seems to get worse since the outbreak of COVID-19. For example, Washington is waging war against Huawei, the Chinese tech giant which is a pioneer in 5G mobile network, and is threatening to ban even TikTok and WeChat, popular social networking services (SNS) that are based in China but have spread worldwide. There are also concerns that the Phase 1 trade deal between the two giants, reached in January 2020, may be annulled, triggering a re-escalation of the trade war. Most Asian economies are small open economies that depend heavily on exports for their economic growth. For most of these economies, China and America are two of the biggest export markets. This means that the US–China trade conflict casts further gloom over their economic prospects, which have already deteriorated sharply thanks to COVID-19.

In summary, the third wave of globalization that dominated the world economy since the end of the Second World War is coming to an end. The onset of COVID-19, which will strengthen nationalism and protectionism, especially in the advanced economies, will transform the retreat from globalization or slowdown of globalization into full-fledged deglobalization. Countries view open borders with much greater wariness and apprehension than ever before. After all, it was open borders and globalization that allowed a new coronavirus from a wet market in Wuhan, China, to wreak havoc on global health and the world economy within a few months. The pandemic also exposed the vulnerability of global manufacturing supply chains to factory closures or other production disruptions in any single location, whether it was Wuhan or northern Italy. Companies, especially those in advanced economies, may opt for shorter and more secure supply chains that are less vulnerable to shocks. Another sign of deglobalization in the post-COVID world is the intense competition for medical equipment and supplies during the pandemic. The third wave of globalization, which brought about a golden era of prosperity in Asia, is clearly on the wane. Deglobalization, which looms on the horizon, will push Asian economies to the brink of the precipice.

4.2. Asia's Looming Demographic Crisis

As explained in Section 4.1, deglobalization will seriously challenge Asia's growth momentum in the post-COVID world. However, slowdown or even reversal of international trade and investment is only one of the several challenges facing Asia's growth in the post-COVID world. Above all, Asia's population, which used to be young, is growing older. As a result, the demographic dividend which has been a major contributor to Asia's growth in the past, is coming to an end. Demographic dividend refers to an acceleration of economic growth associated with a rise in the share of working-age population in the total population. Other things equal, an economy's output will be larger if a larger share of the population is working. The immediate catalyst of the demographic dividend is a decline in fertility rates which causes a corresponding decline in the youth dependency ratio, or the share of youth in total population. According to the life cycle theory of savings, individuals tend to save during their working years and draw down their savings after they retire. Therefore, Asia's demographic dividend has also contributed to the region's high savings and investment rates. The demographic dividend is not an automatic consequence of favorable demographic changes but depends on the ability of the economy to productively use the additional workers. The success of East Asian countries in taking full advantage of their potential demographic dividend by creating a policy and institutional environment that is conducive — e.g. flexible labor markets and promotion of labor-intensive manufacturing — played a major role in the East Asian Miracle.

Unfortunately for Asia, the demographic dividend that lubricated the region's rapid growth is now giving way to older populations in which economically inactive retirees account for a high and growing share of total population. As the large working-age cohort that drove the demographic dividend grows older, population aging sets in. As in other parts of the world, Asia's population aging reflects the combination of two factors — falling fertility and rising life expectancy. As seen in Figures 4.4 and 4.5, compared to other regions of the world, Asia's fertility rate has been decreasing more rapidly while its life expectancy has been increasing more rapidly.

Higher living standards and rapidly changing social conditions such as urbanization enable Asians to live longer and induce families to have fewer children. Other things equal, a fall in the share of the working-age population will lead to a lower output. To some extent,

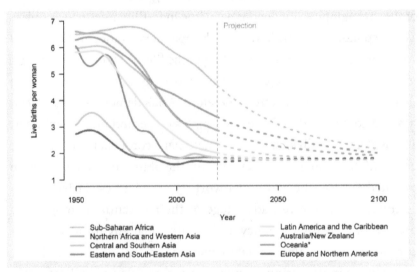

Figure 4.4. Estimated and projected total fertility by region, 1950–2100 (medium-variant projection).

Source: United Nations, Department of Economic and Social Affairs, Population Division (2019). *World Population Prospects 2019.*

* excluding Australia and New Zealand

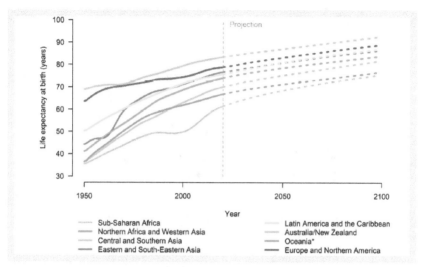

Figure 4.5. Estimated and projected life expectancy at birth for both sexes by region, 1950–2100 (medium-variant projection).
Source: United Nations, Department of Economic and Social Affairs, Population Division (2019). *World Population Prospects 2019.*
* excluding Australia and New Zealand

policies such as opening up to immigration, encouraging higher participation of women in the workforce, and raising the retirement age can compensate for the prospective decline in the labor force, but population aging will nevertheless have an adverse impact on labor supply. Aging also implies that each worker will have to support more and more retirees under public pension and health care systems. All in all, while demographic trends were conducive for economic growth in the past, they will be markedly less so in the future.

Among the subregions, East Asia has the highest proportion of population aged 65 years or above, with more than half the number of developing Asia's older people residing there (Figure 4.6). Within the broader region-wide trend of population aging, Asian economies are

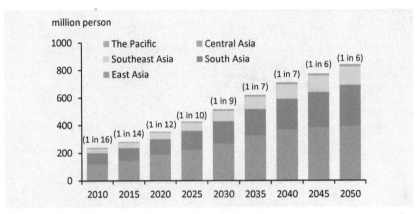

Figure 4.6. Population aged 65 years and above by sub-regions of Asia and the Pacific. *Source:* UN Population Projections (accessed January 15, 2020).

at very different stages of the demographic transition due to large differences in the timing and speed of decline in fertility and mortality rates (Figure 4.7). Broadly speaking, we can divide Asian countries into three groups in terms of the demographic transition. The first group of countries, high-income countries such as Japan, South Korea, and Singapore, are in the advanced stage of population aging. A second group of countries, primarily upper middle-income countries such as China and Thailand, are in the intermediate stage of population aging. Even some lower middle-income countries, most notably Vietnam, are already in this middle stage. Finally, a third group of countries, primarily lower middle-income countries such as India and the Philippines, are in the early stages of population aging. However, even in these younger countries, the demographic transition toward older populations and their journey toward a grayer demographic landscape has already begun.

Notwithstanding their demographic diversity, Asian countries are experiencing important common changes to their age structures. In all countries, the percentage of children in the population is declining or

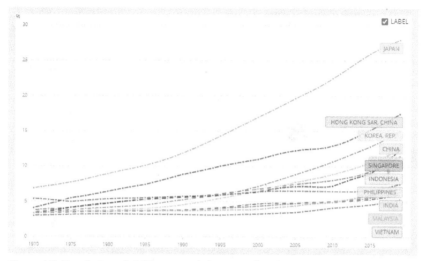

Figure 4.7. Population aged 65 years and above in select Asian economies, 1970–2019.
Source: World Bank's DataBank (accessed August 15, 2020).

has already reached low levels. This is in large part due to a rapid decline in birth rates. The share of the working-age population is increasing or has reached very high levels. Until recently, an increase in working-age population has had a direct and favorable impact on growth in per capita income. However, this is a transitory phenomenon. As seen in Figure 4.8, the share of the working-age population has already started to decline in some East Asian economies. Above all, the share of older population is increasing very rapidly in Asia. The increase has been particularly pronounced in high-income countries in large part because they have very low fertility rates. However, lower-income countries in the region will also experience significant increase in the share of older population in the next few decades. Indeed, as seen in Figure 4.9, Asian economies such as South Korea, Singapore, Taipei,China, Macao, Thailand, and Hong Kong are among top 10 economies that are

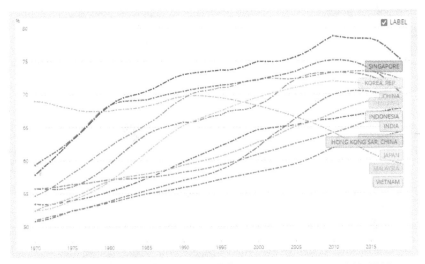

Figure 4.8. Population aged 15–64 years in select Asian economies, 1970–2019.
Source: World Bank's DataBank (accessed August 15, 2020).

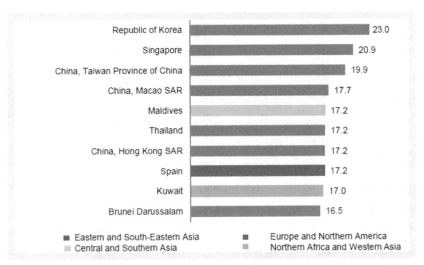

Figure 4.9. Economies with the largest percentage point increase in the share of older persons aged 65 years or over between 2019 and 2050.
Source: United Nations, Department of Economic and Social Affairs, Population Division (2019). *World Population Prospects 2019.*

projected to experience the largest percentage point increase in the share of older persons aged 65 years or over between 2019 and 2050.

As discussed earlier, population aging will have important implications for labor supply, savings and capital formation, and overall economic performance. According to recent studies, an increase in old-age population share hampers economic growth. Furthermore, the negative impact of population aging on economic growth increases as population aging deepens.[5] Aging will also affect the sustainability of publicly funded pension and health care systems, poverty, and intergenerational inequality. Such far-ranging implications have already raised alarm in higher-income Asian countries. In addition, lower-income countries with relatively young populations will be confronting the same kinds of challenges that are now faced by their higher-income neighbors in the not-so-distant future. For Asian policy-makers, population aging gives rise to two major strategic objectives, which sometimes come into sharp conflict with each other. The first is to develop socioeconomic systems that will provide economic security for the growing elderly population. The second is to sustain strong economic growth in the face of population aging over the next few decades. Achieving these two objectives will require policies that promote savings, investment in human capital, well-functioning financial and labor markets, and macroeconomic stability. It will also require avoiding disproportionately large transfer programs for the elderly.

South Korea is perhaps the best country to examine to get a better idea of the huge risk that population aging poses for developing Asia.

---

5   H.-H. Lee, K. Shin, and D. Park (2017). "Population aging and its impact on economic growth," *Economic Analysis*, Vol. 196, pp. 159–179, Economic and Social Research Institute, Cabinet Office, Government of Japan; H.-H. Lee and K. Shin (2019). "Nonlinear effects of population aging on economic growth," *Japan & World Economy*, Vol. 51, No. 100963.

Its transformation into a highly innovative advanced economy within a generation made it a benchmark model for many developing countries. At the same time, it has experienced exceptionally rapid demographic changes. Deglobalization comes at the worst possible time for South Korea, which is already suffering a sharp reduction in long-term potential growth due to low fertility and population aging. South Korea's total fertility rate — or the expected number of children per woman — was 0.92 in 2019, the lowest among all member countries of the Organisation for Economic Cooperation and Development (OECD), an organization of primarily advanced economies. The former managing director of the IMF, Christine Lagarde, is said to have called South Korea a collective suicide society in light of its unprecedentedly rapid population aging. While collective suicide might be too strong a term and even provocative, it is a more or less accurate description of the dramatic demographic changes that are shaking up South Korea.

A peek at the following statistics indicates that Ms. Lagarde had a valid point. As recently as 1970, there were more than a million babies born in South Korea every year. By 1980, the number of births dropped to 860,000 and by 1990, it dropped further to 650,000. By 2002, the number of births fell more than 50% compared to 1970 to 490,000. The sharp decline in fertility shows no signs of slowing down. In 2019, there were only 303,000 births. While it is natural for countries to have declining fertility rates and increasing elderly population as they get richer — the correlation between income and aging seems to be a law-like stylized fact — what is exceptional about the South Korean demographic transition is its sheer speed and scale. South Korea is facing a population cliff. Population aging poses a clear and present danger to the country's economic growth and social stability.

The share of the South Korean population that is aged 65 years or over is steadily on the rise. By 2018, the share surpassed 14%, making South Korea an aged society. At the same time, the share of working-age population — i.e. aged between 15 and 64 years — continued to rise until 2016 but started declining since 2017, as seen in Figure 4.10. As a result, the elderly support ratio, which is the number of elderly per 100 working-age persons, surpassed 10 for the first time in 2000 and continued to rise by 0.5 every year until it reached 20 in 2018. In other words, in 2010, 10 workers had to support 1 senior citizen but by 2018, 5 workers had to support 1 senior citizen. For the working-age population, the economic burden of supporting the elderly has more than doubled in less than two decades. The scale and speed of South Korea's population aging is jaw dropping. No wonder the IMF's Ms. Lagarde used the term collective suicide to describe it.

The dire population cliff facing South Korea today is very similar to the demographic crisis that Japan faced since the early 1990s, which marks the beginning of a prolonged period of economic stagnation. In 1991, the share of the elderly in Japan's population surpassed 12%, and by 1995 the figure topped 14%, pushing Japan into the status of an aged society. On the other hand, the share of the working-age population in the total population started to decline since 1993, as seen in Figure 4.11.

Since the bursting of an asset price bubble in early 1992, when inflated real estate and property prices came crashing down to earth, the Japanese economy grew at a glacial pace for more than 20 years. Japan's long-term economic stagnation became so well known that some economists even coined an unflattering term for long-term economic decline — Japanization. Whenever a major economy showed signs of a long-term stagnation, it was said to be at risk of Japanization.

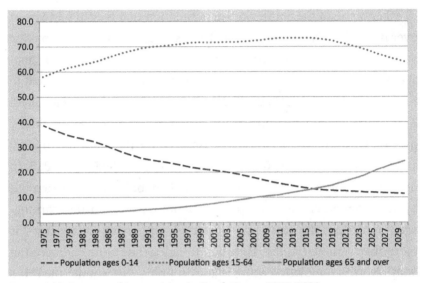

Figure 4.10. Demographic transition in South Korea, 1975–2030.
Source: Authors' graphical representation using data from South Korea Statistical Information Service.

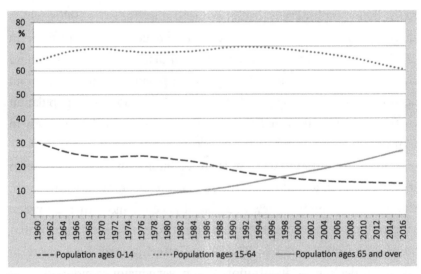

Figure 4.11. Demographic transition in Japan, 1960–2016.
Source: Authors' graphical representation using World Bank's World Development Indicators.

Abenomics, the set of economic policies advocated by Japanese Prime Minister Shinzo Abe since the December 2012 elections, showed some signs of injecting life into the Japanese economy. In particular, two of the three arrows of Abenomics — i.e. monetary easing and fiscal stimulus — helped to keep the Japanese economy afloat. The third arrow — structural reform — was not implemented. In any case, Abenomics may have provided some short-lived temporary relief but it has failed to revive long-lost economic dynamism.

The big concern for South Korea is that it is following in Japan's demographic steps, with a lag of about 20 to 25 years. It is worth recalling that Japan's economic decline began with the bursting of the property bubble in early 1992. The property bubble still shows no signs of bursting but in light of the Japanese experience, the chance of the bubble bursting is on the rise. If you have a fixed number of properties and a shrinking population, then common sense alone tells us that property prices will eventually fall. They may even collapse, as they did in Japan in early 1992. The mostly empty apartments of Japan's ghost towns, inhabited by only few old people, should serve as a stark warning for South Korea.

Of course, bursting of the property bubble is not the only economic risk associated with rapid population aging. As stated earlier, older populations are associated with a broader loss of economic dynamism. For instance, younger people tend to be more innovative, risk-taking, and entrepreneurial, and entrepreneurship is the engine of growth and innovation in any market economy. An iconic example of youthful entrepreneurial energy is Steve Jobs and his friends creating Apple in a garage in a California suburb. Steve Jobs, Jack Ma, and most entrepreneurs generally start young. Therefore, as the population grows older, entrepreneurship and thus economic dynamism declines. In

South Korea, the critical problem of lack of entrepreneurship is further exacerbated by lack of entrepreneurial spirit even among the young. Many, if not most, young South Koreans aspire to become government bureaucrats, even low-level bureaucrats, which does not bode well for the country's economic future.

To make matters worse, South Korea's population aging is set to accelerate further. According to the global population forecasts of the United Nations, South Korea is projected to become the fastest aging country in the world. At the same time, economic growth has continuously declined. Between the 1960s and 1980s, the South Korean economy often grew by double digits — i.e. by more than 10%. However, the South Korean economy shrank by more than 5% in 1998 as a result of the Asian financial crisis before rebounding to a growth of more than 10% in 1999. But since then growth steadily fell until it reached 0.9% in 2009, during the global financial crisis. The economy staged a V-shaped recovery in 2010, growing by 6.8%, but the growth slowdown resumed, barely growing by 2.0% by 2019 (Figure 4.12).

South Korea's secular growth slowdown is due to a wide range of factors. Above all, as a country grows richer, its economic growth decelerates, as the historical experience of advanced countries shows. In that sense, South Korea's slowdown is natural and expected. Indeed, it would be strange and puzzling if South Korea did not slow down; having said that, the sheer speed of the South Korean growth deceleration is exceptional. Just as South Korea's economic rise was unprecedented, so is its slowdown. The most likely culprit for the exceptionally rapid slowdown is the negative impact of South Korea's demographic collapse on the country's potential growth — i.e. growth of long-term productive capacity.

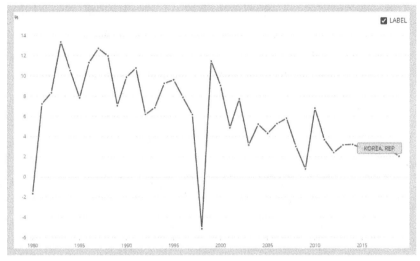

Figure 4.12. GDP growth (annual %) in South Korea, 1980–2019.
Source: World Bank's DataBank (accessed August 15, 2020).

The economy is like the human body in many ways. For one, both consist of countless cells. For a person, aging means that old cells increasingly outnumber young cells. As the number of older cells increase, the supply of oxygen and nutrients to the body is impeded, causing loss of vitality. For the economy, a cell is a person, who is both a producer and a consumer. A person actively produces and consumes goods and services when he or she is young but reduces both production and consumption as he or she grows older. This is why an economy loses its dynamism when the share of the older population increases and the share of the younger population correspondingly decreases. As stated earlier, one important specific channel through which population aging deprives an economy of its dynamism is entrepreneurship, which tends to be associated with younger populations.

In fact, one of our research studies finds that if the share of the population 65 years and older in the total population increases by 10%, the annual economic growth drops by 3.5%. This finding has sobering implications for South Korea's future economic prospects. If the elderly share of population rises from 14% in 2017 to 24% in 2029 (Japan's figure in 2012), unless there are other changes, such as structural reforms, which dramatically boosts productivity, South Korea's economy will begin to shrink rather than expand.

In other words, South Korea is staring straight into Japan's lost decades or Japanization. Furthermore, South Korea may be in a worse position than Japan when the latter faced its population cliff in the early 1990s. At that time, Japan was already a well-established, high-income economy, but South Korea has transitioned from upper-middle income to high income only recently. Furthermore, in the early 1990s, Japan's industrial competitiveness was world class and it enjoyed abundant financial capital. South Korea, on the other hand, finds itself in a much more precarious position and is losing whatever comparative advantage it has on the global marketplace. It is losing its advantage in shipbuilding, steel and chemical industries, and even automobiles and semiconductors to fast-growing emerging markets, especially China. A slew of regulations and red tape is hindering entrepreneurship and the emergence of new high-tech industries.

An earlier book by one of this book's authors, which was published in the immediate aftermath of the 1997–1998 Asian financial crisis, likened that crisis to a stroke suffered by individuals.[6] The immediate cause of that crisis, which began in Thailand and spread to other East Asian countries, was a shortage of foreign currency due to the massive

---

6 C. Harvie and H.-H. Lee (2003). *South Korea's Economic Miracle: Fading or Reviving?* (*Palgrave Macmillan*).

withdrawal of foreign capital invested in South Korea. It was as if a completely healthy person suddenly collapsed due to stroke amid the cold winter winds. However, people who collapse from stroke are often not healthy. Rather, many stroke victims tend to smoke and drink a lot, eat a lot of meat, and do not exercise regularly. As a result, they suffer from high blood pressure and high cholesterol, which increases the chances of a stroke.

Before the outbreak of the Asian financial crisis of 1997–1998, large South Korean corporations invested excessively and diversified into industries outside their core competency areas. Financial institutions were borrowing excessively, a lot of it short-term and in foreign currency. Finally, during the course of South Korea's government-led industrialization process, a lot of inefficiencies associated with cozy ties between politics and business built up. All these factors contributed to the flight of foreign investors and capital from South Korea during the Asian crisis. Yet the South Korean economy was able to stage a V-shaped recovery because the world economy was in good shape. South Korea and the other crisis-hit economies were able to export their way out of the crisis, helped further by currencies which depreciated sharply during the crisis. On top of that, South Korea was a young economy, with the share of population aged 65 years and above standing at only 6.4%.

However, the current COVID-19 health and economic crisis comes at a much worse time. South Korea is already in the midst of a secular stagnation due to rapid population aging. Furthermore, South Korea cannot possibly export its way out of this crisis since the virus has devastated the entire world economy. If the South Korean economy were a person, it would be suffering from an underlying medical condition such as chronic diabetes. It is well known that the COVID-19 fatality rate of young and healthy individuals is quite low. That is, due to strong immune system, a young and healthy person is unlikely to succumb to the virus. The opposite is true for older people with underlying medical conditions. The fatality rate is much higher for such individuals, who account for most of COVID-related deaths. The same is true for economies. Healthy young economies can withstand and overcome even large external shocks. Their intrinsic economic dynamism, e.g. a large reservoir of innovative entrepreneurship, empowers them with a robust resilience.

The problem for South Korea is that it is not a healthy young economy. On the contrary, it is an old economy, akin to an elderly person suffering from underlying medical conditions such as chronic diabetes. The once-in-a-century COVID-19 crisis could not have come at a worse time for South Korea, which also faces the problem of deglobalization. Indeed the post-COVID acceleration of deglobalization will present an unprecedented danger for South Korea, which leveraged globalization to achieve its economic miracle. The sobering lesson for other Asian countries is that population aging will present a formidable challenge for their economic growth. The time for Asia to start preparing for aging is now.

4.3. Asia's Widening Inequality and Polarization

Deglobalization and population aging are not the only major threats to Asia's long-term growth. In particular, worsening income inequality and environmental destruction pose formidable threats to Asia's economic prospects. Let us first discuss income inequality. Asia's economic growth is widely admired around the world because, by and large, it was not only exceptionally rapid and sustained over a long time period but also inclusive. That is, economic growth benefited broad swathes of the population rather than just a small privileged elite. Rapid growth on a sustained basis was only one aspect of the Asian economic miracle, albeit an important aspect. The other significant aspect was the inclusive nature of the rapid growth. The Asian miracle transformed the lives of billions of Asians. The skylines of Bangkok, Kuala Lumpur, Mumbai, Shanghai, Seoul, and countless other Asian cities have changed beyond all recognition. The general living standards of Asians are incomparably higher than those of their parents and grandparents. Asians eat more and better food, wear better clothes, have better homes, have access to better education and health care, and live better.

In addition to the massive improvement in general living standards and upgrading in the quality of billions of human lives, the single biggest benefit from Asia's sustained rapid growth was a historically unprecedented reduction in poverty. That is, the number of poor people in Asia and the share of poor people in the population have decreased at a faster rate than at any time in human history. Poverty rate is usually defined as the share of population living on a certain amount of dollars — e.g. US$1.25 — or less per day, so it is to some extent subjective. Nevertheless, the sheer speed and scale of Asia's poverty reduction was breathtaking testament to the validity of the trickle-down theory — the economic theory which predicts that rapid economic growth will lead to rapid reduction in poverty. Many Asian governments took various specific policy measures to directly help the poor, such as income support for poorer households, but by and large, Asia's poverty reduction miracle was a result of decades of rapid growth. To economists who try to downplay the central role of economic growth in reducing poverty, Asia's experience in the last few decades categorically disproves their argument. Governments of developing countries can do more to directly tackle poverty, e.g. by expanding and improving the access of the poor to health care and education, but the most powerful weapon against poverty is economic growth.

Zhuang[7] analyzes and compares the performance of different regions of the developing world in terms of economic growth and poverty reduction. The comparative analysis resoundingly confirms the notion that Asia's poverty reduction miracle was driven and made possible by Asia's economic growth miracle. Figure 4.13 shows that developing Asia grew much faster than other parts of the world — sub-Saharan Africa, Latin America and the Caribbean, and Middle East and North Africa — between 1990 and 2017. The figure is consistent with conventional wisdom of a dynamic Asia racing ahead while other developing regions are stagnating and falling behind. Asia's sustained rapid growth uplifted general living standards and catapulted the region from the periphery of the world economy to its front and center. A huge consequence of Asia's rapid growth during an extended period was a historical reduction in poverty. Asia enjoyed a far greater reduction of poverty than the other parts of the developing world.

---

7   J. Zhuang (2018). *"The recent trend of income inequality in Asia and how policy should respond,"* *Working Paper, G-24 and Fiedrich-Ebert-Stiftung, New York.*

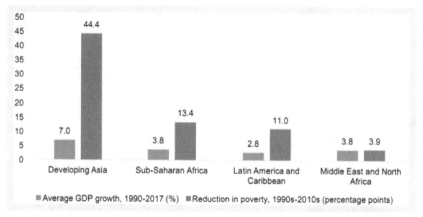

Figure 4.13. Average annual GDP growth and poverty reduction, 1990–2017.
Source: J. Zhuang (2018). "The recent trend of income inequality in Asia and how policy should respond," Working Paper, G-24 and Fiedrich-Ebert-Stiftung, New York.

While general living standards improved and poverty rates decreased dramatically in Asia due to rapid growth for an extended period of time, the region now confronts a new problem, namely widening inequality. During the 1960s and 1970s, Asia's rapid growth was accompanied by relatively low levels of inequality. This benign mix of rapid growth and moderate inequality was especially evident in East Asian NIEs, which is why they are seen as benchmarks for other developing countries. However, in more recent decades, many Asian countries experienced deterioration of income inequality, as seen in Figures 4.14 and 4.15.

Figures 4.16 and 4.17 particularly show that income inequality worsened sharply in both China and India between 1980 and 2015. The two Asian giants were the world's fastest growing big economies during this period. But the figures suggest that the acceleration of economic growth came at the cost of deterioration in equity. Widening inequality coincided with the adoption of market forces that propelled

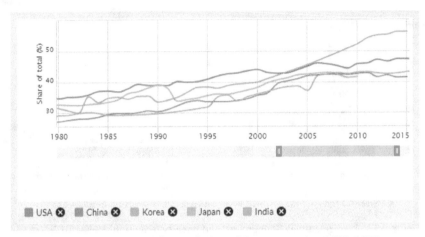

Figure 4.14. Top 10% income shares of selected Asian countries, 1980–2015.
Source: World Inequality Database (accessed August 15, 2020).

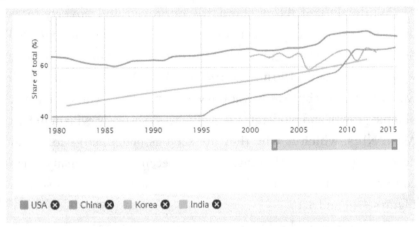

Figure 4.15. Top 10% wealth shares of selected Asian countries, 1980–2015.
Source: World Inequality Database (accessed August 15, 2020).

growth. In China's case, the market reforms kicked off by Deng Xiaoping in 1978 to move the economy away from central planning explains both world-beating economic growth and widening inequality. In India's

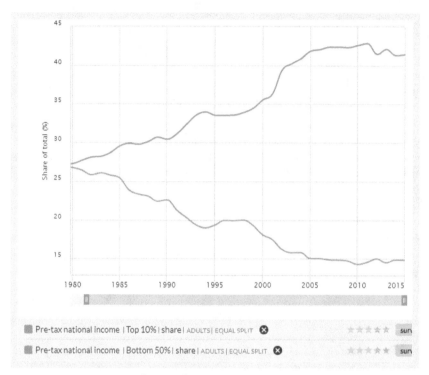

Figure 4.16. Income inequality in China, 1980–2015.
Source: World Inequality Database (accessed August 15, 2020).

case, the economic liberalization of 1991 under Finance Minister Manmohan Singh unleashed rapid growth but worsened the income gap between the rich and the poor. The figure shows that India's income inequality widened sharply since the early 1990s, which was when the economy was liberalized to allow for a much larger role of market forces.

A study by Thomas Piketty, a world-class economist who specializes in analysis of inequality, and two Chinese co-authors finds that in China, income inequality increased substantially between 1978, the year that kicked off China's transition from socialism to a market economy, and

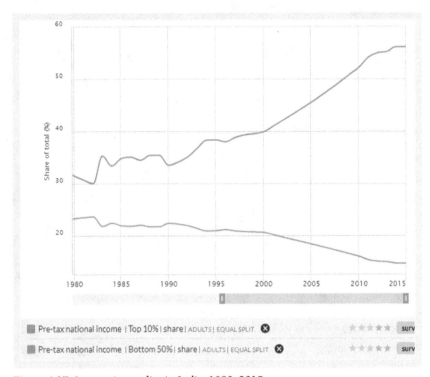

Figure 4.17. Income inequality in India, 1980–2015.
Source: World Inequality Database (accessed August 15, 2020).

2015.[8] More specifically, they find that the share of national income earned by the richest 10% of the population grew from 27% in 1978 to 41% in 2015, while the share earned by the poorest 50% fell from 27% to 15%. That is, the top 10% of the population used to have about the same income share as the bottom 50%, but now their income share is 2.7 times greater. The level of inequality in China in the late 1970s used to be less than the European average — closer to those observed

---

8　T. Piketty, L. Yang, and G. Zucman (2017). *"Capital accumulation, private property and rising inequality in China,"* NBER Working Paper No.23368.

in Sweden and other Nordic countries, egalitarian countries with extensive social welfare systems — but they are now approaching a level that is almost comparable with the US.

Let us look at the case of South Korea. The South Korean economy took off in the early 1960s and grew rapidly to become a high-income economy with a per capita income of more than US$30,000. However, in recent years, social and economic polarization due to worsening income inequality has reached serious levels, bordering on social conflict. As seen in Figure 4.18, the share of income accruing to the richest 10% was 30% in 1990. However, this figure grew steadily to reach 43% by 2016, the highest among major Asian countries. Moreover,

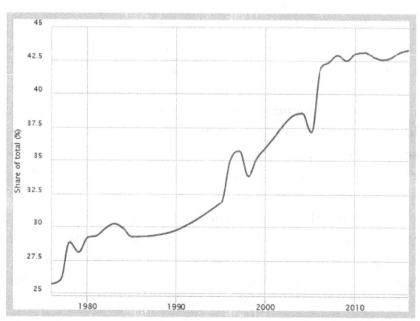

Figure 4.18. Top 10% national income share in South Korea, 1976–2016.
Source: World Inequality Database (accessed August 15, 2020).

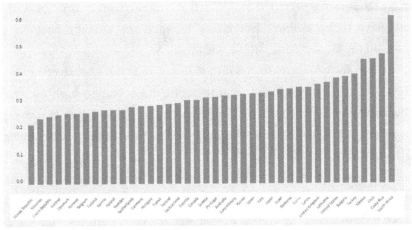

Figure 4.19. Gini coefficients of OECD members, 2019 or latest available.
Source: OECD, Income Inequality Database (accessed August 15, 2020).

among the 29 members of OECD, an organization of mostly high-income countries, South Korea was the 11ᵗʰ most unequal country (Figure 4.19).

Perhaps the most serious problems facing young South Koreans is the limited scope for upward mobility. Even if they study hard, work hard, and save money, most of them cannot hope to achieve higher socioeconomic status. Poor but talented youth find it increasingly difficult to climb up the socioeconomic ladder based on their efforts alone. The South Korean people are angry and resentful at widespread media reports of the rich and politically well-connected elite's abuse of their power to further enrich themselves and secure all kinds of privileges, from slots at top universities for their children to exemptions from military service for their sons. The South Korean public despairs at the common sight of the elite passing on their wealth, honor, and power to their children. South Korea is characterized by ever-worsening inequality of opportunity. In South Korea, chances and opportunities in life are pre-determined at birth rather than based on talent or hard work.

The ladder of upward socioeconomic mobility has been truncated. For young South Koreans, getting a good job is akin to winning the lottery. On top of this, the sharp escalation of housing prices means that they cannot even dream about leaving their parents' homes and becoming financially independent. The South Korean youth of today is the "give up" generation. Many of them are forced to give up on marriage, buying a house, and having children. Above all, they are forced to give up hope. In a sense, South Korea's collapse in fertility rate and the consequent demographic crisis is a result of socioeconomic polarization and loss of hope among the youth. Hopelessness is also reflected in a severe lack of entrepreneurship among South Korean youth. Entrepreneurs are inherently bold optimists who believe that they can succeed against all odds. Despair and lack of hope explains why South Korea has the world's highest suicide rate. In South Korea, as in the rest of the world, COVID-19 is further exacerbating income inequality, which was already high before the pandemic. Many poorer South Koreans have lost their jobs or suffered loss of income. In addition, the already bleak job market for South Korean youths has worsened due to the pandemic.

Asia is not alone in the trend toward greater income inequality. The income gap between the rich and the poor is widening across the world, not just in Asia. While high and growing inequality is not unique to Asia, Asia does no better than the rest of the world in reducing income inequality. There have been many explanations for the ever-widening income gap between the rich and the poor. Thomas Piketty, for example, produces evidence which indicates that wealth grows faster than economic output over time. This implies that the income gap between factory owners — i.e. capitalists or owners of capital — and factory workers — i.e. owners of labor — will widen over time. At a broader level, unfortunately, many factors that contribute to economic growth also contribute to greater inequality. For example, technological progress is a powerful driver of economic growth but it benefits skilled workers more than unskilled workers; the former are better able to work with new technologies than the latter. Likewise, globalization benefits some groups more than others. Firms and industries that can compete in the global marketplace will thrive, while those that cannot will wilt.

High and growing inequality presents a major risk to Asia's future economic growth, along with population aging and deglobalization. What drives economic prosperity and technological progress in a capitalist economy is entrepreneurial capitalism, which is the greatest invention in human history. Capitalism is far from perfect as an economic system, but common sense alone tells us that it is incomparably more productive and efficient than socialism, the other main alternative economic system. A comparison of South South Korea versus North South Korea proves the point. Another example is the spectacular economic miracle that transformed China and dramatically improved the lives of more than a billion Chinese since the Asian giant threw off the yoke of socialism and embraced capitalism in 1978. Yet another example is India's economic takeoff from its abysmal economic stagnation, widely ridiculed as Hindu rate of growth, since it jettisoned socialism in 1991.

What gives capitalism its unparalleled productive capacity is entrepreneurship. Innovative entrepreneurs like Steve Jobs and Jack Ma create socially useful products and technologies, driving growth, fueling technological progress, and creating jobs. Entrepreneurship is the heart and soul of a well-functioning capitalist economy. A clear distinction has to be made between entrepreneurial capitalism of Steve Jobs and Jack Ma versus the greed-crazed financial capitalism of Wall Street, which adds little social value and lies at the global financial crisis of 2008. The natural role of finance — banks and stock and bond markets — is to channel resources to entrepreneurs, firms, industries, and households. An efficient financial system does a good job of identifying and extending credit to future Apples and Alibabas. However, the modern financial system, especially in rich countries, has become a leviathan which serves itself rather than the real economy. When its reckless greed causes a crisis, it cries out for help from taxpayers! Many opponents of capitalism have this capitalism — i.e. financial capitalism — in mind when they denounce capitalism. We too denounce this kind of capitalism, of Wall Street serving itself rather than Main Street.

But the benign, high-value, productive kind of capitalism — i.e. entrepreneurial capitalism — is much closer to the original vision of socially useful capitalism laid out by Adam Smith. Entrepreneurs who compete furiously with each other to capture consumer hearts and wallets based on the quality of their products and technologies are the star players and main actors of a well-functioning capitalist economy. Those entrepreneurs capture the Schumpeterian paradigm of new and superior products and technologies driving out old and inferior products and technologies in a never-ending process of dynamic competition. Competition is the key to entrepreneurship, and entrepreneurship is the key to benign and socially useful capitalism. This explains why high and growing inequality poses the single biggest threat to entrepreneurial capitalism in Asia and the world.

Current levels of income inequality, which are unacceptably high and growing wider, are eroding the political, social, and moral legitimacy of capitalism. Popular support for capitalism always rested on the popular belief that anybody with talent, creativity, and determination could succeed and become rich through hard work and a dose of good luck. However, the past few decades of a tiny elite getting richer while the rest of the population stagnate or even fall behind has left a sour taste in the public's perception of capitalism, both in Asia and the rest of the world. In fact, there is a growing popular backlash against capitalism. People are increasingly angry at what they view as an unfair economic system.

Democratic capitalism or merit capitalism is being replaced by elite capitalism or hereditary capitalism. The steady erosion is driven by the cancer at the heart of today's capitalism — wide and worsening income inequality between the rich and the poor. Under democratic capitalism, one's wealth is due to one's contribution to the economy, e.g. by inventing a socially useful new product or technology; i.e. wealth is based on merit. Under the other, less benign kind of capitalism, the children of self-perpetuating elites inherit their wealth from their parents, who are rich, politically powerful, or both. You are rich because your parents are rich. You do not earn your wealth, you inherit it. The difference between the two types of capitalism is stark, to say the least.

Going forward, the erosion of popular support for capitalism due to unacceptable income inequality presents a huge danger to Asia's economic growth. Entrepreneurial capitalism is what drove Asia's prosperity in the past, and entrepreneurial capitalism is what Asia needs to continue to prosper in the post-COVID world. For example, notwithstanding the widespread misunderstanding of China's economic model as state capitalism, which is probably one of the biggest economic myths in history, China's economic miracles were mostly made in the private sector. Bold, visionary, risk-taking entrepreneurs are the true heroes and the driving force behind the Chinese miracle. If growing public anger at growing inequality led Asian governments to rein in entrepreneurial capitalism, it would be a monumental mistake, killing the golden goose that drove Asia's economic miracle. Yes, Asian governments must do more to tackle inequality, but impeding and harassing entrepreneurs is not part of the solution.

4.4. Asia's Environmental Degradation

Environmental destruction and climate changes presents yet another significant danger to Asia's economic growth in the post-COVID period. The COVID-19 pandemic itself underscores the risk to mankind's very survival stemming from reckless destruction of the environment. Mankind's relentless intrusion into the natural habitat has brought it into more frequent contact with wildlife, which plays a major role in the transmission of viruses from wildlife to humans and then from humans to humans. This explains the emergence of not only COVID-19 but also earlier outbreaks of other coronavirus pandemics such as SARS and MERS. The unprecedented, once-in-a-century nature of COVID-19, which has triggered a global health and economic crisis, should serve as a stark warning for Asians to take better care of their environment or face catastrophic consequence.

In truth, given Asia's laser-like focus on growth, the region paid relatively little attention to environmental degradation until relatively recently. According to ADB, rapid industrialization, more material and energy consumption, and larger population combined with urbanization, took a heavy toll on the environment.[9] Asian governments pursued a "grow first, clean-up later" growth strategy in which environmental considerations took a backseat to economic growth. Predictably, this growth strategy degraded forests, soil quality, biodiversity, freshwater ecosystems, ocean health, and air quality. The environmental cost is evident in millions of premature deaths from pollution each year, declining natural capital to sustain future production, increased ecosystem fragility, and other environmental imbalances. Furthermore,

9 Asian Development Bank (2020). Asia's Journey to Prosperity: Policy, Market, and Technology over 50 Years (Manila: ADB).

Asia faces challenges in meeting growing demand for water, energy, and food.

The high environmental cost of the Asian economic miracle has adversely affected the quality of life. For example, according to ADB, the majority of Asia's densely populated and rapidly growing cities experience air pollution which poses a significant health hazard.[10] More specifically, the study reports that 61% of large Asian cities and 52% of medium-sized Asian cities are classified as poor to critical in terms of air pollution and health implications. Schraufnagel *et al.* find that air pollution is linked to respiratory and cardiovascular disease, miscarriage, premature birth, neurological pathology in children, and dementia among the elderly.[11] A sobering environmental statistic is that indoor and outdoor air pollution prematurely kill four million people in urban and rural Asia each year. Children, the poor, the sick, and the elderly are especially vulnerable to suffering severe health effects from Asia's worsening pollution.

Climate change has become as a core global issue in recent years, particularly after the UN Conference on Environment and Development in Rio de Janeiro in 1992. Asia's sustained rapid growth required a large and growing mobilization of fossil fuel resources, including coal, contributing to the sharp global rise in emission of greenhouse gases, which contributes to climate change. In some Asian countries, deforestation has also been a major source of increased emissions. Historically, developing Asia was not a major source of greenhouse gas

10 Asian Development Bank (2019). *Asian Development Outlook 2019 Update: Fostering Growth and Inclusion in Asia's Cities* (Manila: ADB).

11 D. E. Schraufnagel, J. R. Balmes, C. T. Cowl, S. D. Matteis, S.-H. Jung, K. Mortimer, R. Perez-Padilla, M. B. Rice, H. Riojas-Rodriguez, A. Sood, G. D. Thurston, T. To, A. Vanker, and D. J. Wuebbles (2019). "Air pollution and noncommunicable diseases: A review by the Forum of International Respiratory Societies' Environmental Committee, Part 1: The damaging effects of air pollution," *Chest* Vol. 155, No. 2, pp. 417–426.

emissions on a per capita basis. However, in line with its rapid growth and development, Asia's emissions have grown much more rapidly than the global average.[12] This is partly because Asia's energy systems have become more carbon intensive. As of 2014, developing Asia accounted for 42% of global carbon dioxide equivalent emissions, which exceeded its share of global GDP, which was 23%. Climate change, which exacerbates resource degradation and water stress, poses an additional risk to Asia's natural resources. Asia is vulnerable to extreme weather events such as droughts, hurricanes, and flooding, in addition to rising sea levels, loss of glacial water reserves, and coastal erosion.

In response to the growing costs of environmental degradation and climate change, Asian governments have begun to pay much greater attention to protecting the environment than before. Growing at all costs and ignoring environmental effects is no longer an option. Asian governments are now increasingly aware that protecting the environment is indispensable for sustainable development. That is, Asian countries cannot continue to grow on a sustained basis unless they safeguard their environmental resources. More specifically, many Asian countries are making a concerted effort to protect the environment, mitigate greenhouse gas emission, and adapt to climate change. Key environmental policy measures such as legislation for environmental frameworks, air and water quality standards, and safeguard policies are on the rise across the region. Nevertheless, unless Asian countries do much more to protect their environment, lack of environmental resources will seriously harm their long-term growth prospects. In their rush to grow as rapidly as possible, Asians tended to take air, water, land, and other environmental resources for granted, as if they were free. These

---

12 *Asian Development Bank (2020). Asia's Journey to Prosperity: Policy, Market, and Technology over 50 Years (Manila: ADB).*

resources are indispensable for the region's continued growth, a fact that is not lost any more on the region's policy-makers. A business-as-usual policy approach to the environment will be costly for both the environment and the economy.

Economists traditionally measure happiness with a concept called utility. Utility is determined by the amount of goods and services consumed. This explains why economists traditionally focused on maximizing economic growth. That is, economists prioritized producing and consuming goods and services, which maximizes happiness. But in truth, my happiness does not depend solely on my own consumption. It also depends on my neighbors' consumption. If my neighbor drives a new Ferrari while I drive a secondhand Honda Civic, that makes me unhappy. If my neighbor can afford to take vacation trips to the French Riviera while I cannot take any vacation trip at all, I am bound to be unhappy. Furthermore, material consumption is not the only determinant of happiness; it also depends on clean air and water, as well as peace of mind and a grateful, positive outlook on life.

It is true that COVID-19 has temporarily improved Asia's air quality. However, prior to the pandemic, dust storms and fine dust made it difficult for many Asians to even breathe without a face mask. This explains why wearing a face mask has become second nature to Asians, which served most Asian countries well in the fight against the coronavirus. Environmental degradation has filled up many rivers in Asia with green algae and other unhealthy organisms, making it impossible for fish to survive. As a result of growth that depended heavily on fossil fuels, China, India, Japan, and South Korea were among the biggest consumers of primary energy in the world in 2019, as seen in Figure 4.20.

In the Climate Change Performance Index that was announced in early 2020, four Asian economies, namely Chinese Taipei, South Korea,

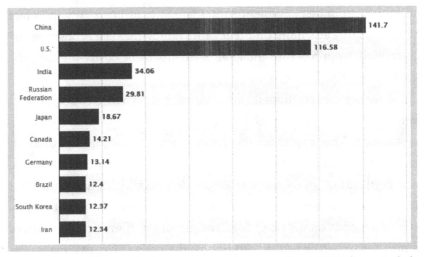

Figure 4.20. Top 10 countries in primary energy consumption in 2019 (in exajoules).
Source: Statista (accessed August 15, 2020).

Malaysia, and Japan, ranked among the bottom 14 performers. According to Global Footprint Network, many Asian countries are currently putting more ecological pressure than their biocapacities. Asian countries with the greatest ecological deficit (i.e. ecological footprint exceeding biocapacity) are Singapore, South Korea, Japan, China, India, the Philippines, Pakistan, Thailand, Vietnam, and Bangladesh. For example, Figure 4.21 shows that South Korea's per capita ecological footprint grew rapidly since the late 1960s when the country embarked upon industrialization. By 2016, the footprint has come to exceed more than six times the country's biocapacity. In other words, the energy used by South Koreans and the waste and pollution they produce is more than six times what South Korea's land mass can handle. Quality of life depends on income as well as living harmoniously with others in a clean and green environment.

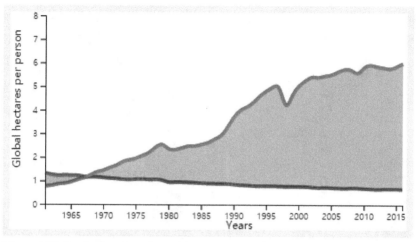

Figure 4.21. South Korea's ecological footprint per person vs. biocapacity per person, 1961–2016.

Note: The red line represents ecological footprint per person while the green line represents biocapacity per person.

Source: Global Footprint Network (accessed August 15, 2020).

According to the 2020 World Happiness Report published by the United Nations Sustainable Development Solutions Network (SDSN), the world's happiest countries include Finland, Denmark, Switzerland, Iceland, Norway, Netherlands, Sweden, New Zealand, and Austria. All these countries not only have high incomes but clean environments. South Korea, on the other hand, ranked only 61st despite having the world's 27th highest per capita income. While the overriding priority of South Korean policy-makers is post-COVID economic recovery, they must also reduce economic inequality and foster environmental sustainability. Unless they do so, growth and development will not be sustainable. Other Asian countries too must work simultaneously on growth, inequality, and environment in order to prolong Asia's economic miracle into the post-COVID period.

Chapter 5

The Fourth Industrial Revolution and the Fourth Wave of Globalization

5.1. Outward-looking Growth is a Necessity, Not a Choice

T he story of Asia's economic miracle is one of outward-looking, export-oriented growth strategy. The extent to which Asian countries leveraged trade and foreign investment to drive their growth differed from country to country but overall, the region benefited more than any other part of the world from globalization. As noted earlier, Asia is no longer just riding the coattails of globalization but is now at the front and center of the world economy and globalization. According to a September 2019 McKinsey report,[1] Asia's role in

---

1 O. Tonby, J. Woetzel, W. Choi, K. Eloot, R. Dhawan, J. Seong, and P. Wang (2019). "The future of Asia: Asian flows and networks are defining the next phase of globalization," Discussion Paper, September, McKinsey Global Institute.

globalization is large and growing. Asia has seen its share of global goods trade rise from 25% in 2007 to 33% in 2017. The region accounts for 23% of international capital flows in 2017, compared to 13% in 2007. Asia also accounts for 65% of worldwide patents in 2017, compared to 52% just 10 years ago. Asia now also accounts for no less than 62% of global container shipping traffic. Whatever indicator of globalization you look at, you get the same story — Asia's imprint on globalization is growing rapidly. In fact, the report highlights the fact that global cross-border flows are shifting toward Asia in seven out of the eight dimensions that it examines — trade, capital, people, knowledge, transport, culture, resources, and the environment.[2] Asia's growing role in globalization closely mirrors its growing role in the world economy. Asia has seen its share of global output rise from 32% in 2000 to 42% in 2017, and the share is projected to reach 52% by 2040.[3] We are witnessing the dawn of the Asian Century.

Globalization, more specifically export-oriented industrialization, enabled East Asian countries to transform themselves from low-income to middle-income and, in the case of Korea and the other NIEs, even high-income economies in a relatively short period of time. They closely followed the footsteps of Japan, which industrialized much earlier than the rest of Asia by virtue of its opening up to advanced Western technology and foreign trade during the Meiji Restoration in the second half of the 19th century. Indeed, by importing Western technology and absorbing it effectively, Japan was able to become an honorary Western power. It became the dominant economic, technological, and military power of Asia by virtue of having modernized much earlier than the

---

2   *The only flow that declined was waste flows.*
3   *The shares are in purchasing power parity (PPP) terms, which takes into account the fact that non-traded services such as haircuts tend to be cheaper in poorer countries.*

rest of the region. Japan became so powerful that it used its newfound supremacy to invade other Asian countries before and during the Second World War, leaving a bitter historical legacy. On the other hand, Japan directly and indirectly benefited other Asian countries by serving as a central hub of trade, investment, and technology for the entire region.

China's spectacular economic rise since opening up and liberalizing its economy in 1978 and joining the World Trade Organization (WTO) in 2001 is another powerful testament to the transformational impact of globalization on Asian economies. Market reforms that did away with inefficient, sclerotic socialist planning and economic globalization which linked the hitherto closed Chinese economy to global trade and global financial markets were the twin engines of the Chinese miracle. The entry of foreign firms from more advanced Western and East Asian countries brought in not only capital but also technology, managerial expertise, and marketing networks abroad. China was able to leverage foreign technology to develop its own technological capability and its own manufacturing industries, just like Meiji Japan did in the 19th century. It is difficult to overstate the role of globalization in China's stunning ascent. However, the positive impact of globalization on Asia is not confined to the two giants of China and Japan. Whether it is Korea's high-tech manufacturing exports, India's IT services exports, or the remittances of Filipino workers working abroad, globalization played a major role in economic growth and development of many Asian countries.

Unfortunately, as explained earlier, the golden age of postwar globalization is coming to an end. Protectionism is on the rise worldwide, most notably in America, where the Trump Administration makes no bones about its intention to use tariffs and other protectionist tools to promote both economic and geopolitical objectives. In particular, America, the incumbent superpower, is turning to protectionism as a major weapon in its budding rivalry with China, the rising superpower. While it is tempting to blame American protectionism on one person, namely President Donald Trump, in truth it is a symptom of a much bigger and deeper force, namely growing popular discontent and anger at globalization, especially in rich Western countries. The upshot of an increasingly inward-looking, "America First" America is that the postwar era of globalization led and presided over by a benign superpower — i.e. Pax Americana — is coming to an end and may even have already ended. Pax Americana was overall marked by objective, reasonable, and impartial rules of the game set by multilateral organizations such as International Monetary Fund (IMF) and WTO. The end of Pax Americana leaves a big vacuum in the global economic landscape.

The trillion-dollar question facing Asian economies, which benefited hugely from globalization, is "How do we cope with the retreat from globalization and outright deglobalization?" The vacuum left behind by the end of Pax Americana will persist for some time to come. China is not yet strong enough to lead and preside over a Pax Sinica. More importantly, there is no concrete evidence that China is poised to become a largely benign superpower, as America was during Pax Americana. To the contrary, China's increasingly assertive nationalism, evident in its actions in the South China Sea, is sowing doubts about the feasibility and desirability of a Pax Sinica. But for Asia, economic openness and outward-looking growth is a necessity, not a choice. The region cannot afford to close its economies and turn inward. That would amount to economic suicide.

Most Asian economies are small open economies that depend heavily on trade to survive and thrive. It is true that China is a large continental economy in which domestic demand plays a much bigger role in growth. Contrary to the popular myth of China as an export-dependent economy, it is in fact a continental economy dominated by domestic demand, much like America. Common sense alone tells us that China could not have possibly grown by more than 9% in 2009, the peak year of the global financial crisis when the economies of US and other advanced economies shrank by 3%, if China's growth depended mainly on exports rather than domestic demand. Even China, despite its huge domestic market and domestic demand-led economy, cannot go it alone. Huawei's struggles in the face of the Trump Administration's attempts to strangle it is just one example of China's interdependence with the world. This is true even for Japan, the world's third largest economy.

Asia finds itself at the end of Pax Americana, which greatly benefited the region. America is increasingly unable and unwilling to lead the world. At the same time, Asian countries outside China find themselves facing an assertive rising superpower in the form of China. So going forward, what must smaller Asian countries do to survive and thrive in the post-COVID world? Again, inward-looking autarky is not an option for Asia's small open economies, unless they want to reduce themselves to the grinding, inhumane poverty of small closed economies like Cuba or North Korea. The good news is that they do not have to look far for salvation. Going forward, their own region may hold the key to the growth of Asian countries. As noted earlier, Asia is now at the front and center of the world economy and globalization. In fact, Asia has already the world's largest regional economy, with 42% of global GDP in 2017, far bigger than Europe's 22% share or North America's 18%. Asia's next wave of globalization is likely to take the form of greater flows of goods, services, capital, and people with Asia, as we will explain in the Section 5.2.

A brief excursion into the history of Korea, the poster child for the huge economic benefits of globalization, vividly confirms why globalization is a necessity, not a choice, for Asian countries. For much of their 5,000-year history, the Korean people were subject to waves of foreign invaders and lived mostly in poverty. The most recent kingdom on the Korean Peninsula was the Chosun dynasty, which was a semi-vassal state of China that was invaded by Manchus, Japanese, and others. The preceding Koryo dynasty was ransacked by the Mongol hordes. In the late 19th century, the Chosun dynasty was wracked by political infighting among different factions. Partly as a result, the kingdom lost a golden opportunity to modernize and globalize when Western forces knocked on its door. Korea missed the globalization boat, an event that would later deprive the country of its freedom and sovereignty when it was annexed by Japan, which did not miss the boat.

In sharp contrast, Japan entered into the Japan and US Treaty of Peace and Amity or the Kanagawa Treaty in 1854. The treaty effectively ended Japan's self-isolation policy and opened the ports of Shimoda and Hakodate to American ships. In 1858, Japan opened itself up even further, concluding commercial treaties with America, Britain, Russia, Netherlands, and France. In the Meiji period, Japan reformed itself and rapidly caught up with Western countries, becoming Asia's pre-eminent power. In 1910, Japan annexed Korea and started a brutal colonial rule of 35 years. For Koreans, the 1910–1945 period of Japanese colonial rule was a time of humiliation and despair, particularly because Korea had traditionally looked down upon Japan as culturally backward.

When Korea was finally liberated in 1945, after Japan was defeated by the US in the Second World War, the Korean Peninsula was divided into a communist, Soviet-backed North and a capitalist, American-backed South. The Korean War, which was kicked off by North Korea's invasion of South Korea in June 1950, left the Peninsula in utter ruins. Both Koreas were easily among the poorest countries on the planet. However, the economy of South Korea, or the Republic of Korea (henceforth Korea), began to grow and develop at a historically unprecedented speed under the export-oriented industrialization growth strategy of President Park Chung-Hee in the 1960s. President Park, like China's Deng Xiaoping and Singapore's Lee Kuan Yew, was a transformational leader and the father of the Korean economic miracle. Korea's per capita GDP exploded from US$94 in 1961 to US$1,000 in 1977, US$5,000 in 1989, US$10,000 in 1994, and US$20,000 in 2006. Finally, Korea's per capita GDP reached US$31,762 in 2019, firmly entrenching the country as a high-income, advanced economy. Based on per capita GDP, Korea is now the 28th richest country in the 200-strong community of countries. In terms of the size of the economy, measured by GDP, Korea ranks 12th.

Korean companies like Samsung, LG, and Hyundai are recognized as world-class companies. Furthermore, the Korean economy is now dominated by high-tech manufacturing and has become one of the most innovative economies in the world, investing heavily in research and development (R&D) and manufacturing many new products and cutting-edge technologies. In addition to a world-class manufacturing sector, Korea now boasts globally influential soft power. The Korean Wave or K-Wave, which includes drama, movies, music, and online games, is hugely popular not only in Asia but also worldwide. According to 2020 Henry Passport Index announced by CNN Travel, Korea has the third most powerful passport — meaning you can visit countries without visas and other administrative hassles — in the world, along with Germany, right behind Japan and Singapore. Korea's transformation from the ruins of the Korean War into a highly successful economy is nothing short of miraculous.

The miraculous transformation would not have been possible without the blood, sweat, and tears of the great generation who drove the industrialization of the 1960s and 1970s. This generation spearheaded the government's export-oriented industrialization amid appalling living conditions and working environments. They made untold personal sacrifices, working in the mines, construction sites, and factories, from light industries such as clothing and footwear to heavy industries such as steel, shipbuilding, and chemicals. They are the true heroes of the Korean economic miracle. They also sacrificed their own well-being so that their children could get a better education and a better life. As a result of their sacrifices, Korea now has one of the world's best educated and skilled workforces.

Export-oriented industrialization is fundamentally a growth strategy of using foreign loans and foreign aid to build factories and import inputs to produce and export manufactured products. If successful, export-oriented industrialization results in the following virtuous cycle — exports bring in US dollars, which are used to build more factories and import more inputs, which makes it possible to produce and export more products. A growth strategy of more exports, more factories, even more exports, rapid industrialization, and rapid economic growth seems all too sensible now. However, in the 1960s, dependency theory, which envisaged developing countries as being enslaved to advanced countries in a state of dependency, dominated the thoughts of policy-makers in many developing countries. For example, Latin American countries turned to inward-looking, import substitution growth strategy, which led to rampant corruption and chronic foreign debt crisis, plunging them into poverty and stagnation.

The fact that Korea, which had no natural resources to speak of unlike most Latin American countries, chose outward-looking, export-oriented industrialization as its growth strategy was a stroke of good luck and visionary leadership of President Park Chung-Hee. Singapore's Prime Minister Lee Kuan Yew, who embraced foreign investment long before the leaders of other developing countries, was also a visionary leader who transformed his country by opening up to the world. Countries like Korea and Singapore were able to succeed in export-oriented industrialization because they were able to ride the wave of the third, postwar golden age of globalization. Korea missed the globalization boat in the 19th century while Japan got on it, but Korea was not about to make the same huge mistake twice.

Unfortunately for countries like Korea and Singapore, the golden age of globalization is in its terminal phase. Countries like America and China, which are blessed with huge domestic markets, can recover from mega-shocks such as the COVID-19 crisis even in the face of deglobalization. Korea, Singapore, and the other small open economies of Asia do not have such luxury. They cannot prosper unless they are able to sell what they produce in global markets. Therefore, coronavirus or not, deglobalization or not, US–China Cold War or not, Asia's small open economies have no choice but to continue to pursue outward-looking growth. For these economies, outward-looking growth is a necessity, not a luxury. But to pursue globalization in a productive way, Asia must stand at the forefront of the fourth wave of globalization and the Fourth Industrial Revolution. If Asian countries collectively rise to this difficult task, they may preside over and lead the post-COVID world. Pax Americana would give way to Pax Asiana. Just as a Great

Generation led Korea's industrialization in the 1960s and 1970s, another Great Generation must emerge to capitalize on the upcoming new waves of globalization and industrialization in the 2020s. And the same is true for the rest of Asia. History will be kind to today's Asians if we succeed in meeting this formidable challenge.

5.2. Asia as the Agenda Setter of the New Wave of Globalization

It was noted earlier that Asia's share of the world economy is on the rise, as is Asia's role in globalization. Whereas Asia was largely a follower in the third wave of globalization, it is poised to become a leader and agenda setter in the upcoming fourth wave of globalization. In particular, given that Asian economies are rapidly integrating with each other, they are set to enter a new stage of globalization — i.e. regionalization. Global value chains, which are an integral part of Asia's globalization, are giving way to regional value chains. According to a 2019 McKinsey report,[4] five structural shifts are reshaping the global value chains. First, the trade intensity — i.e. the ratio of exports to output — is falling in almost all goods-producing value chains. Second, the role of services in global value chains is growing. Third, trade driven by low labor costs is declining. Fourth, global value chains are becoming more knowledge intensive. Fifth, value chains are becoming more regional and less global. A major driver of the ongoing transformation of global value chains is the shift of global demand from advanced economies to emerging markets, especially China and other Asian economies. Emerging markets will consume almost two-thirds of manufactured goods such as cars, building materials, and machinery by 2025 and account for more than half of global consumption by 2030. The stereotype of global value chains as low-wage factory workers in emerging markets producing goods for rich consumers in advanced countries is increasingly outdated. Asian now consumes a lot of what it produces.

---

4 S. Lund, J. Manyika, J. Woetzel, J. Bouhin, M. Krishnan, J. Seong, and M. Muir (2019). *"Globalization in transition: The future of trade and value chains,"* McKinsey Global Institute.

According to another 2019 McKinsey report,[5] the worldwide reduction of trade intensity in goods-producing value chains is more evident in Asia than elsewhere. The global pattern of services trade growing faster than goods trade is also more pronounced in Asia. The fundamental factor reshaping Asia's role in globalization — more specifically the shift from globalization to regionalization — is Asia's transformation from producer to consumer. Asia is no longer just the Factory of the World, it is also becoming the Consumer of the World. In line with its growing share of global production, Asia's share of global consumption is rising rapidly, from 23% in 2000 to 28% in 2017 and a projected 39% in 2040. In all the eight dimensions analyzed by the report — trade, capital, people, knowledge, transport, culture, resources, and the environment — Asian countries are becoming more integrated with each other, and there is a clear trend toward greater regionalization. For example, 60% of Asian trade is now between Asian countries, 71% of Asian investment in startups and 59% of foreign direct investment (FDI) is intra-Asian, and 74% of Asian travel takes place within Asia. Today's prosperous and self-confident Asians are no longer content to sell what they produce to Americans and Europeans. They can increasingly afford to buy and consume what they produce.

Driven by rising living standards and growing purchasing power, regionalization is thus gradually replacing globalization as the central motif of Asia's openness and cross-border trade and investment. One additional factor that will further promote regionalization is the diversity and heterogeneity of Asia. Asian economies are not only highly

---

5 O. Tonby, J. Woetzel, W. Choi, K. Eloot, R. Dhawan, J. Seong, and P. Wang (2019). "The future of Asia — Asian flows and networks are defining the next phase of globalization," McKinsey Global Institute.

diverse but also highly complementary. That is, the strength of some Asian economies can help address the weakness of other Asian economies. For instance, as noted earlier, while Asia as a whole is aging, Asian economies differ greatly in the speed and scale of aging. Some countries — e.g. India and the Philippines — are still young whereas others — e.g. Japan and Korea — are facing an immediate demographic crisis. Yet others — e.g. China, Thailand, and Vietnam — are somewhere in between. What this means is that there is plenty of scope for mutually beneficial economic interaction between demographically diverse Asian countries. For instance, Japan and Korea may import young Filipino health care workers to provide long-term care for their growing army of the elderly and very elderly. Of course, immigration is a politically sensitive issue, so it is unlikely that older countries will open their doors to younger workers from younger countries. However, there are channels besides immigration which enable Asian countries to capitalize on their demographic diversity. For example, older richer countries with abundance of capital but shortage of labor, such as Japan and Korea, can invest in younger poorer countries with abundance of labor but shortage of capital, such as India and the Philippines.

At a broader level, aside from demographics, Asia is not a monolithic region but a region with a great deal of economic diversity. The difference of income level between India and Japan, for instance, is like night and day. There are four groups of Asian countries based on income and development level as well as other key economic characteristics. One group is high-income, capital-abundant, globalized, technologically advanced economies, which consists of Japan, Korea, Taipei, Hong Kong, and Singapore. We can also throw in Australia and New Zealand into this group due to their geographic proximity to Asia. The second group is China. Its characteristics are broadly similar to the first group except that it is much poorer and much bigger. In fact, China is the dominant economy of the region and the only systematically important economy — i.e. it is the only economy that can significantly affect the rest of Asia. China is the region's one and only economic superpower.

The third group is the emerging markets of ASEAN or Southeast Asia. They vary widely in income and development levels, from Malaysia and Thailand at the top to Indonesia, the Philippines, and Vietnam in the middle, to Myanmar, Cambodia, and Lao People's Democratic Republic (PDR) at the bottom. These countries are well integrated into the world economy and also with each other. That is, they trade extensively with the rest of the world and with each other. The fourth group of Asian economies consists of the frontier markets of India, other South Asian countries such as Bangladesh and Pakistan, and Central Asian countries such as Kazakhstan and Uzbekistan. These countries vary widely in income levels — from poor Bangladesh to upper middle-income Kazakhstan — although they generally tend to be poorer than the three other groups. Their key common denominator is that their level of integration with the world economy and with each other — among South Asian economies and among Central Asian economies — is limited. In general, the emerging markets of Southeast Asia are more developed, industrialized, and globalized than the frontier markets of South and Central Asia.

The immense heterogeneity of Asia provides many opportunities for win-win partnerships among Asian economies. Asia is slowly but steadily evolving toward a coherent economic bloc like Europe. This is not to say that Asia will reach the deep, close, and sophisticated level of integration achieved by Europe, where 19 countries even share a common currency, the euro. Furthermore, in contrast to Asia, Europe's economic integration was driven largely by similarities among Western European countries that pioneered and led European integration in income and development levels as well as cultural values, rather than by differences and diversity. More specifically, much of Europe's intra-regional trade — trade among European countries — is intra-industry trade among rich countries — e.g. Germany selling Audis to France and France selling Peugeots to Germany. Of course, some of Europe's economic integration is driven by differences among countries. For example, German firms have invested heavily in poorer Eastern European countries such as the Czech Republic, Slovakia, and Poland to take advantage of lower labor and overall costs. More importantly, the point is not that Asia can replicate European levels of integration in the foreseeable future. Rather, it is that Asia, like Europe, can become a powerful economic bloc which trades and invests much more within itself, rather than the rest of the world. That would make Asia much less vulnerable to protectionist and other economic threats, whether from America or anywhere else.

In fact, regionalization is already well under way in Asia. As noted earlier, economic globalization is increasingly giving way to economic regionalization in Asia, driven by rising consumption power and diversity among Asian countries. In this context, one especially notable and significant trend is the emergence of intra-Asian manufacturing supply chains. Unlike the global value chains which characterized the globalization of Asia, especially East Asia, Asian countries (and not Western countries) are the consumers of the final product, whether it is a car, a computer, or a shirt. China, which has seen a rapid escalation of wages and a growing shortage of unskilled labor due to rising incomes and aging population, is shifting away from low-tech, labor-intensive manufacturing toward high-tech, skill- and knowledge-intensive manufacturing. Some of the low-tech, labor-intensive manufacturing is migrating to emerging markets and frontier markets.

More generally, the growth of Asia's regional supply chains for manufacturing goods is driven by the growth of trade and investment between high-income Asian economies and China on one hand and Asia's emerging and frontier markets on the other hand. High-income Asia and China account for around two-thirds of emerging Asia's exports and two-thirds of its imports. In addition, they account for around half of emerging Asia's FDI inflows and outflows. The emerging markets of ASEAN are also growing rapidly in their own right. This means that the regional supply chains that are linking ASEAN, China, and high-income Asian countries are contributing to the emergence of a self-sufficient economic bloc, much like Western Europe; not self-sufficient in the sense of economic autarky but in the sense that the bloc largely consumes what it produces. The frontier markets of South Asia and Central Asia are not yet integrated with high-income Asia and China. However, India in particular has a lot of potential due to its young, large population but it needs to improve its connectivity as well as energy and other infrastructure, reduce bureaucratic red tape, and create a more business-friendly environment if it wants to ride the wave of Asia's economic regionalization.

There is yet another major reason to be optimistic about the future of Asian regionalization, which will be the region's next phase of globalization, namely technology and innovation. Japan remains Asia's technologically most advanced country, but Korea and China have been rapidly catching up. Nowadays, Asia's most innovative world-class manufacturing companies, such as Samsung Electronics and LG, are Korean rather than Japanese. More recently, China has emerged as a global technological powerhouse, leading the world in state-of-the-art technologies such as fifth-generation (5G) wireless telecommunications technology and artificial intelligence. The three East Asian heavyweights all invest heavily in R&D and other innovative activities. Furthermore, high-income Asia and China are the leading investors in startups in emerging and frontier Asia. According to the above-mentioned September 2019 McKinsey report, Asia's share of patents filed worldwide rose from 52% in 2007 to 65% in 2017. Asia's share of global startup funding rose from 16% in 2013 to 47% in 2018, and 70% of the region's venture capital funding is intra-regional. Asia is no longer a region that imports superior technology from Western countries. Rather, it is now an innovative region that is at the front and center of global innovation, with countries of all income levels pursuing innovation.

Yet another dimension of Asia's economic regionalization is evident in the flow of people and culture. To a large extent, the increased flow of people is a consequence of the region's rising wealth. Just a generation ago, few Asians could afford to travel abroad. Now international travel has become a part of everyday life for Asians. The rapid expansion of middle classes with substantial discretionary purchasing power means that millions of Asians are traveling by air for the first time and enjoying their first overseas trips. In 2009, Asia had 150 million international airline passengers, a figure which rose to 415 million by 2018. The region is home to 11 of the world's 25 largest airports. Chinese tourists are welcome around the world for their big wallets. In 2018, they spent a total of US$277 billion abroad, more than any other nationality and almost twice as much as the US$144 billion spent by American tourists, the second biggest spenders. Furthermore, much of the growth in Asia's travel and tourism is driven by intra-regional travel and tourism. Chinese tourists sunbathing in Southeast Asian resorts, such as Phuket in Thailand, or Bali in Indonesia, are a common sight now, as are Thai and Malaysian tourists enjoying their first experience of snow in Korean ski resorts. In the past, Asia was largely a recipient market of Hollywood movies and American pop music. However, Asia is now producing and consuming large amounts of cultural content. Korean pop culture, also known as K-wave, is now a global force, with a huge following in Asia and beyond. Similarly, India's huge movie industry, especially Bollywood, has long been an influential player in the global movie landscape.

To sum up, Asia is rapidly moving toward its next phase of globalization, i.e. regionalization. Dramatic shifts are under way on the ground, in trade, investment, innovation, flows of people, and flows of culture, that are linking Asian economies ever closer with each other. Asia is becoming like Europe, an economic bloc that can stand on its own, without undue dependence on America. However, unlike Europe, Asia lacks the institutional, inter-governmental framework for economic integration. European integration and the formation of the European Union was spearheaded by the joint leadership of two big powers, namely France and Germany, and their common desire for peace and prosperity in the aftermath of the Second World War. In striking contrast, the three big powers of East Asia — China, Japan, and Korea — have never been able to reach a historic rapprochement after the Second World War. In particular, the bitter historical legacy of Japanese wartime aggression continues to divide China and Korea from Japan. Yet if those three countries come together and initiate an Asian integration project, like the European project led by France and Germany, they will be able to lay a firmer foundation for Asia's economic integration. The institutional framework will first bind high-income Asia, China, and the emerging markets of ASEAN, and subsequently bring in India and other frontier markets. Institutional integration will further cement the de facto regional integration that is already well under way.

The third wave of globalization has been in retreat since the global financial crisis of 2008 but the COVID-19 crisis is pushing the world into outright deglobalization. While the post-COVID world presents a lot of risks for the Asian economy, it also presents a lot of opportunities. This is because the Fourth Industrial Revolution, along with greater digitalization, will kick off the fourth wave of globalization. All Asia had to do to benefit from the third wave of globalization was to get on the boat. However, for Asia to benefit from the fourth wave of globalization, Asia must be at its forefront and help set its agenda.

The third wave was centered on manufacturing and a global value chain based on face-to-face contact. That is, the global value chain was a physical supply chain. But now we are on the cusp of the Fourth Industrial Revolution and the fourth wave of globalization. Virtual global supply chain based on online contact is set to play a larger role. The virtual global supply chain is made possible by the new technologies of the Fourth Industrial Revolution, including artificial intelligence (AI), big data, cloud computing, digital platform, e-commerce, and FinTech. Internet of things (IoT) will generate big data, which are stored in clouds and analyzed by AI. Manufacturing production will be carried out by robots and 3D printers. Sales will be carried out by e-commerce that utilize digital platforms, and payments will be processed by FinTech. In short, the global supply chain will be smart and virtual.

In the fourth wave of globalization, the key assets will be ideas and information, and they will generate economic activity and benefits across borders. For example, computer programmers will collaborate online while they live and work across the world. Up to now, Western universities received hundreds of thousands of foreign students from China, India, and other countries. The tuition and living expenses paid by those students were a major source of income for the universities and the economies of the regions which hosted those universities. Going forward, online education will play a larger role, and studying abroad will mean taking online courses from a foreign university rather than studying and working abroad. Furthermore, a wide range of online services, including remote medicine or telemedicine, will become more widely available and connect the world.

COVID-19 crisis alerted global companies to the vulnerability of global supply chains to big shocks. Global companies will now reconfigure their global supply chains, which the crisis has proven to be too risky. They are likely to reshore a lot of their production to their home countries. Furthermore, American companies may move production to foreign countries closer to home, most notably Mexico, and Western European companies may shift production to nearby Eastern Europe or Turkey, in a process called near-shoring. At the same time, they will seek to diversify their global supply chain production, which had relied too heavily on China, to other Asian countries. That is, global companies have the option of moving a large part of the production process back home, to nearby countries, or to other countries besides China.

Then the question arises: which countries are most likely to be favored by global companies as the relocation destinations? For American firms, Mexico might seem to be the logical choice. Mexico borders America, has abundant cheap labor, and is a natural geographical bridge to the rest of Latin America. However, a corrupt and incompetent government, exacerbated by the pervasive presence of powerful drug cartels, rules out Mexico. India is another potential choice. It has a huge population and a potentially huge domestic market. In addition, most educated Indians speak English, and the country boasts perhaps the world's largest pool of information technology (IT) talent, such as

IT programmers and engineers. However, poor infrastructure and excessive bureaucracy make for an unattractive business environment. An additional deterrent is social instability due to gaping economic inequality and social polarization.

Therefore, the most appealing candidate for global companies seeking to relocate their production is ASEAN countries. While these countries vary a lot in terms of skillsets — e.g. Vietnam has a disciplined, technically competent, hardworking workforce who make excellent manufacturing workers whereas friendly Filipino workers are better suited for service industries requiring good people skills — they have good transport connections to the world and with each other, good infrastructure, pro-business government, and an overall business-friendly environment. However, they are technologically backward and not yet an integral part of the Fourth Industrial Revolution. Therefore, while ASEAN countries are ideal candidates for low-tech and medium-tech manufacturing production, Korea and other NIEs are possible locations for high-tech manufacturing production. Korea has a highly skilled workforce and is among the world's most advanced IT countries. Korea is also geographically close to large markets in China and ASEAN. Furthermore, Korea's world-class success in tackling the COVID-19 pandemic suggests that it is less vulnerable to and more resilient against even big shocks, and is thus a safe production location.

Nonetheless, there is a lot of work that needs to be done by both ASEAN countries and NIEs to improve their business environments. For example, there is scope for deregulation and rationalizing outdated regulations to make it easier for domestic and foreign companies, as well as entrepreneurs, to do business. Furthermore, high-income Asian countries, China, and the ASEAN countries must further strengthen their trade cooperation. Furthermore, Asian countries should foster a free environment for trade and investment within the Regional Comprehensive Economic Partnership (RCEP), which encompasses all of East Asia. Furthermore, Asian countries should join Comprehensive and Progressive Agreement on Trans-Pacific Partnership (CPTPP). By actively promoting and taking part in these diverse regional cooperation mechanisms, Asian countries can cement and strengthen trade and investment links with each other and the rest of the world.

As explained earlier, well before the outbreak, global companies were reshaping the focus of global value chains from low labor costs to Fourth Industrial Revolution technologies such as digital platform, IoT, robots, and AI. This transformation of the global value chain will accelerate in the post-COVID world. Therefore, the new global supply chain will aim to achieve high quality at optimal cost rather than low-cost mass production. In order for Asian countries to promote domestic and foreign investment and benefit from the upcoming fourth wave of globalization, they must stand at the front and center of the Fourth Industrial Revolution. Even technologically backward countries, such as those of ASEAN, must rapidly upgrade their technological capability by investing in science, engineering, and technical human capital.

As noted earlier, the global leadership status of America will decline in the age of the Fourth Industrial Revolution in the post-COVID world. America's catastrophic mishandling of the pandemic and, more fundamentally, its growing self-isolation and unwillingness to lead the world, has greatly diminished its standing in the community of nations. Nor is America now viewed as a benign leader of the world in most countries. At the same time, China is neither strong enough nor widely viewed as a benign power to replace America as the world's leading superpower. Furthermore, China's authoritarian political system puts it at odds with countries with more pluralistic political systems.

Therefore, instead of a single superpower leading the world, as happened during the Pax Americana, which is now coming to an end, what we are likely to see is a Cold War between the two superpowers. In practical terms, America and China are unlikely to fight each other directly but will battle through their proxies, in a series of proxy wars. The polarization of the world into pro-US and pro-China camps makes multilateral cooperation all the more imperative for small Asian countries. Collectively, Asian countries play a bigger leadership role in multilateral organizations such as the United Nations, WTO, World Bank, and IMF. If Asian countries overcome their differences and collectively rise to the challenge of leading the next wave of globalization, advocating and leading globalization on the global stage will be an integral part of Asia's benign leadership. In this way, the vacuum left behind by the end of Pax Americana can be filled up by Pax Asiana. This makes perfect sense in light of Asia's growing share of the world economy. However, in order for Asia to fulfill its potential leadership role, it must be able to develop and propose creative ideas and solutions for mankind's common challenges.

5.3. Asia Must Ride the Wave of the Fourth Industrial Revolution

According to Wikipedia, the Fourth Industrial Revolution is "the ongoing automation of traditional manufacturing and industrial practices, using modern smart technology. Large-scale machine-to-machine communication (M2M) and the internet of things (IoT) are integrated for increased automation, improved communication and self-monitoring, and production of smart machines that can analyze and diagnose issues without the need for human intervention."[6] Karl Schwab, the executive chairman of the World Economic Forum (WEF), first introduced the concept of the Fourth Industrial Revolution in a 2015 article in Foreign Affairs[7] and a 2016 book.[8] According to Schwab, the cornerstones of the revolution are technologies that combine hardware, software, and biology (i.e. cyber-physical systems) and advances in communication and connectivity. Some specific breakthrough technologies include robots, AI, nanotechnology, quantum computing, biotechnology, IoT, the industrial IoT, decentralized consensus, 5G technologies, 3D printing, big data, machine learning, and fully autonomous vehicles.

Wikipedia states that: "In essence, the Fourth Industrial Revolution is the trend towards automation and data exchange in manufacturing technologies and processes which include cyber-physical systems (CPS), the internet of things (IoT), industrial internet of things (IIoT), cloud computing, cognitive computing, and artificial intelligence."[9]

---

6   *https://en.wikipedia.org/wiki/Fourth_Industrial_Revolution. Accessed August 15, 2020.*
7   *K. Schwab (2015). "The Fourth Industrial Revolution," Foreign Affairs, December 12.*
8   *K. Schwab (2016). The Fourth Industrial Revolution (New York: Crown Publishing Group) (published 2017).*
9   *https://en.wikipedia.org/wiki/Fourth_Industrial_Revolution.*

That is, the core essence of the revolution is greater automation and data exchange in manufacturing. One key example is the smart factory in which cyber-physical systems communicate and cooperate with each other and with factory workers. A smart factory is more productive and efficient than a normal factory. Another example is predictive maintenance, based on IoT sensors, which allows machine owners to perform cost-effective maintenance. For example, a company in Osaka can assess whether a machine in Bangkok is running normally or needs to be repaired. Yet another example is 3D printing, which can physically reproduce 3D objects. 3D printing is still an evolving technology so its true potential is not yet fully known but it is already useful for reproducing spare parts and installing them locally. Finally, smart sensors are devices that take inputs from the physical environment and use built-in computing resources to perform pre-defined functions and then process the data before passing it on. They are the driving forces of a wide range of smart megatrends, including smart production.

Let us delve deeper into smart factories to get a better understanding of what the Fourth Industrial Revolution actually means for manufacturing. Germany was the birthplace of the concept of the smart factory. Germany has long been Europe's manufacturing powerhouse, but its manufacturing industries were facing difficult challenges in recent years. These included rapid technological progress, the diversification of consumer preferences, population aging, and a decline in the skill level of the workforce. The consequent search for a fundamental paradigm shift in manufacturing resulted in an industrial strategy called Industrie 4.0, which was first proposed at Hannover Messe in 2011. After extensive discussions among business, government, and academia, Industrie 4.0 became Germany's official national strategy. In practice, smart factory can be defined as the digitalization and networking of all processes, products, and resources. That is, all data related to production is digitalized and shared. New technologies such as IoT and smart sensors enable the digitalization of data, which facilitate their networking and sharing. The smart factories of Nobilia, a German kitchen manufacturer, highlight the huge productivity potential of factory smartization. Kitchens are inherently customized rather than mass produced. Yet through extensive smartization, Nobilia factories share over million pieces of data every day. Crucially, it takes only 100 milliseconds to process one piece of data. Due to smartization, Nobilia has become Europe's biggest kitchen manufacturer, producing 2,600 kitchen sets with just two factories.

In Asia, Korea is at the forefront of the smart factory movement. Like Germany and Japan, Korea is a high-tech manufacturing powerhouse which traditionally has a stronger comparative advantage in manufacturing than in services. The Korean manufacturing sector too is beset by a number of difficult challenges, including rapid population aging and catch-up by China, which is technologically upgrading at a rapid pace. Following Germany's lead, the Korean government is pursuing factory smartization as a core strategy to boost the competitiveness of its manufacturing industries. In the case of Korea, government support for factory smartization began in 2014. The government has proposed a target of 30,000 smart factories by 2022. According to a 2019 Korea Development Institute (KDI) study[10] based on a survey of 1,000 Korean manufacturing firms, despite such concerted policy support, there remains significant scope for further smartization. The survey indicated that smartization rate of factories was 0.31 in 2015 and 0.37 in 2017. Analysis of 1,000 factories indicates

10 M. Kim, S. Chung, and C. Lee (2019). "Effects and policy implications of smart factories," Korea Development Institute (KDI) Research Report 2019-01 [in Korean].

that, overall, smartization has a positive and significant impact on factory productivity and efficiency. The positive effect of factory smartization on firm performance suggests that it can help enhance the competitiveness of Korean manufacturing firms.

It is instructive to look at Korea's prospects in the Fourth Industrial Revolution. While Korea is technologically far ahead of the emerging markets of ASEAN and the frontier markets of India and South Asia, nevertheless, Korea's opportunities and challenges provide plenty of lessons for all Asian countries. As explained earlier, the Korean economy was already losing its dynamism even before the outbreak of the coronavirus, which will further accelerate deglobalization. The Korean economy is facing a here-and-now crisis. The one silver ray of hope is that COVID-19 will speed up the Fourth Industrial Revolution. If Korea can be at the forefront of that revolution, the current crisis may turn into a great opportunity.

The research of Professors Acemoglu and Restrepo, world-class economists in the field of economic growth, finds that among countries with old populations, countries that are forcefully introducing robotics and other automation technologies grow faster than countries which do not.[11] Their research only looked at robotics and automation, but if we also take into account AI, big data, 3D printing, and all the other breakthrough technologies of the Fourth Industrial Revolution, there is scope for dramatic improvements in productivity and economic growth. Therefore, Korea can offset the loss of productivity due to population aging with productivity gains due to the technologies of the Fourth Industrial Revolution. Moreover, if Korea manages to become

---

11 D. Acemoglu and P. Restrepo (2017). "Secular stagnation? The effect of aging on economic growth in the age of automation," American Economic Review, Vol. 105, No. 5, pp. 174–179.

a leader, rather than just a participant, in the revolution, it has a golden opportunity to become one of the world's leading countries.

As one of the world's most advanced information and communication technology (ICT) countries, Korea has a great deal of upside potential in the upcoming post-COVID digitalization of the world economy. However, in the list of the world's top 100 digital tech companies announced by *Forbes* magazine, there were only 4 Korean firms, compared to 39 American firms, 12 Japanese firms, and 9 Chinese firms. More worryingly, there is a lack of new tech startups — future potential Apples and Alibabas — in Korea. Of the world's top 500 tech startups, 155 were American, 27 were Japanese, 25 were United Kingdom, 19 were Canadian, 13 were Australian, 12 were French, 11 were German, 7 were Israeli, and 5 were Singaporean. Korea only had one, a startup called Platum.[12] According to CB Insight, of the world's top 100 AI firms in 2020, 65 were American, 8 were Canadian, another 8 were British, 6 were Chinese, and 3 were Israeli. There was not a single Korean firm.[13]

While semiconductors are the current mainstays of the Korean economy, Korea desperately needs new companies and industries that will lead the country through the Fourth Industrial Revolution and the fourth wave of globalization based on digital data and information. Without the emergence of such companies and industries, Korea risks being left behind. The country cannot live on semiconductors forever and it needs new champions which can master the new technologies and add value with the new technologies. The economy urgently needs an entrepreneurial ecosystem which enables the birth of many new

12 *Startup Ranking, https://www.startupranking.com/top. Accessed August 15, 2020.*
13 *CB INSIGHTS (2020). "AI100: The artificial intelligence startups redefining industries," March 3.*

startups that leverage the Fourth Industrial Revolution in their business models.

The fundamental problem is dismal lack of entrepreneurship among Korean youths, many of whom prefer to spend many years studying for civil service exams to become government bureaucrats, mostly low-level bureaucrats, rather than try their luck at a new business. This bodes very ill for the future of the Korean economy. No country ever got rich by growing the government or expanding the number of bureaucrats. While there are many reasons why bold, risk-taking, visionary, innovative entrepreneurship is dead among Korean youths, irrational and excessive regulation and red tape is one main barrier. There is a famous (or infamous) saying: if the world's top 100 digital tech firms came to Korea, half would be illegal due to Korea's many red tapes. Similarly, if the world's top 500 tech startups came to Korea, well over half would be illegal.

According a survey result reported in the 2019 edition of the Global Entrepreneurship Monitor (GEM), Korea ranked 42nd out of 50 countries in terms of the ease of starting a new business.[14] In Asia, only Japan, another country where the entrepreneurial spirit is dead, ranked lower. In Europe and North America, only Slovakia, Russia, and Latvia ranked lower than Korea. The Korean government should change the positive regulatory system of the Third Industrial Revolution to a negative regulatory system in the Fourth Industrial Revolution. That is, unless explicitly banned, all activities must be allowed. In 2018, the Korean government set forth a so-called comprehensive negative regulation system, which allowed the entry of new technologies and business models but subjected them to subsequent review and

---

14 GEM (2020). *Global Entrepreneurship Monitor — 2019/2020 Global Report.*

regulation "if necessary." While plausible, the devil is in the details. The clause "if necessary," which is arbitrarily determined by the government's political self-interest, imposes a huge risk on entrepreneurs and startups. For example, the government initially praised Tada, Korea's answer to Uber, as an innovative ride-hailing platform. However, due to the opposition of the taxi industry, the parliament blocked the company at the last minute, nullifying massive investment of capital and labor.

While Uber is a fact of everyday life in other countries, Tada's failure to get off the ground in Korea in the face of political opposition by vested interest groups — i.e. taxi industry — explains why Korea produces so few digital startups despite its world-class ICT infrastructure and high-quality human capital. The so-called comprehensive negative regulation system must be replaced by an explicit negative regulation system. The arbitrary "if necessary" clause, which causes a lot of uncertainty among entrepreneurs and imposes a high cost on them, must be eliminated. Only then can we expect Korea to give rise to more digital startups and entrepreneurs. And, only when we see more young Korean entrepreneurs create startups and new businesses can we become more confident about Korea's economic future.

This is not to say that Korea or other Asian countries should do away with regulations together. Rather, what entrepreneurs and startups need to thrive is a rational, stable, and predictable regulatory environment which gives them clear and transparent guidance on what they can do and what they cannot do. The best analogy comes from traffic systems. Well-functioning traffic light and speed limit systems help to make traffic flow more smoothly while dysfunctional traffic light and speed limit systems often exacerbate traffic jams. A high-quality regulatory system regulates areas which need to be regulated in a strict and rigorous manner. On the other hand, for areas where the case for regulation is much weaker, a good regulatory system applies only light regulations or none at all. At all times, the regulations must be enforced in an impartial, objective, and transparent way. Enforcement must not be based on the subjective whims of the regulator. Subjective, arbitrary enforcement creates a great deal of uncertainty for startups and entrepreneurs, and many of them will be deterred from starting a business in the first place. Subjective enforcement also creates opportunities for corruption. If the Korean government is serious about improving the business environment, it must thoroughly reform the regulatory system so that it provides clear, predictable, and objective guidance for entrepreneurs and other stakeholders. Phrases like "review and regulation *if necessary*" will definitely discourage new firms and new investments.

In the hyper-competitive business environment of the Fourth Industrial Revolution, only firms that offer the best value for money will survive. Digital technology has drastically reduced the cost of entry for new entrepreneurs. Because a new firm does not need a brick-and-mortar store and other physical facilities in the digital age, the cost of starting a new business has declined sharply. While this bodes well for aspiring entrepreneurs, it also implies a much more competitive business environment. In manufacturing, the way forward is the smart factory, which was described earlier. Consumption too must move toward smart consumption, which requires FinTech and digital platforms supported by fast and robust internet infrastructure and sound and conducive regulatory framework. The mix of smart factories and smart consumption will be a big step toward a smart economy.

The defining feature of the Fourth Industrial Revolution is constant, relentless innovation. Critically, innovation refers not only to new technologies but also new business models based on new technologies, especially digital technology. New business models based on digital technology are not confined to advanced countries. For example, Grab has emerged as Southeast Asia's top ride-hailing app, food delivery service, and cashless payment solution all rolled into one. Indonesia's Gojek, an on-demand multi-service platform and digital payment technology firm which started out as a motorcycle-hailing app, is another example of an innovative business model. Innovation, which is the core ingredient of the Fourth Industrial Revolution and fourth wave of globalization, is a fundamentally human endeavor. Therefore, the key to prospering in the Fourth Industrial Revolution is to nurture creative human talent. Creative life and creative education hold the key to nurturing creative human talent.

Unfortunately, it is difficult to see how the current lives and schools of the Korean people can promote creativity. Most Koreans live in square-shaped apartment buildings in cities. Korean schools too are squared-shaped buildings, surrounded by a square-shaped wall. The only other structures that share this design are prisons. How can we expect the Korean youth, who are locked up in such uniform, monolithic homes and schools for 12 years to be creative and innovative entrepreneurs? To be the next Steve Jobs, Elon Musk, or Jack Ma, Korea needs a revolution in the layout of homes and schools if it wants to thrive in the Fourth Industrial Revolution.

Each individual must marshal the will power to change. Everybody will soon realize that the post-COVID world will be radically different from the pre-COVID world. The Fourth Industrial Revolution will sweep away all remnants of the old analog world and usher in a hyper-connected, hyper-digital world. The Fourth Industrial Revolution may kill off as many as half of today's jobs and professions.

New jobs and professions will pop up and take their place. Today's best jobs and professions may disappear or be relegated to second-rate jobs and professions in the era of the Fourth Industrial Revolution. Korean youths must give up dreams of becoming government bureaucrats, lawyers, medical doctors, and accountants, all professions which may disappear. In particular, far too many Korean youths aspire to become bureaucrats. Yet it is entrepreneurs who innovate, create jobs, and drive technological and economic progress, not bureaucrats. Without a complete overhaul of social and individual values, it is hard to see Korea doing well as the Fourth Industrial Revolution unfolds.

Finally, talented young Koreans would do well to give up their dreams of joining a large corporation. Instead, if the Korean economy is to thrive, more young Koreans should aspire to become the next Steve Jobs or Jack Ma. Half of Korea's biggest companies by market capitalization may disappear within 10 years. Tech giants like Amazon, Apple, Facebook, Google, and Microsoft barely existed a generation ago but they are now among the world's most valuable companies. Similarly, the Fourth Industrial Revolution will give rise to a slew of new tech giants that do not even exist today. A lot of education that today's Korean youths receive may become useless by the time they graduate. Only global talent who can add value in the hyper-connected, hyper-digital post-COVID world will do well in the future. Nobody can predict what tomorrow's best jobs and professions will be. What we do know is that tomorrow's top talent must have creativity and diverse skills. Therefore, Korea needs an education revolution that teaches students how to think outside the box and be proficient in diverse skills. At the same time, students must have strong literacy, numeracy, and ICT skills. There is no shortcut to creativity.

We looked specifically at Korea's prospects in the Fourth Industrial Revolution. But the Korean case holds plenty of valuable lessons for other Asian countries. While most Asian countries lag behind Korea technologically, they too can benefit from the technological progress if they create innovative and entrepreneurial societies. The core ingredients for such societies are same regardless of a country's income level. Above all, such societies require a strong yet flexible education system that produces a large pool of potential innovators. They also require a sound and conducive entrepreneurial ecosystem that enables innovative entrepreneurship to flourish and produce useful new products.

5.4. Lessons from Countries at the Forefront of the Revolution

The world is in the cusp of the Fourth Industrial Revolution and the fourth wave of globalization which will accompany the revolution. As explained in Section 5.3, in order for Asia to continue to prosper in the post-COVID world, it must not only ride the technological revolution but also spearhead the technological revolution. Simply getting on and riding the boat, as Asia did during the third wave of globalization that began after the end of the Second World War, delivered an unprecedented economic boom for the region. However, that will no longer be sufficient. For the upcoming industrial revolution and globalization, Asia will have to innovate more and innovate better. Innovation, especially entrepreneurial innovation, holds the key to sustaining Asia's growth in the post-COVID world. This is true for all groups of Asian countries — high-income Asia, China, the emerging markets of Southeast Asia, and the frontier markets of South Asia and Central Asia.

The Asian Development Bank's annual flagship report Asian Development Outlook 2020 "What Drives Innovation in Asia," released in April 2020, takes an in-depth look at the current state of innovation in Asia and what the region must do to foster more and better innovation.[15] Broadly speaking, innovation refers to new or significantly different products and processes that improve productivity and benefit users. Innovation encompasses a wide range of activities carried out by a variety of actors. Some innovations such as mobile phones replacing landline phones are game changers. But marginal innovations, such as more and better features on mobile phones, are much more common.

---

15 Asian Development Bank (2020). *Asian Development Outlook 2020: What Drives Innovation in Asia?* (Manila: ADB).

And while first-in-the-world "frontier" innovations like driverless cars grab most of the headlines, it is the first-in-your-context "catch-up" innovations that are occurring all across developing Asia, and which matter greatly for development. We tend to associate innovation with state-of-the-art innovations like AI or 3D printing but in fact, much of innovation, especially in developing countries, are not such revolutionary, first-in-the-world innovations which push the global technology frontier but marginal, first-in-the-country innovations that push the national technology frontier. But what matters for the firms and consumers of Bangladesh or Nepal, for example, is the Bangladeshi or Nepali technology frontier. Marginal and localized innovations are more relevant for improving the productivity of firms and welfare of consumers in those countries.

Sound education systems can contribute to a larger pool of innovators. The link between education and innovation is not automatic. A pre-requisite for a well-educated workforce that can innovate is quality education in literacy, numeracy, and other basic skills. In countries that fail to deliver, the education system must be reformed thoroughly with the objective of drastically improving the quality of basic skills education. Shifting toward more student-centered teaching can foster creative and innovative thinking. Finally, a mix of different skills is key to driving innovation. While Science, Technology, Engineering and Maths (STEM) clearly provides key competencies that promote innovation, it is just as important to develop non-cognitive abilities such as creativity, critical thinking, collaboration, and grit, which are just as critical for the innovation process.

High-quality entrepreneurship is associated with innovation and strong institutions. While entrepreneurship is important for innovation, quality matters more than quantity. Only a very small minority of entrepreneurs, known as gazelles, account for the bulk of innovation and job growth while most entrepreneurs are neither innovative nor create jobs. Whether a country can foster gazelles is largely determined by the country's institutional conditions such as rule of law, property rights protection, and ease of business registration. Finally, the rapid advancement of ICT has revolutionized the entrepreneurial ecosystem by sharply reducing the cost of innovative entrepreneurship, especially via new business models using frontier technology platforms such as the Global Positioning System (GPS) — witness the successes of Grab and Gojek, for example.

There are three countries that can give valuable lessons for all Asian countries when it comes to leading the Fourth Industrial Revolution and more generally, becoming a more innovative economy. Two of them are fellow Asian countries — China and Singapore — and the other is Israel. Up to now, America remains the leader of the Fourth Industrial Revolution and the world's technologically advanced country. However, China is rapidly catching up and seeking to overtake America. China lagged America by a sizable margin during the Third Industrial Revolution, but it has ambitions to lead the Fourth Industrial Revolution and thus become the world's pre-eminent superpower. According to the World Intellectual Property Organization (WIPO), China was the runaway global leader in the number of patent applications in 2018, with 1,393,815 applications, which was about five times more than the applications of the runner-up, America, which had 285,095 applications. Korea came in at fourth with 162,561 patent applications.

China has the world's biggest mobile payment system and big data as well as the world's best face recognition technology. In fact, China has become an almost cashless economy, with most payments made by WeChat or Alipay. In China, you can even give alms to street beggars by swiping your mobile phones on their QR codes! The government's cyber control, which was based on world-class digital technology, played a major role in relatively effective containment of COVID-19. China's central bank, the People's Bank of China (PBOC), has already introduced central bank digital currency (CBDC) as a legal tender, on an experimental basis, in the Agricultural Bank of China, one of the country's four big state-owned banks. It is likely that China will be the first country in the world to adopt digital currency as legal tender. For the time being, digital currency will only be used for domestic transactions, but in due course, it will also be used for foreign trade payments and remittances abroad. Such technological advances will place the Chinese yuan in a much stronger position to vie with the US dollar as the world's dominant currency and the reserve currency of the world's central banks. What is notable about the Chinese government's attitude to new ideas is its bold willingness to plunge headfirst into new technologies and new ways of doing things.

In order to overcome the severe economic downturn due to COVID-19, the Chinese government announced a national plan for the construction of seven major new infrastructure areas. More specifically, China plans to invest 50 trillion yuan in 5G mobile telecommunications network, industrial internet (robotics, cloud computing, smart sensors), big data center, AI, extra high-pressure equipment, alternative energy automobiles, and urban railroads. The huge investment, which is around US$7 trillion, amounts to half of China's total output in 2019. The new infrastructure plan is a prime example of China thinking big, investing in itself, and investing in the Fourth Industrial Revolution. It also reflects the government's hopes for reviving the economy in the short term while preparing China for the Fourth Industrial Revolution in the long term.

In addition to China, there are two much smaller countries that provide valuable lessons for Asian countries — Israel and Singapore. Israel is a small state of 22,000 km² and 9 million people, surrounded by hostile enemy states. Prime Minister Shimon Peres played a decisive role in the reforms that transformed Israel from a small, weak country (except militarily) to a small, strong power (including economically). When Peres became the prime minister in 1984, Israel suffered from annual inflation approaching 400% and a stock market collapse. After taking office, Peres shifted the basic paradigm of the Israeli economy from sclerotic socialism to a more market-oriented system based on consensus between business and labor, kicking off rapid economic growth. In the latter part of his political life, Peres played a key role in turning Israel into a world-class innovation hub and a cradle of successful tech startups. The visionary, transformational leadership of Peres helped Israel pioneer nuclear power safety technology, cybersecurity technology, and USB drives.

In 2018, the ratio of venture capital investment to GDP reached 1.75% in Israel, compared to 0.64% in America and only 0.36% in Korea. Of the 6,000 startups that were founded in Israel, 90 were listed on Nasdaq, compared to only 2 each from Japan and Korea. The world's top venture capital firms flock to Silicon Wadi, Israel's answer to Silicon Valley. While governments around the world have tried to create CyberThis or CyberThat and SiliconThis or SiliconThat, the vast majority have failed miserably because the key to creating successful digital business is innovative entrepreneurship, not detailed bureaucratic "guidance." Government bureaucrats could not create a Silicon Valley if their lives depended on it! In Silicon Wadi, which is attracting high-tech venture capital into automobiles, IT, bioindustries, agriculture, and other fields, the Israeli government created a business environment which enabled creative entrepreneurs to network and bounce ideas off each other. As with entrepreneurship in general, digital entrepreneurship thrives when the government steps aside after creating the right broader environment, and lets bold, creative, innovative, visionary, risk-taking entrepreneurs take center stage. As noted earlier, Israel boasts 7 of the world's top 500 startups, compared to only one for Korea. In addition, among the 50 top cities for startups, Valuer ranked Tel Aviv, Israel's largest city and tech mecca, as the second best.[16]

The Southeast Asian city-state of Singapore has long been viewed as one of the world's best places to do business in. The city-state's founding father, Lee Kuan Yew, was a visionary leader who embraced foreign investors while other developing countries denounced them as legacies of Western colonialism and imperialism. He also made English the multi-ethnic country's official language, both to foster inter-ethnic harmony and to better position Singapore as Southeast Asia's business hub. In 2014, Singapore launched the Smart Nation project, with the aim of promoting a smart economy that grows on a sustained basis. Singapore has consistently garnered the top stop in polls of world-class smart cities. For example, in 2017, Singapore ranked first in a smart city performance index compiled by Juniper Research of UK. Singapore was honored as the "Smart City of the Year" in a smart city expo hosted by Barcelona in 2018. Valuer's ranking of top cities for startups ranked Singapore 12th among 50 global cities.

In 2018, Singapore replicated the entire city-state as a 3D (three-dimensional) virtual reality (VR). The virtual version of Singapore not only encompasses roads, buildings, and other major facilities but such

---

16 Valuer, 50 Best Startup Cities in 2019. Other Asian cities were Bengaluru, India (5th), Singapore (12th), Beijing, China (19th), Tokyo, Japan (20th), Hong Kong (28th), Shanghai, China (31st), and Seoul, Korea (36th).

details as trees and benches in a public park. The government is utilizing virtual Singapore in its planning in construction, transportation, environment, energy, public safety, and other areas. In addition, in 2017 Singapore invited NuTonomy, an MIT spin-off technology startup that makes software to build self-driving cars, to start a robo-taxi service — i.e. on-demand, driverless, self-driving taxi service. If you input your location and your desired destination in your smart phone, the NuTonomy car nearest to you will pick you up and take you to your destination. Singapore is also exploring the commercial deployment of self-driving buses. Singapore's active pursuit of innovation is made possible by the commitment of the Singaporean government to creating the best possible business environment for companies and the best quality of life for its residents.

Launch pads, the collaborative networks of private companies formed in 2011, also played a major role. Almost 800 startup firms are now taking part in launch pads and developing a wide range of innovative technologies. The goal of launch pads is to turn Singapore into a regional and global innovation hub. Partly due to launch pads, the world's top 500 startups include 5 Singaporean companies. A coronavirus outbreak among unskilled foreign laborers living in crowded, run-down dormitories shows that the Singaporean model is far from perfect. However, smart companies and smart residents, led by a smart government, are building a smart innovative country.

Both Singapore and Israel are small countries. Singapore's population is less than six million and it is a city-state. Israel's population is less than 9 million, crammed into 22,000 km². Neither country has any natural resources to speak of. But against all odds, they managed to become two of the richest countries on the planet by building innovative knowledge-based economies. In 2019, Singapore was the

8th richest country in the world, with a per capita income of US$63,987. Israel came in at 19th, with a per capita income of US$43,823. Both are richer than Korea, which is ranked 27th with a per capita income of US$31,762. The only resource that Singapore and Israel have is human resources. What turns a human being into economically productive human capital is the education. The Jewish people who dominate Israel are world-famous for their education system which inculcates creativity. Their creative, questioning educational culture underlies their disproportionate success in global commerce, politics, culture, arts, and science. It also explains their disproportionate representation among Nobel laureates. Singapore, for its part, boasts world-class universities. According to 2021 rankings by highly respected UK university evaluation organization Quacquarelli Symonds (QS), two Singaporean universities, National University of Singapore (NUS) and Nanyang Technological University (NTU) ranked as world's 11th and 13th top universities, respectively. They ranked even higher than University of Pennsylvania (16th), Yale (17th), Cornell (18th), and Columbia (19th).[17]

Like Singapore and Israel, Korea's only natural resource is human resource. During the Third Industrial Revolution and third wave of globalization, Korea engaged well-educated workers to process imported natural resources into manufactured goods and exported them to global markets. Exports generated foreign exchange, which allowed Korea to import more natural resources, which its well-educated

---

[17] *Other Asian universities ranked among top 50 universities were: Tsinghua University (15th), University of Hong Kong (22nd), Peking University (23rd), University of Tokyo (24th), Hong Kong University of Science and Technology (27th), Fudan University (34th), Seoul National University (37th), Kyoto University (38th), Korea Advanced Institute of Science & Technology (39th), Chinese University Hong Kong (43rd), Shanghai Jiao Tong University (47th), and City University Hong Kong (48th).*

workers turned into manufactured exports, which allowed more imports. Very roughly, this is how Korea grew rapidly in the past few decades. However, prospering and thriving in the Fourth Industrial Revolution requires creativity and innovation, which requires human talent that possess these skills. To emphasize again, innovation is and will always remain an intrinsically human endeavor, born of the ingenuity and imagination of the human mind.

Strong basic numeracy, literacy, and IT skills are a pre-condition for a nimble flexible mind that can think outside the box and innovate. Yet shockingly, 1 in 3 10-year-old children in Asia cannot read adequately, according to ADB.[18] Therefore, in low- and middle-income Asian countries, the first step toward nurturing potential innovators must be to reform and strengthen education systems. There is no shortcut to creativity. You cannot fly before you can walk. In upper middle-income and high-income Asian countries such as Korea, students already have strong basic skills. Therefore, in those countries, education reform must prioritize creativity and diversity — i.e. molding young minds that are not only strong in reading, writing, and math but also can think outside the box and constantly ask new questions and seek new answers; i.e. to add "software" to students who are already equipped with the "hardware." In all Asian countries, education reform holds the key to producing a large pool of innovative entrepreneurs, who will determine whether country will sink or swim in the upcoming torrent of technological progress in the Fourth Industrial Revolution.

---

18 Asian Development Bank (2020). *Asian Development Outlook 2020: What Drives Innovation in Asia?* (Manila: ADB).

5.5. Beyond Smart Cities to Smart Countries

In recent years, there has been growing interest in smart cities among policy-makers and governments around the world. There is no universally agreed-upon definition of a smart city, and it means different things to different people. "The conceptualization of smart city, therefore, varies from city to city and country to country, depending on the level of development, willingness to change and reform, resources and aspirations of the city residents. A smart city would have a different connotation in India than, say, Europe. Even in India, there is no one way of defining a smart city."[19] While it is tempting to associate smart cities with rich, technologically advanced countries, in fact countries of all income levels are pursuing smart cities even though rich countries do account for most smart-city initiatives. Out of 153 cities worldwide with official smart-city strategies, 111 were in high-income countries, 22 in upper-middle income countries, and 20 in lower-middle income countries. Furthermore, 35 were in Asia, 60 in Europe, 37 in North America, and 21 in other regions. Within Asia, China and India accounted for most of the smart-city strategies.[20] Of course, we can expect the level of smartization to be lower in poorer countries.

But exactly what is a smart city? Precisely because there is no universally accepted definition of a smart city, we dug into the internet — more precisely, Google — to get some clues about the definition of a smart city so that we can at least get some broad idea as

19 *Smart Cities Mission website of Ministry of Housing and Urban Affairs, Government of India* (http://smartcities.gov.in/content/innerpage/what-is-smart-city.php).
20 R. Berger (2019). *The Smart City Breakaway: How a Small Group of Leading Digital Cities is Outpacing the Rest. Munich, ROLAND BERGER GMBH.*

to what a smart city means. According to one definition,[21] "A smart city is a municipality that uses information and communication technologies (ICT) to increase operational efficiency, share information with the public and improve both the quality of government services and citizen welfare. While the exact definition varies, the overarching mission of a smart city is to optimize city functions and drive economic growth while improving quality of life for its citizens using smart technology and data analysis. Value is given to the smart city based on what they choose to do with the technology, not just how much technology they may have." From the definition, it is clear that the core bedrock technology of smart cities is ICT, although newer technologies also play a role.

Here is an alternative, more detailed definition of a smart city, from Wikipedia.[22] "A smart city is an urban area that uses different types of electronic Internet of things (IoT) sensors to collect data. Insights gained from that data are used to manage assets, resources and services efficiently; in return, that data is used to improve the operations across the city. This includes data collected from citizens, devices, buildings and assets that is then processed and analyzed to monitor and manage traffic and transportation systems, power plants, utilities, water supply networks, waste, crime detection, information systems, schools, libraries, hospitals, and other community services. Major technological, economic and environmental changes have generated increased interest in smart cities, including climate change, economic restructuring, **coronavirus**, move to online retail and entertainment, ageing populations, urban population growth and pressures on public finances."

---

21 *IoT Agenda website (https://internetofthingsagenda.techtarget.com/definition/smart-city).*
22 *https://en.wikipedia.org/wiki/Smart_city. Accessed August 15, 2020.*

Interestingly and significantly, the last sentence implies that COVID-19 will speed up the advent of smart cities. At a broader level, this is intuitively plausible since as we emphasized many times earlier, intensive digitalization will be the defining feature of the post-COVID world. To repeat, while ICT is not new — it has now been with us for a generation — COVID will force us to fully leverage ICT's transformative potential. During the COVID lockdowns, we could not have worked at home without ICT, shopped without ICT, entertained ourselves without ICT, learned without ICT, and lived our lives without ICT. Up to now, we only scratched the surface of the enormous potential of digital technology. COVID will change that forever. Therefore, it is only natural that the concept of digital cities — although the above definitions suggest that smart cities are much more than just digital cities — gained more traction since the pandemic. In other words, the growing prominence of smart cities is part and parcel of a much more digital post-COVID world.

The strong link between smartization of cities and the post-COVID world is evidenced by how cities deployed smart technologies to contain the pandemic. More specifically, in many cities, governments deployed smart technologies to track the pandemic and support the implementation of medical strategies. The Korean experience during the pandemic illustrates the power of smart technologies. The government deployed the Smart City Data Hub system, which enabled it to use data from cameras and other sensors to conduct high-tech contact tracing.[23]

As a result, Korea is one of the few countries which managed to rapidly reduce infection rates even without a complete lockdown. Smart technologies have proven their immense value in Korea's containment of COVID-19 but even beyond the pandemic, they will help shape the

23 *Oxford Business Group website (https://oxfordbusinessgroup.com/news/what-future-smart-cities-after-covid-19). Accessed August 15, 2020.*

future of smart cities. For example, smart traffic lights which react quickly to changing traffic flows and specific traffic situations can reduce road congestion by as much as 25%.[24] Given that new cars are equipped with smart devices and mobile phones are equipped with tracking features, upgrading the traffic infrastructure will make it possible to steer traffic lights more intelligently. Less traffic due to smart traffic lights can free up more lanes for pedestrians and bicycles, which contribute to lower pollution and greenhouse gas emissions.

As explained earlier in connection with use of smart technology to effectively contain COVID-19, Korea is one of the most advanced countries in the world in the field of smart cities. Due to the pandemic, many people around the world are involuntarily taking part in an involuntary experiment in which digital technology is radically altering the way we work, study, shop, and entertain ourselves. The experiment's results are an unqualified success. We can work productively without face-to-face meetings or after-work dinners and drinks with our colleagues. In addition, we can save on commute time and cost as well as rent for office space. While both online and offline learning have their pros and cons, offline classes are not patently superior to online classes, which offer many advantages, such as reducing unproductive time and providing more substantive learning content.

The more fundamental problem of everyday life in Korea during COVID-19 is our home or living space. Thanks to the pandemic, Koreans were locked up in matchbox apartments for 24 hours a day. The matchbox is blocked on all sides. Residents are afraid to annoy their neighbors on upper and lower floors so they dare not engage in even light exercise such as skipping ropes. People sometimes take walks

---

24 DW.COM website (https://www.dw.com/en/how-covid-19-could-speed-up-smart-city-visions/a-53654217). Accessed August 15, 2020.

inside their apartment compounds or neighboring parks but they are fearful of physical contact with others, who are seen as viral vectors rather than human beings. Due to cabin fever, family members fight each other more often and many come down with a new kind of depression called the corona blues. Therefore, we long desperately for a small outside space where we can take in fresh air and have a cup of coffee. But most Korean apartments do not have a verandah, which were done away with to increase living space. The grey city which stares at us outside our windows makes us even more depressed.

During the age of industrialization, people from all over the country flocked to Seoul and other major cities to become the frontline workers of Korea's industrial revolution. Concentrating capital and labor in a few major cities, especially Seoul, was an optimal strategy since it maximized both agglomeration (i.e. clustering) and economies of scale benefits. Furthermore, apartments could be mass produced in a limited area so they were the perfect living space for densely populated Korean cities. The result was a grey concrete forest of matchbox apartments. On the other hand, the countryside degenerated into hollowed-out semi-deserts where only old people remained after a massive exodus of younger people to the cities.

In the post-COVID world, the Fourth Industrial Revolution will touch every nook and cranny of our daily lives. Online work will replace offline work, online education will replace offline education, and so forth. The reason that Koreans lived in matchbox apartments, which were habitually as an accepted fact of everyday life, was their convenience as places to sleep after being out all day, whether at work or at school. With the outbreak, the inconvenience of spending a lot of time with family members in a confined space begins to outweigh the convenience of a place to sleep.

A few years ago, the BBC aired a story about young people who did high-tech business all over the world using high-speed internet work from their base in Bali, Indonesia. They had ditched Silicon Valley for Silicon Bali. Those young workers of a high-tech company preferred the relaxed, easygoing, inexpensive lifestyle of Silicon Bali to the stressful, harried, expensive lifestyle of Silicon Valley. Rapid advances in ICT make it possible for you to access the global market from Bali, Indonesia.

The Economist published an interesting article which predicted that future history will be divided into BC (Before Coronavirus) and AD (After Domestication).[25] That is, the working at office era (BC) will give way to the working at home era (AD). In May 2020, Twitter announced that it will allow its workers to work from home indefinitely. Similarly, Facebook predicted that half of its employees will work from home within 10 years. In the AD era, we can expect to see a growing number of people leave their Seoul matchbox apartments in favor of a house with a garden in the countryside. For example, a typical office worker may end up commuting to the office just twice a week and work from the countryside home the remaining three days. Taking in the smell of the soil and enjoying the scenery of green forests will not only improve the quality of life but also lift productivity.

Working at home and social distancing will greatly reduce Koreans' preference for crowded big cities and monolithic apartment blocks. At the same time, more Koreans will head for the outskirts of cities and even the countryside. In this context, the government should pursue a housing policy that targets the whole country rather than just Seoul and major cities. In the digital post-COVID world, the connection of virtual online networks matters more than the physical clustering of

---

25 The Economist (2020). "Working life has entered a new era: Farewell BC (before coronavirus). Welcome AD (after domestication)," May 30.

people. Therefore, Korea must equip itself with an internet infrastructure which connects every corner of the country with a high-speed digital network. In this way, Korea can aspire to make itself a smart country, rather than just create smart cities here and there. In addition, the living conditions of rural areas must be drastically upgraded. As indicated earlier, a massive exodus of young people from rural areas has left behind a hollowed-out, semi-deserted countryside. Improved education and health care in particular will improve the quality of rural life. Rural development must become an integral part of the government's national land development strategy.

Korea can also take this opportunity to transform its Seoul-centric, apartment-centric living culture to a living culture which embraces the whole country and coexists harmoniously with nature. Were this to happen, the heavy concentration of people and money in Seoul will spread itself out more evenly across the country. An influx of people to rural areas will help resolve the growing problem of empty, unoccupied homes in those areas. COVID-19 can be a blessing in disguise for Korea if it helps to revitalize Korea's many dying areas outside Seoul — i.e. provincial cities and countryside — and promote a more balanced national development which benefits the whole country rather than just Seoul, especially Gangnam. This can be a win-win trend that alleviates the over-crowding, pollution, and other problems of Seoul while injecting new life into the rest of the country, especially stagnant small cities and rural areas that are left behind. Such win-win balanced national development is a blueprint for other Asian countries as well since they too suffer from excessive concentration of people and money in a few dynamic urban hubs coexisting with stagnation and hopelessness in large swathes of the country.

Chapter 6

Sustainable Development in Post-COVID Asia

6.1. Thinking Outside the Box to Overcome the Population Crisis

We saw earlier that Asia as a whole is aging, although the speed and scale of aging differs substantially across subregions and countries. According to a popular saying among economists, demographics is destiny, implying that population aging is a powerful force in the face of which countries cannot avoid economic stagnation. As such, it is basically a pessimistic prediction of a negative automatic link between demographic change and economic growth. However, Asian countries are not powerless to alter their demographic destiny. In fact, there are many measures they can take to mitigate the adverse economic impact of population aging. Asia's transition to a grayer demographic landscape poses two huge strategic challenges for the region — sustaining economic growth in the face of less favorable demographics and delivering adequate, affordable, and sustainable old-age income support for the large and growing numbers of older Asians. Meeting the demographic challenge will be a formidable task but it can be overcome with concerted efforts by the government and society of Asian countries.[1]

In the first instance, Asian countries must maintain a healthy population growth. While it is difficult to define the optimal rate of population growth, clearly it is too high in very poor regions such as sub-Saharan Africa, which is suffering from the toxic combination of explosive population growth and weak economic growth. When there are too many mouths to feed, each child will only get little food and education. On the other hand, population growth is clearly too low in some high-income countries, including rich Asian countries such as Japan and Korea. These countries are facing a here-and-now population cliff and demographic crisis, with the fertility rate too low to replenish the population. Roughly speaking, optimal population growth must be somewhere in the middle: not too rapid so as to impoverish the country yet not too slow so as to deprive the country of youthful energy and even raise the specter of depopulation.

Given Asia's demographic diversity, however, there is no one-size-fits-all population policy, and the policies must be tailored to each country's demographic circumstances. Societies in advanced stages of the transition should consider pursuing pro-natalist policies — i.e. policies that promote births — to revive fertility rates. Korea and the other newly industrialized economies (NIEs) are following in Japan's demographic footsteps and have already reached advanced stages of

---

1 For an excellent and comprehensive discussion of how Asia can tackle its looming demographic challenge, the reader is referred to: D. Park, S.-H. Lee, and A. Mason (eds.) (2012). Aging, Economic Growth, and Old-Age Security in Asia (Edward Elgar), Cheltenham, UK.

population aging. Specific policies include fiscal incentives that encourage childbearing and providing a supportive overall environment, e.g. more and better childcare. Opening up to immigration can also help to offset fertility declines, as the experience of Singapore shows. Economies in the middle of the transition should carefully reassess outdated population policies that may lead to exceptionally rapid population aging. The PRC's one-child policy was perhaps the most well-known example. Given the region's rapidly changing demographic landscape and the risk of exceptionally rapid population aging, birth control policies that contributed to growth in the past may exacerbate population aging in the present and need to be reassessed. Finally, younger Asian countries in the early stages of demographic transition may need to retain population policies that seek to limit population growth. Indeed in some of the region's countries in the early stages of aging, there may be a case for introducing or retaining policies that seek to control fertility rates.

Of course, one way to cope with growing shortage of workers is by mobilizing older workers and female workers. Today's Asians are living much longer and healthier than they were one generation ago. This means that the concept of working age has to be re-defined and updated. Retirement ages that made sense 30 years ago make much less sense today. The obvious policy implication, especially in countries in the advanced and middle stages of the transition, is to increase the retirement age or remove it altogether. Furthermore, governments may need to step in with active labor market policies to remove employer prejudice and discrimination against older workers. Population aging strengthens the case for training and re-training older workers. The low income of older Asian workers is partly due to their low productivity and hence low wages. Therefore, there is a case for governments to promote investment in the human capital of older workers. Training and re-training older workers will not only be beneficial for the workers themselves but also augment the quantity and quality of the workforce. Population aging strengthens the case for promoting female participation in the workforce. The participation of women in the labor force in Asia is visibly lower than in comparable economies. In Japan and the Republic of Korea, for example, their participation rate is lower than that of most other OECD countries. Governments can take various measures to encourage employers to hire more women and to encourage more women to look for work. For example, more and better childcare facilities and generous maternity and paternity leaves can have a positive effect on female participation in the workforce.

Sustaining growth in the face of less benign demographics — i.e. fewer younger workers, more older retirees — is one of the two strategic challenges that population aging poses for Asia. In the past, Asia benefited greatly from favorable demographics — i.e. large share of working-age population in the total population — but demographic dividend is now dwindling and even turning into a burden in older countries. Broadly speaking, more productive workers can offset the loss in output due to fewer workers. That is, even if the number of workers decreases, if each worker becomes more productive, the higher output per worker can compensate for the decline in the number of workers. In this context, education, worker training, and skill-building, and more generally, human capital investment, become pivotal for Asian countries to sustain growth as the workforce growth rate slows down or the workforce shrinks. We already noted that education reform is key to Asia's quest to thrive and prosper amid the relentless technological advances of the Fourth Industrial Revolution and fourth wave of globalization. Although the specific priorities of education reform will inevitably differ from country to country, the common goal must be to produce workers who have strong basic numerate, literate, and IT skills as well as creative, nimble, inquisitive minds that are capable of innovating. Science, Technology, Education, and Math (STEM) is vital for innovation, but so are soft skills and people skills. Schools must evolve from degree factories to incubators of skills that employers need. That is, reducing the skills mismatch between what the schools produce and what the economy needs must be central to Asia's efforts to improve worker productivity.

In addition to sustaining growth, the other strategic challenge posed by population aging is providing economic security for Asia's large and growing elderly population. There are two important avenues for improving old-age economic security. First, Asian countries must build strong national pension systems. Despite the region-wide demographic transition to older populations, many economies do not yet have efficient and effective national pension systems. Therefore, pension reform that ultimately delivers affordable and sustainable systems with adequate benefits for a wide segment of the population is an urgent region-wide priority for old-age economic security. Second, governments should help individuals to make sound financial decisions for retirement. The first step toward adequate old-age support, especially in younger countries, is to raise public awareness about the need to save for retirement. Although financial education and literacy are critical, governments should try to provide a broader overall environment in which individuals are better informed and have stronger incentives to make sound financial decisions. This is a relatively inexpensive way for governments to strengthen old-age support.

Finally, there are a number of opportunities for the region to leverage its demographic diversity through intra-regional cooperation and integration. In addition to sharing knowledge, intra-regional immigration and investment offer potentially large returns. There is a growing shortage of workers in some aging Asian countries, which will only become more acute in the coming years. Geographical proximity and cultural affinity in some cases make intra-Asian labor movement a promising area for cooperation. Malaysia and Singapore have, for example, relied on foreign workers to alleviate their labor shortages.

It is instructive to look at the demographic challenges confronting Korea, a rich country facing a here-and-now population crisis. In Korea, the fertility rate and number of births fell from 0.98 and 327,000 in 2018 to 0.92 and 303,000 in 2019, respectively. Even in Japan, which is the world's most aged society, the corresponding figures were 1.37 and 864,000 in 2019. That is, the number of annual births in Korea is only one third that of Japan.

A major reason for Korea's alarming collapse of fertility rate is that many young Koreans neither have good or stable jobs nor can they afford to buy a home if they get married. A further deterrent to having children is the astronomical education costs and the hyper-competitive, hyper-stressful academic environment the children face in Korea. Furthermore, parents, especially mothers, are often forced to give up their jobs or suffer career setbacks if they give birth to and raise a child. Korea's fertility crisis is thus due to a complex combination of job market, housing, education, and childrearing factors.

One potential policy to encourage marriages and births is to give extra points to newly married young Koreans when they apply for civil service and other public sector jobs. These types of government jobs are clearly NOT what Korea needs for economic dynamism, nevertheless, they can encourage young Koreans to marry and have children. Of course, the fundamental solution for a more dynamic economy is youth entrepreneurship and better jobs for the youth. Another idea is to give newlywed couples mortgage loans of up 100 million Korean won (around US$85,000) at no interest for 20 years. Even if the Korean government gives out such zero-interest, long-term mortgages to 300,000 newlywed couples, the fiscal cost is a manageable 900 billion won. In addition, why not build much more public housing and rent them to the public? In Singapore, one of the world's freest free-market economies, housing ownership is around 90% but 80% live in public apartments built by the government's Housing Development Board (HDB).

However, encouraging marriage alone is not enough to boost fertility. Married couples must want to have children. In this context, the example of Australia, which is maintaining fertility rate of 1.8 through policy support for births and childrearing, is worth a second look. Through a system called the Family Tax Benefits (FTB), the Australian government provides up to a maximum of AU$5,916 per child per year from birth to 19 years, depending on the family's circumstances, such as income.[2] The government also provides a wide range of additional benefits for birth and childrearing, including medical fee support, subsidies for childrearing, and tax credits.

Korea should seriously consider paying the education costs of all future children and making public universities tuition-free. The government can pay for this expenditure by switching all its substantial financial support for private universities to public universities. At the same time, in exchange for withdrawing financial support from private universities, the government should give them full autonomy and

---

2 *Specifically, the maximum rate for each child per fortnight (FTB Part A) is: AU$189.56 for a child aged 0–12 years, AU$246.54 for a child aged 13–15 years, and AU$246.54 for a child aged 16–19 years who meets the study requirements.*

minimize its interference. Coincidentally or not, advanced countries which have relatively high fertility rates, such as Germany, Norway, and Finland, have had tuition-free public universities for a long time.

The policies outlined above are just a few examples of outside-the-box policies for preventing Korea's demographic catastrophe. Low birth rate and aging is not only a family and social issue but also affects education, national defense, housing, and industry. Therefore, Korea's current presidential committee,[3] which is led by civic society and hosted by a low-level government division, is woefully inadequate for dealing with the catastrophe. What Korea needs is an entire government ministry — Ministry of Population — with the most capable civil servants dedicated to fighting the country's population crisis. The sheer magnitude of the crisis demands no less. The ministry should set a target fertility rate of 2.0, which would keep the population stable, and pursue a holistic set of policies that will boost fertility. A potential model is Japan's government agency set up in 2015 with the objective of keeping Japan's population at a minimum of 100 million even 50 years from now.

Realistically, there is a clear limit to what government policies can achieve in terms of encouraging people to have more children. Many advanced countries tried to boost fertility and reverse demographic decline, but with only marginal success. A few thousand dollars is not going to make people want to have more children. The best way forward for Korea and other Asian countries facing a demographic disaster is to create dynamic and vibrant societies and economies in which optimism and positive thinking prevail. Optimistic people become entrepreneurs because they believe they can make it against heavy odds;

---

3   *The Presidential Committee on Ageing Society and Population Policy.*

they also have more children because they believe tomorrow will be better than today. The key to optimism is the self-belief that you can succeed on your own if you have talent and work hard. If Korea and other Asian countries create fundamentally fairer societies with equality of opportunity for everybody, not just those with political connections or inherited wealth, that would be the single best way to create dynamic and optimistic societies, i.e. societies in which young people want to marry and have children, even lots of children.

6.2. An A-system of Sustainable Development Unique to Asia

The COVID-19 crisis is truly an unprecedented, once-in-a-century public health and economic shock. Mankind is at war against an invisible, insidious, and intractable enemy. The highly contagious nature of the virus has spread fear and anxiety around the world. People are rightfully worried about being infected, losing their lives, and losing loved ones. The pronounced economic impact of the pandemic has left millions jobless and sharply reduced the income of millions. Never before in our living memory has a disease caused such extensive damage to our health and economy. The economic downturn due to COVID-19 is expected to be much worse than the Great Recession in the aftermath of the global financial crisis in 2007–2008.

The COVID-19 crisis is, in the first instance, a human tragedy that is causing a great deal of human suffering, misery, and pain worldwide. As of October 20, 2020, over 40 million people have been infected around the world, and the total number of deaths has surpassed 1.1 million. The tragic pictures of the large numbers of human corpses being dumped into hastily dug mass graves or shipping containers painfully reveal the sheer scale of the human tragedy inflicted by the virus. However, COVID-19 has not been an equal-opportunity cause of misery. To the contrary, it has had a disproportionate adverse impact on the poor and disadvantaged. In America, for example, blacks and Latinos, who occupy the lowest rung of the socioeconomic ladder, have been hit disproportionately hard both health wise and in economic hardship. More specifically, they account for a disproportionate share of COVID infections, deaths, unemployment, and business closures. Although the immediate catalyst of the social protests sweeping

America, which unfortunately degenerated into looting and violence in some cases, was the senseless killing of a black man by police officers in Minneapolis, it would be naïve to think that public anger at broader American inequality, especially anger at fundamental inequality between blacks and whites, did not play a major role in the social explosion.

In Asia too, the economic fallout of COVID-19 threatens to undo a lot of the remarkable progress that the region has made in reducing poverty in recent years. Asia would have experienced a continuous reduction in poverty rates in the absence of the pandemic. As emphasized repeatedly, dramatic poverty reduction is the single most significant by-product of Asia's sustained rapid growth. According to a report by Asian Development Bank (ADB),[4] a 5% reduction in annual per capita consumption expenditure due to COVID-19 would push 89 million Asians into poverty, defined in 2020 as living on US$3.2 or less per day. A 10% or 20% reduction in poverty would push 183 million and 399 million people into poverty, respectively. The numbers are equally sobering for extreme poverty, defined as living on US$1.9 or less per day. A 5%, 10%, and 20% reduction in consumption would push 34 million, 78 million, and 185 million Asians into extreme poverty, respectively. Such sharp reversals in poverty reduction are likely to threaten Asia's social and political stability which, in turn, laid the foundation for the region's growth and development.

COVID-19 thus highlights the need for governments and governance systems that place a higher priority on inclusive growth that benefits the entire population rather than a small privileged elite. Business-as-usual (BAU) is no longer a viable approach for governments

---

4 *J. Bulan, R. Hasan, A. Martinez, and I. Sebastian (2020). "COVID-19 and poverty: Some scenarios." Unpublished note prepared for Economic Research and Regional Cooperation Department, Asian Development Bank.*

in post-COVID Asia. The irrelevance of BAU governments and governance systems is even more evident in the environment. The pandemic should serve as a stark warning to mankind to take better care of our environment and planet. There is a growing scientific consensus that the increasing prevalence of pandemics, which is triggered by viruses spreading to humans from wildlife such as bats, civets, and monkeys, is largely due to mankind's invasion into natural habitat that was previously cut off from human contact. For example, deforestation and construction of logging roads clears up deep jungles and brings humans and wildlife into closer contact than ever before. More generally, Asia has to pursue a cleaner and greener environment if it is to succeed in the post-COVID world. While the pandemic has temporarily improved the quality of Asia's environment, e.g. by keeping cars off the road and factories closed, there is a risk that Asia will go back to BAU and continue destroying the environment in the name of economic growth. However, if Asia wants to sustain growth over the long haul, as opposed to growing rapidly for a few years before the environmental destruction exacts a heavy price on growth, a BAU approach to the environment is not a viable option.

To summarize, Asia must pursue economic growth that benefits the entire population, while not destroying the environment. In other words, Asia must pursue sustainable development. As a matter of fact, sustainable development must become mankind's vision for the future. Humans must coexist with and respect other humans and nature. The notion of sustainable development was first laid out in 1987 in the United Nations report "Our Common Future."[5] The essence of the concept is that sustainable development, which benefits not only

---

5   World Commission on Environment and Development (1987). "Our Common Future," United Nations.

us but also our future generations, is possible if and only if we simultaneously achieve economic growth, social equity, and environmental protection.

However, it is extremely difficult to promote growth, equity, and environment at the same time. To the contrary, the three objectives tend to collide with and contradict each other. For instance, prioritizing economic growth often harms social equity and the environment. On the other hand, prioritizing social equity and environmental protection often harms economic growth. This is what we call *trilemma of sustainable development*. How can we resolve this difficult trilemma?

Asia should embrace inclusive growth and green growth as the two engines of sustainable development. Inclusive growth is a growth strategy which aims to simultaneously achieve economic growth and social equity, while green growth aims to achieve a win-win partnership between economic growth and environmental protection, as illustrated in Figure 6.1. This is what we call the *A-system of sustainable development* — which can help Asia achieve sustainable development and become a showcase for the rest of the world.

In the following Sections 6.3 and 6.4, we will discuss how best Asia can design and implement inclusive growth and green growth strategies. It is worthwhile to emphasize that there is no one-size-fits-all approach to the A-system of inclusive growth and green growth for sustainable development. The shift from BAU economic growth to an inclusive and environmentally sustainable growth will necessarily differ from country to country. But, critically, all Asian countries will have to make such a shift if they are to succeed. China may have its unique C-system, India may have its unique I-system, Vietnam may have its unique V-system, and so forth. In short, Asian countries must abandon BAU governance systems in favor of more sustainable governance

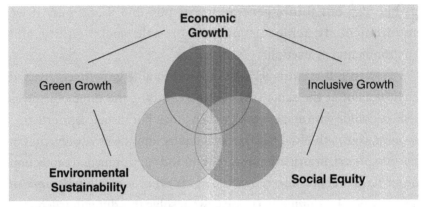

Figure 6.1. A-system of sustainable development.
Source: Authors' drawing.

systems better suited for the post-COVID world. Each will navigate its own specific route rooted in its own culture, history, and circumstances but the destination will be the same — environmentally sustainable and inclusive growth — i.e. sustainable development.

For a long time, Western countries asserted that the only avenue to economic growth and prosperity was the mix of a democratic political system and a market economy. That is, liberal democracy and unfettered markets were thought to be the ingredients of success. The US, with the European Union (EU) at its side, stood at the front and center of this worldview. However, America's astonishingly catastrophic mishandling of the COVID-19 crisis, evident in its world-leading number of infections and deaths as well as shortages and hoarding of face masks and tissues, has rudely disabused us from any notion that this combination was perfect. America's coronavirus disaster is a reminder of not only the weakness of its manufacturing sector but also its entire economic system and social protection system. Moreover, America's glaring failure can be attributed to the lack of a competent and effective government response; i.e. the massive COVID-19 failure is mainly a massive government failure. In addition to government failure, the irresponsible and inconsiderate behavior of millions of Americans contributed to the crisis.

In striking contrast to America's bungling response, China was able to contain the pandemic very quickly and effectively despite having been its original epicenter. Some interpret China's success in tackling COVID-19 as proof of the superiority of China's unique model that combines political authoritarianism with economic capitalism. In addition, China's massive investments in artificial intelligence (AI) and big data, which allowed the country to become a global leader in those technologies, contributed to its successful fight against the virus. Beijing is able to collect and monitor data from every nook and cranny of the society, which allows it to control the mixed system of political authoritarianism and market economy. However, lack of transparency and tight control of information is sowing the seeds of distrust of China in the international community. The Chinese model confirms that a society in which the government controls individuals' information and private life runs the risk of becoming a panopticon society governed by the Big Brother. Whether China, which lacks in transparency and credibility, can spearhead the Fourth Industrial Revolution and fourth wave of globalization is uncertain at best. Above all, Western countries will not accept China's authoritarian model of government.

At this point, it is instructive to take a look at K-system or Korea's governance system. Like China, Korea was able to contain the pandemic quickly and effectively after it became the second country in the world to suffer a major outbreak, in late February 2020. Yet unlike China,

Korea did not impose draconian lockdowns domestically or blanket bans on flights from specific regions or countries. Korea's transparent and effective quarantine system has won praises from around the world. The foreign press is attributing Korea's success to transparency, open communications, and close cooperation between government and society.

According to a *New York Times* op-ed entitled "Post-COVID world" by the world-famous Israeli historian Yuval Harari, mankind finds itself at the crossroads of two critical choices. On one hand, mankind must choose between totalitarian surveillance and civic capability. At the same time, mankind must choose between nationalistic self-isolation or globalization. Korea's success in tackling COVID-19 without draconian restrictions has shown mankind that civic capability may be superior to totalitarian surveillance and open globalization many be superior to nationalistic self-isolation.

Even before COVID-19, K-pop, an integral part of K-wave or globally popular Korean entertainment, was a globally successful Korean product. BTS, a Korean boyband which is said to have the world's biggest fandom since the Beatles, debuted on YouTube, not terrestrial network TV. As such, BTS became a potent symbol of the Fourth Industrial Revolution and fourth wave of globalization. The Beatles ruled the world via terrestrial network TV during the Third Industrial Revolution, but BTS rules the world online through YouTube. In addition, BTS sings their songs in Korean, not English. During the third wave of globalization, which was the period of Pax Americana presided over by America, the benign superpower, globalization meant Americanization. America set global standards, and English became the world's common tongue. In the Fourth Industrial Revolution, uniquely Korean products like BTS can become global products.

According to the Secretariat of the Davos Forum, also known as the World Economic Forum, this is the biggest lesson of BTS' global popularity in the Fourth Industrial Revolution.[6]

During the third wave of globalization, Korea was a follower and a passive recipient of the rules and standards set by America and other Western countries. Futurologist Professor Jim Dator requested Korea to be no longer content to just follow the lead of Western countries but to take a stronger leadership role. In the fourth wave of globalization, which will emerge in the post-COVID world, the K-system, a governance system unique to Korea, must strive to show the way forward for all of mankind. The same is true for the governance systems of other Asian countries, whether it be Singapore's S-system, Thailand's T-system, or Pakistan's P-system. Each Asian country must find its unique path to an inclusive and environmentally sustainable future while seeking to provide at least some valuable lessons for the rest of the world. In the new world of Pax Asiana, Asia must be willing and prepared to lead, rather than just free ride on the leadership and initiative of Western countries. Asia is no longer a small part of the world and world economy but its largest and fastest-growing center. In Pax Asiana, Asia must play a leadership role commensurate with its outsized economic weight.

---

6 P. Vanham (2018). "Here's what a Korean boy band can teach us about globalization 4.0." World Economic Forum website (accessed August 1). https://www.weforum.org/agenda/2018/12/here-s-what-a-korean-boy-band-can-teach-us-about-globalization/.

6.3. Inclusive Growth for Sustainable Development

We saw earlier that Asia is confronted with a growing income gap between the haves and the have-nots. The residents of high-income and low-income neighborhoods of major cities in Asian countries, whether it is Shanghai in China, Mumbai in India, Jakarta in Indonesia, Tokyo in Japan, Seoul in Korea, or any other major city in any other Asian country, might as well be living in different countries. For sure, they are living in different worlds. The residents of luxurious, chic, elegant, and rich neighborhoods have almost nothing in common with the residents of decaying, desolate, drab, and poor neighborhoods of Asian cities. This is similar to how the residents of affluent, pleasant, leafy, largely white American suburbs have very little in common with the impoverished, rundown, desolate, largely black inner cities of urban America, and how the glorious, breathtaking splendor of central Paris is a completely different universe from the grim and grimy banlieues — i.e. outer suburbs — populated by Arab and African immigrants. Growing inequality is therefore a global social and economic problem, rather than a problem that is unique to Asia. However, the fact that income inequality is not just an Asia-centric problem does not lessen the urgency of tackling inequality in Asian countries. In fact, in order for the Asian economic miracle to continue in the post-COVID world, Asian countries must tackle inequality with full force. Tackling inequality head-on and pursuing more inclusive growth must be a top priority for all of Asia.

One of the authors, Park, argues in his recent book that capitalism is an intrinsically unequal and unfair economic system.[7] The basic tenet

---

7   D. Park (2019). *Capitalism in the 21st Century: Why Global Capitalism is Broken and How It Can Be Fixed* (Singapore: World Scientific).

of capitalism is that each of us earns according to our ability and enterprise. Some of us are more talented than others, some of us work harder than us, and some of us are luckier than others, so it is only natural that some of us are richer than others. Nobody would begrudge the huge personal fortune of innovative entrepreneurs like Steve Jobs or Jack Ma, who became rich by producing socially useful products beloved by consumers. Of course, this is not to say that inequality is good. To the contrary, most people would agree that inequality is bad, especially if it is extreme and getting worse, as it is happening around the world today. For one thing, vast income gaps between the rich and the poor fuel discontent and resentment among the poor, who see the rich feeding steaks to their pet dogs while they fight starvation. The resulting social instability, which sometimes fuels social explosions such as violent riots, sours the business climate, discourages investment, and harms economic growth. Furthermore, severe inequality is bad even for the rich. A few millionaires surrounded by a sea of desperate and destitute masses are bound to feel a paranoid sense of insecurity and anxiety, constantly looking over their shoulders.

Inequality is a classic example of what economists call "market failure." Left to themselves, the markets sometimes fail to produce socially desirable outcomes, such as tolerable income gaps between the rich and the poor. Market failures are grounds for government intervention and in fact, redistributing income from the rich to the poor through taxation and income transfers to reduce income inequality is one of the key roles of the government in market economies.

Economic vitality matters greatly for social vitality, which, in turn, encourages people to be more optimistic about the future. As noted earlier, social optimism encourages people to engage in socially beneficial behavior, such as having children. At the same time, a society which experiences environmental destruction and social polarization due to unacceptably high inequality cannot possibly be a happy society. Humans must coexist with and respect other humans and nature. Only this kind of an economy can deliver a happy society in which all individuals can aspire to lead happy and fulfilling lives. A number of research studies from the Organisation of Economic Co-operation and Development (OECD), International Monetary Fund (IMF), and others document a negative impact of income inequality on economic growth.[8] However, we do not need such academic research to tell us the obvious. If there is no equality of opportunity and a realistic hope that anybody with talent and drive can aspire to become the next Steve Jobs or Jack Ma, there will be far fewer wealth- and job-creating innovative entrepreneurs. Both the economy and society will stagnate due to the lack of entrepreneurship.

It is now time for inclusive growth rather than growth for the sake of growth or growth which only benefits a small privileged elite. Equality of opportunity and widespread entrepreneurship hold the key to such a growth. An inclusive growth strategy aims to simultaneously achieve economic growth and social equity. Equality of opportunity, where poor but talented and hardworking individuals have a good shot at succeeding in business and in life, holds the key to inclusive growth. Equality of rewards, which is like paying Lionel Messi the same salary as the 22nd best reserve player on the Barcelona football team, leads to poverty and misery for all, as evident in pre-Deng China or today's North Korea or Cuba. The catastrophic failure of socialism as an economic and political system is all too clear throughout recent history

---

8   See, for example, E. Dabla-Norris, K. Kochhar, N. Suphaphiphat, F. Ricka, and E. Tsounta (2015). "Causes and consequences of income inequality: A global perspective," IMF Staff Discussion Note SDN/15/13, International Monetary Fund.

so we will not dwell further on it here, except to repeat that it is the single biggest manmade disaster in human history, with the possible exception of climate change, which mankind needs to tackle soon.

To promote equality of opportunity, Asian governments should invest more in education and health.[9] Public spending on education and health are powerful means of leveling the playing field between the rich and poor since education and health are among the most important determinants of earning potential. The rich have greater access to private education and health care than the poor. Furthermore, education and health contribute to a country's stock of human capital, and thus promote equity and economic growth. However, as noted earlier, the region spends less on education and health relative to not only advanced economies but also Latin America. Therefore, although governments in the region have been investing more in recent years, they need to invest more.

Inequality of opportunity perpetuates income inequality and passes it from one generation to the next. The children of the rich become rich and the children of the poor become poor. However, inequality of opportunity affects much more than just income gaps between the rich and the poor. Indeed, it weakens the very foundation of entrepreneurial capitalism, which is the foundation of economic growth. Inequality is a permanent fact of life, which means that the playing field can never be completely level. Nevertheless, some government intervention can help make the playing field more level.

In this context, the best way for governments to foster equality of opportunity is to build good public education and health care systems. Education is the most important avenue for upward social mobility, or

---

9　See, for example, D. Park, S.-H. Lee, and M. Lee (2015). *Inequality, Inclusive Growth, and Fiscal Policy in Asia* (New York: Routledge).

moving up the socioeconomic ladder. However, the cost of education can prevent bright but poor youngsters from going to school, which is why there is a strong case for the government to subsidize education. Good public schools are probably the single best use of taxpayer money. By equipping the poor to better compete with the rich, good public schools reduce inequality *and* strengthen entrepreneurial capitalism and thus economic growth. They expand the size of the pie *and* divide up the pie more fairly, thereby providing the best of both worlds.

To repeat, inclusive growth requires equality of educational opportunity. All students must be given access to quality education regardless of how rich their families are or in which neighborhood they live. Equality of opportunity, especially between men and women, must accompany equality of educational opportunity. Both sexes must contribute to housework, and women's careers must not be disrupted too much by childbirth and childrearing. Another good use of taxpayers' money is public health care, for exactly the same reason. Health is as important as education in determining a person's chances of succeeding in life.

Another key component of Asia's quest for more inclusive growth is an intelligent competition policy to create a more level playing field for all firms, including new startups and small and medium enterprises (SMEs). In the case of Korea, for example, the corporate landscape is characterized by severe inequality between a few innovative, high-tech, highly efficient, globally competitive conglomerates, such as Samsung, LG, and Hyundai, and a large mass of relatively inefficient and unproductive SMEs. A well-thought-out and implemented competition policy can, of course, foster more competitive environments in which innovative and efficient newcomers and small companies can compete fairly with the conglomerates and become the new Samsungs, LGs, and

Hyundais. In America and China, tech companies such as Apple and Alibaba, which did not even exist a generation ago, have become industry giants. Korea does have some successful tech companies of its own, most notably the search engine Naver, but it needs far more Navers if it is to do well in the digital post-COVID world. Korea's current competition policy, unfortunately, appears to be largely random punishment of large conglomerates. It is most definitely not smart competition policy based on a strategic blueprint for leveling the playing field to promote the emergence of more Navers. As such, the Korean competition policy needs to be thoroughly upgraded to selectively target instances in which large firms are clearly abusing their market power to hinder newcomers or small firms. This requires a very high level of expertise, which means that the government must allocate the best bureaucrats to the competition authority and train them adequately.

Fiscal policy, especially public spending, can make a visible dent in inequality. International experience, especially the experience of the advanced economies, indicates that fiscal policy can be a powerful tool for reducing inequality. One result that emerges consistently from research studies that is applicable to both advanced and developing economies is that public spending has a bigger impact on reducing inequality than does taxation. According to a study by IMF,[10] public expenditures contributed more to income redistribution than did taxes. The general pattern is also true in developing Asia.[11]

Expanding public transfers, especially conditional cash transfers (CCTs), can protect the most vulnerable and disadvantaged groups.

---

10 *International Monetary Fund (2014). "Fiscal policy and income inequality," IMF Policy Paper, Washington, DC.*

11 *I. Claus, J. Martinez-Vasquez, and V. Vulovic (2014). "Government fiscal policies and redistribution in Asian countries," In R. Kanbur, C. Rhee, and J. Zhuang (eds.) Inequality in Asia and the Pacific: Trends, Drivers, and Policy Implications (London and New York: Routledge; Manila: ADB).*

Public transfers, or transfers from the government to households, in developing Asia lag behind the advanced economies and Latin America. Yet the empirical evidence indicates that public transfers can have a significant effect on inequality in the region. This suggests some scope for expanding transfers but transfers, unlike education and health, do not inherently contribute to economic growth. One promising option is to make transfers conditional on the recipient making investments that augment their human capital — e.g. sending children to school or receiving specific medical care. Such CCTs have proven relatively effective in Latin America.

Korea is an interesting case study because during the initial phase of its remarkably successful industrialization and development, income inequality remained at manageable levels. Therefore, Korea was widely admired as an example of economic growth that did not sacrifice equity. However, in the last two decades, Korea's economic growth has steadily slowed down (Figure 6.2). At the same time, the Korean society became polarized due to growing income inequality (see Figure 4.18 in Chapter 4), and environmental degradation has made it difficult to even breathe sometimes (see Figure 4.21 in Chapter 4). As in other countries, the economic paralysis due to the pandemic is further exacerbating economic inequalities. Unskilled, low-wage workers and small firms are the hardest hit. Worryingly, the post-COVID advent of the Fourth Industrial Revolution and its companion, the fourth wave of globalization, is likely to further exacerbate income inequality and social polarization.

Since coming to office in 2017, the Korean government of President Moon Jae-In has pursued a so-called income-led growth strategy. The government defines income-led growth as growth which creates jobs, increases long-term potential, and makes income distribution more equal by expanding household income and strengthening social safety nets and social welfare. In short, the policy aims to foster economic growth and more equal income distribution by increasing the income of low-income households, whose spending will boost total consumption and demand. Common sense alone tells us this kind of growth strategy is rooted in economic illiteracy. If income-led growth strategy worked, then populist, so-called socialist banana republics, such as Venezuela under the Chavez–Maduro regime, would lead the world in economic performance. Instead, the country has degenerated into a complete basket case, with millions of Venezuelans fleeing to neighboring countries to escape crushing poverty and hardship.

Let us leave aside Venezuela and go back to Korea. The policy that epitomizes the Moon government's so-called income-led growth was the drastic increase in the minimum wage. In 2017, the minimum wage was 6,470 Korean won, or roughly US$6. In 2018 and 2019, the minimum wage was increased by 16.4% and 10.9%, respectively. That is, the minimum wage rose by a staggering 29% in just two years. In addition, labor laws were amended to reduce weekly working hours from 68 hours to 52 hours. The law went into effect in July 2019 in private businesses and government offices with more than 300 workers. Since January 2020, it went into effect in workplaces with 50 to 300 workers.

Let us first take a look at the impact of the new labor policies on Korea's economic growth. A country's potential GDP, or its long-run productive capacity, is determined by the quantity and quality of its land, labor, and capital, as well as its technological capacity. Korea's land area is fixed. Working-age population, which refers to population aged 15 to 65 years, fell by around 110,000 from 37.6 million in 2017 to 37.5 million in 2019. With land area fixed and the workforce shrinking, Korea can increase its potential GDP only by either augmenting its capital — i.e. investment — or by improving its technology. A good indicator of capital accumulation is plant and equipment investment — i.e. investment in factories and machines — and a good indicator of technological development is production of intellectual property. Plant and equipment investment grew by 16.5% in 2017 but shrank by 2.4% in 2018 and 7.7% in 2019. The corresponding figures for intellectual property production are 6.5%, 2.2%, and 2.7%. That is, since the introduction of income-led growth policies, the pace of technological progress slowed down sharply and capital investment shrank outright. As a result, GDP growth rate fell from 3.2% in 2017 to 2.7% in 2018 and further to 2.0% in 2019, as seen in Figure 6.2.

Thus income-led growth policies have patently failed to promote economic growth. So did they at least promote more equal income

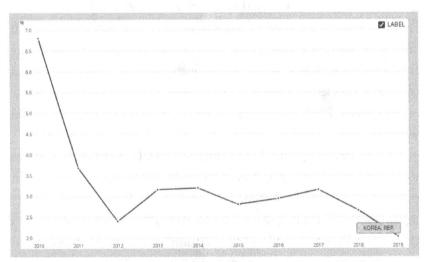

Figure 6.2. GDP growth (annual %), Korea, 2010–2019.
Source: World Bank's DataBank (accessed August 15, 2020).

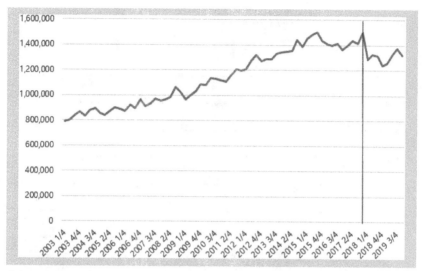

Figure 6.3. Total income of poorest 20% of Korean households (average, won), 2003–2019.
Source: Authors' drawing using data from Korean Statistical Information Office.

distribution? Figure 6.3 shows total income of the poorest 20% of households. In the fourth quarter of 2017, their income stood at 1,504,820 Korean won but dropped sharply to 1,286,702 won in the first quarter of 2018, when the minimum wage rose by 16.4%. This is a staggering decline of 14.5%. The income loss is even more dramatic if we look at labor income, which is the largest component of total income (Figure 6.4). Labor income fell from 681,446 won in the fourth quarter of 2017 to 472,914 won in the first quarter of 2018, a jaw-dropping decline of 30.6%. Labor income continued to fall until the second half of 2019, when it recovered a little, but it is still below the level of the first quarter of 2018. The second biggest source of income for the poorest 20% households, business income, also fell by 17.2%, from 226,746 won to 187,813 won (Figure 6.5).

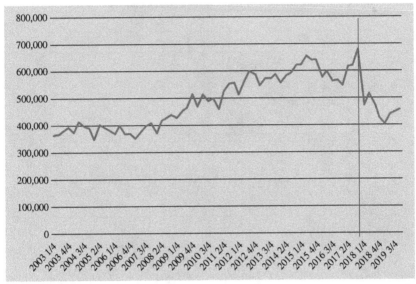

Figure 6.4. Labor income of poorest 20% of Korean households (average, won), 2003–2019.
Source: Authors' drawing using data from Korean Statistical Information Office.

In sum, the alleged goal of the current Korean government's income-led growth strategy was win-win inclusive growth that benefits both growth and equity but it failed on both accounts. Indeed it reduced economic growth and worsened income inequality. Many Korean economists had expressed serious doubts about whether the drastic increase in the minimum wage and more broadly, income-led growth strategy would improve the income and consumption of low-income households. They also doubted whether Korean companies would invest more and produce more, fostering economic growth. But, as we saw earlier, the minimum wage hike brought about a reduction, rather than expansion, of the income of poorer households. Due to drastically higher minimum wages, mom-and-pop stores like convenience stores and restaurants had to close or suffer big reduction in profits.

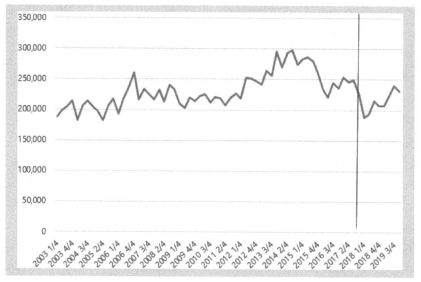

Figure 6.5. Business income of poorest 20% of Korean households (average, won), 2003–2019.
Source: Authors' drawing using data from Korean Statistical Information Office.

These small businesses had no choice but to cut back on workers, which reduced the number of jobs available for the poor.

In retrospect, the drastic increase in the minimum wage, which is the core of the current Korean government's income-led growth strategy, had the effect of decreasing rather than increasing equality of opportunity. By reducing rather than expanding the poor's income, the strategy had the effect of slowing growth and worsening inequality, the worst of both worlds.

When it comes to social inequality, what matters is not only income distribution but also wealth distribution. In this context, the skyrocketing housing prices of major Asian cities have exacerbated wealth inequality and hence social inequality between people with and without their own homes and between major cities and the rest of the country. Soaring housing prices make it impossible for poorer urban residents from even dreaming of owning a home and deter non-city residents from moving to cities.

Furthermore, consumption is not only a function of income but also wealth. Therefore, even if the wages of low-income workers rise rapidly, social inequality will widen further due to soaring housing prices. The poor's share of consumption is likely to fall rather than rise in this scenario. Income inequality is, to a large extent, due to difference in skill levels across workers and thus inevitable. However, the widening inequality of wealth due to escalation of housing prices is not due to hard work or entrepreneurship. The increase in housing wealth of those who are fortunate enough to have a home is pure unadulterated unearned income, which will be widely viewed as unfair by those without a home. The likely result is social polarization fueled by growing inequality of wealth between home owners versus home renters.

Capital cities and large major cities enjoy a concentration of good jobs and economic opportunities. In addition, the quality of transportation, education, health care, culture, and other social infrastructure is superior to that of the rest of the country. This explains the sky-high housing prices in major cities. However, taxpayers pay for social infrastructure. Therefore, it is only fair to tax the increase in housing prices, which reflects superior social infrastructure paid for by taxpayers.

Social polarization is likely to increase between people who can adapt to and thrive in the Fourth Industrial Revolution and people who cannot do so. On the other hand, there is also scope for the revolution's new breakthrough technologies to promote more inclusive growth. For example, in Korea, English ability is a major determinant of a person's life chances. At a global level, English has become the de facto global language due to the third wave of globalization, which turned the world into a single economic bloc. However, English ability depends heavily on one's circumstances. In particular, if you were born rich, you are more likely to have lived abroad or learned from a native-speaking tutor. That is, you would have a decisive advantage if you have rich parents, which implies inter-generational transmission of inequality.

However, new real-time automatic translators allow a person to speak and understand most major languages of the world. For example, with a Birgus voice translator device in your hand, you can communicate in 70 languages, which cover 95% of mankind. Birgus has an accuracy rate of 98%. In 2020, Google launched the Pixel Buds 2 wireless earphone, which not only has the typical functions of smartphone earphones but also uses Google translators to translate 40 languages in real time. Also in 2020, Microsoft launched the Surface Earbuds earphone which can translate more than 60 languages in real time. In principle, the emergence of such revolutionary translation devices can reduce income inequality due to differences in mastery of English and other foreign languages. Furthermore, if all production processes from research and development (R&D) to production to marketing is digitalized and work from home becomes the norm, it will become much easier for women and the elderly to work. This will reduce sexism and ageism while improving the economy's productivity and mitigating the shortage of workers. In that sense, building fast and reliable internet networks and creating a regulatory framework that is conducive to the digital revolution and working from home is very much an integral part of an inclusive growth strategy in the post-COVID world.

To fully benefit from the Fourth Industrial Revolution and fourth wave of globalization, Asian countries must create an industrial ecosystem that is conducive for smart entrepreneurship. This is the overriding pre-condition for Asian countries to prosper in the post-COVID world. The increasingly digital world of the post-COVID era will provide many opportunities for job-creating, growth-promoting entrepreneurship. In any economy, the central ingredient of economic and technological progress is entrepreneurship. The cost of digital entrepreneurship is only a fraction of traditional, offline entrepreneurship.

6.4. Green Growth for Sustainable Development

Humans must coexist with and respect nature. Time is running out for mankind to save the environment and the only planet we have. When it comes to global environmental destruction, Asia is an integral part of problem and it must be an integral part of the solution. Free riding on the efforts of advanced countries is no longer a viable option. Although European countries are at the forefront of global efforts to protect the environment and fight climate change, America has abdicated its leadership role on environmental issues. Since the advent of the Trump Administration in January 2017, the decline of America's role as a benign superpower presiding over a peaceful and prosperous world — i.e. Pax Americana — has accelerated. Perhaps nowhere is the decline as pronounced as it is in climate change. In fact, in June 2017, the US announced that it would unilaterally withdraw from the Paris Agreement on climate mitigation. The Paris Agreement, which was signed by 197 countries and went into effect in November 2016, set out a global framework to prevent dangerous climate change by limiting the global average temperature rise in this century to well below 2°C, while pursuing efforts to limit the temperature rise to 1.5°C. Whatever its shortcomings, the agreement was a concrete symbol of the global community's commitment to tackle climate change, so America's announcement of withdrawal came as a rude shock.

Above all, Asia must tackle climate change out of pure self-interest. Whatever indicator you use, Asian cities and countries invariably appear among the world's most polluted cities and countries. For example, in terms of PM2.5, a widely used indicator of air pollution, Asia was home to 8 of the 10 most polluted countries and 12 of the

20 most polluted countries in the world in 2019.[12] According to a research study by ADB, a large majority of Asia's cities, which are densely populated and rapidly growing, suffer from poor air quality, which poses a substantial risk to health.[13] Air quality can be categorized as poor to critical in 61% of large Asian cities and 52% of medium-sized Asian cities. The evidence from research studies links polluted air to miscarriage, premature birth, neurological conditions in children, respiratory and cardiovascular disease, and dementia in the elderly. The poor, weak, and elderly are particularly vulnerable to pollution. Given that urban air pollution is rooted in many sources, including energy and heat generation, transport, and construction, tackling it is a highly complex process. Therefore, Asian cities must take a holistic and integrated approach which involves sound urban planning and strong environmental governance for monitoring air quality and enforcing regulations.

To a large extent, Asia's environmental degradation is a consequence of its sustained rapid growth. Asia is a victim of its own success, in a sense. If drastic poverty reduction, which allowed hundreds of millions of Asians to live more dignified lives, was the most significant gain from Asia's stunning economic miracle, then destruction of the environment was perhaps the biggest loss. It is worth remembering that just a generation ago, Asia was an impoverished and stagnant region. The lack of pollution was primarily a reflection of Asia's largely rural and agricultural economy, which may have delivered a clean environment but also delivered crushing poverty for billions of Asians. Massive

---

12 IQAir, *World's most polluted countries 2019 (PM2.5)*. *https://www.iqair.com/world-most-polluted-cities*.

13 *Asian Development Bank (2019). "Fostering growth and inclusion in Asia's cities," Theme chapter of the Asian Development Outlook 2019 (Manila: ADB).*

export-oriented industrialization, especially in East and Southeast Asia, transformed Asia's economic landscape and enabled its rapid economic growth and development. However, industrialization, which was driven primarily by energy from traditional fossil fuels, inflicted serious damage on the environment. The rapid expansion of the urban middle class has also dramatically expanded consumption, which is harming the environment as much as industrialization. Hundreds of millions of Asians now have their own cars, which is a major source of carbon emissions. Millions of Asians are flying, which also has a sizable carbon footprint. Asian countries use colossal amounts of disposable plastic products and throw away colossal amounts of plastic waste, accounting for more than half of the 8 million tons of plastic waste that ends up in the oceans every year.[14]

According to Asian Development Outlook 2016,[15] Asia is already a huge part of the global climate change problem and, in the absence of big changes, it will play an even bigger role. Asia is the world's biggest source of carbon dioxide emissions. More specifically, emissions from the region have risen rapidly, from 25% of the global total in 1990–1999 to 40% in 2012. Unless Asia gets serious about fighting climate change and implements strong climate policies, Asia will generate nearly 50% of all greenhouse gas emissions by 2030, and these emissions will double in volume by 2050. Asia must change its ways and pursue green growth, both for its own sake and for the rest of the world. Fossil fuels account for over two-thirds of Asia's carbon dioxide emissions. Therefore, the region's transition to a low-carbon economy must begin with the energy sector.

---

14 Mongabay (2019). "Southeast Asian countries pledge to tackle marine plastic waste crisis," June 27.

15 Asian Development Bank (2016). "Asian Development Outlook 2016: Meeting the low-carbon growth challenge."

Rapid carbon emissions reduction requires massive investment in clean energy. Achieving the 2°C goal of the Paris Agreement will require Asia to invest a tremendous amount of money on clean power-supply technology and infrastructure such as renewable power, carbon capture and storage, smart grids, and energy storage. The cost of switching to a low-carbon economy can be modest. A low-carbon transition requires economic adjustment and substantial new investment in energy-efficient infrastructure and low-carbon energy generation.

Low-carbon transition requires four sets of policies. These are: (1) pricing carbon emissions, (2) putting in place conducive regulations, (3) supporting clean energy investments, and (4) international coordination. What causes the overproduction of carbon emissions is the failure of the market to fully reflect the economic, social, and environmental cost of greenhouse gas emissions. Reducing the gap between the market cost and true cost of emissions involves removing costly subsidies, imposing carbon taxes, and promoting emissions trading. Government regulations such as mandates on use of renewable energy sources, vehicle emission standards, and energy efficiency standards for consumer products, buildings, and industry are indispensable for promoting clean energy and energy efficiency. Asian governments can support clean energy projects by, for example, offering risk guarantees and taking equity stakes. In addition, governments can offer private lenders incentives such as interest subsidies for green loans. Finally, given that climate change is a global problem requiring a concerted global effort, Asian countries must cooperate closely with each other and with the rest of the world.

Given that climate change, carbon emission, and environmental degradation reflect the failure of the market to appropriately price the environment, governments have to take the lead in promoting green growth. However, according to ADB,[16] given the government's limited resources and expertise, Asia's private sector will have to do its part in the region's low-carbon transition. In fact, the private sector is playing a large and growing role in the region's renewable energy, energy efficiency, greenhouse gas mitigation, pollution abatement, and material recycling. The region's environmental market and trade is growing faster than other regions, with Japan and China being the largest contributors. Furthermore, Asian countries are leaders in green innovation, accounting for 44% of global exports of climate change mitigation technologies such as solar panels and efficient lighting. They filed more high-value patents for these technologies than Europe and Latin America together. Market demand for environmental goods, services, and technologies is growing rapidly across the region.

Within the private sector, innovative entrepreneurs are likely to hold the key to developing new ingenious technologies which will move us toward cleaner and greener technologies. As is the case with the economy in general, so it is with green growth — the primary role of the government is to provide a sound and conducive environment for green entrepreneurs to thrive and blossom. When it comes to developing innovative and socially useful products and technologies, the government is usually the supporting actor and the bold and visionary entrepreneur is the star player. One such green entrepreneur is Elon Musk, the founder of Tesla Motors, who has become synonymous with electric cars. It remains to be seen whether he will fulfill his audacious ambition of becoming the Henry Ford of electric cars — i.e. mass-producing electric cars at affordable prices. If he succeeds, that

---

16 Asian Development Bank (2020). *Asia's Journey to Prosperity: Policy, Market, and Technology over 50 Years* (Manila: ADB). *https://www.adb.org/publications/asias-journey-to-prosperity.*

will not only be good for Tesla Motors, it will be good for the environment and for mankind.

A less well-known but no less inspiring example of a bold green entrepreneur is Boyan Slat, a 26-year-old Dutch inventor and entrepreneur.[17] A former aerospace engineering student, he is the CEO of the green startup The Ocean Cleanup. Amazingly, he came across his big idea — his apple falls on Isaac Newton's head moment — in 2011, when he was only 16 years old. Slat has devised an ingenious system for cleaning up plastic waste from the world's oceans. His passive cleanup system uses ocean currents to gather and trap plastic debris, of which there are massive amounts floating around the Pacific, Atlantic, and Indian Oceans. Over the past three decades, millions of tons of plastic have contaminated the oceans, and around 10% of the almost 300 million tons that is produced each year eventually ends up in oceans.

The Ocean Cleanup is a perfect storm of entrepreneurship, environmentalism, and technology. Slat's innovative idea attracted thousands of volunteers, especially after his TEDx talk "How the Oceans Can Clean Themselves" went viral. The strong wave of popular enthusiasm led to a crowd funding campaign which raised US$2.2 million and provided The Ocean Cleanup with the seed money to finance its pilot projects. In October 2019, Slat tweeted that his startup's 600 meter-long, free-floating boom captured and retained plastic debris from what is known as the Great Pacific Garbage Patch, a gigantic plastic flotsam one and half times the size of the US. It took him six years, millions of dollars, and a lot of trial and error but he finally devised a working system that can even pick up 1-millimeter

---

17 D. Park (2019). *Capitalism in the 21*ˢᵗ *Century: Why Global Capitalism is Broken and How It Can Be Fixed* (Singapore: World Scientific).

microplastics. While Greta Thunberg, a fiery activist with plenty of passion but no concrete solution, gets all the media attention and Nobel Prize nominations, it is the daring, visionary entrepreneurs with innovative ideas who think big, like Boyan Slat, who move us much closer to a greener world. The role of Asian governments is to create an environment that is conducive for Asian Boyan Slats and Asian Elon Musks and be good supporting players to the star player, who is the visionary and innovative entrepreneur.

Let us now take a closer look at the Korean experience with green growth. In Korea's case, green growth has been on the policy agenda for quite some time. While inclusive growth aims to achieve a win-win partnership between economic growth and social equity, green growth seeks to do the same for economic growth and environmental protection. In August 2008, then-President Lee Myung-Bak proclaimed that his government will pursue low-carbon green growth as the new growth strategy, which led many people to believe that Korea is some kind of a model or benchmark for green growth. The Lee Administration's centerpiece of green growth strategy was pursuit of the Four Big Rivers Project, which was centered on the country's Han River, Nakdong River, Geum River, and Youngsan River. Overall, the project has received a lot of criticism for causing a deterioration of water quality. Others criticized the project as a development project rather than a conservation project. As a result of the controversial Four Big Rivers Projects, many Koreans have come to view green growth unfavorably.

In truth, green growth was first put forth by Professor Paul Ekins in a 1999 book.[18] In March 2005, at an Asia-Pacific Ministerial Conference on Environment and Development hosted by the United

---

18 P. Ekins (1999). *Economic Growth and Environmental Sustainability: The Prospects for Green Growth* (Routledge), Abingdon-on-Thames, UK.

Nations Economic and Social Commission for Asia and the Pacific (UNESCAP), the UNESCAP member states adopted green growth as a growth strategy. As a matter of fact, at that time, one of the authors — Lee — was a senior environment officer in UNESCAP's Environment and Sustainable Development Division (ESDD), which was in charge of green growth strategy. The author helped to define the basic concept of green growth as well as implementation plans for achieving green growth.

The author had objected to the Four Big Rivers Project due to reservations about its environmental impact. A better strategy might have been to first clean up Youngsan River, which was relatively short in length and suffered from terrible water quality, before possibly cleaning up other rivers. A gradualist strategy of evaluating the results of the Youngsan River cleanup before moving on to the other three rivers would have been more sensible. Be that as it may, the failure of the river project, or at least lack of any strong proof of success, has given green growth a bad name in Korea. This is in stark contrast to the growing attention to green growth in the global community. International organizations that actively embrace green growth as a core concept in sustainable development include Global Green Growth Institute (GGGI), OECD, World Bank, IMF, and ADB. In addition, when China rolled out its latest 13th Five-Year Plan (FYP) in 2016, green growth was one of the two central focuses, along with rural infrastructure.

The basic concept underlying green growth is fostering economic growth and job creation while at the same time improving environmental sustainability. For example, renewable energy such as solar power, wind power, and biomass energy and new green technology industries such as electric cars can be developed as new engines of growth. Provision of financial support and a regulatory environment that is conducive to green growth can support not only the new industries but also demand for their products. At a broader level, the Fourth Industrial Revolution is itself a powerful force for green growth since its core technologies such as AI and big data are more environment-friendly than traditional manufacturing industries, which tend to be energy- and pollution-intensive. Not only that, smart deployment of AI and big data can drastically reduce the energy requirements of cities and the amount of waste they produce.

In addition, the post-COVID expansion of online work, online education, online shopping, and online meetings can sharply reduce transportation. Digital technology can spread population more evenly, reducing the over-concentration of population in few major cities, enabling more balanced development between major cities versus other cities and between cities versus the countryside. Going forward, just as China and Korea deployed smart digital technology to effectively contain COVID-19, the technology can be used to prevent and contain pandemics that are expected to arise in the future. Many health experts predict that COVID-19, as frightening as it is, will not be the last pandemic to torment humanity. As such, in order for us to coexist with pandemics, it is imperative for Asian governments to learn from the Chinese and Korean experiences so that they too are ready to leverage digital technology for contact tracing and other containment mechanisms when the next pandemic strikes. Therefore, in a fundamental sense, government support for speeding up the Fourth Industrial Revolution can also be viewed as core elements of the green growth strategy.

Yet another important policy tool for promoting green growth is green tax reform. Instead of raising environmental taxes while keeping total tax revenues fixed, the government can consider reducing income taxes at the same time. For example, in 1999, Germany passed new environmental legislation which increased taxes on fossil fuels and energy use. However, the government used the additional revenues from the green taxes to finance employment subsidies, which reduced labor costs and thus improved the German industry's international competitiveness. These types of intelligent and carefully designed policies contributed to Germany's mix of strong growth and clean environment. In order for Asian countries to achieve sustainable development which delivers economic growth, social equity, and environmental protection, they must grow in an inclusive and green way. By doing so, Asia can show the way forward to sustainable development to the rest of the world. Serving as a model of inclusive and environmentally sustainable development for the rest of the world will be another dimension of Pax Asiana.

6.5. An Asian New Deal Based on Three Axes

By fully embracing globalization during the wave of globalization of the postwar era, Asia was able to grow much faster than the rest of the world. In fact, in recent years, Asia had become the main engine of growth for the world economy, accounting for much of global growth. Asia was the biggest beneficiary of Pax Americana, presided over by a benign superpower which spearheaded a golden age of globalization. Overall, Pax Americana was based on rules of the game set in multilateral frameworks such as the GATT–WTO global trade regime which oversaw a dramatic expansion of international trade. The IMF monitored global financial stability while the World Bank set the development agenda of the poor Global South. By pursuing largely sound and conducive macroeconomic and structural policies, Asia leveraged the huge opportunities opened up by international trade and investment to catapult itself from the periphery of the world economy to its front and center. In fact, Asia is now the biggest economy in the world, and its share of the world economy will continue to expand in the coming years.

Yet Asia now finds itself at a critical crossroads since the COVID-19 outbreak. Even before the pandemic, formidable challenges emerged and loomed largely on Asia's horizons after its long period of sustained rapid growth. In particular, since the global financial crisis of 2008, there has been a tangible slowdown in the momentum of globalization, evident in key indicators such as international trade and investment. The retreat from globalization was further fueled by growing resentment toward globalization from the losers of globalization — e.g. factory workers who lost their jobs due to cheaper imports from developing countries with plenty of low-wage workers. The resentment was especially pronounced in advanced economies. This wave of growing popular anger against globalization contributed to the shocking election of Donald Trump as the US president in November 2016. President Trump launched a full-scale trade war against China, which has subsequently morphed into a broader economic conflict between the two giants. The US–China trade war epitomizes growing protectionism around the retreat from globalization.

As if the specter of growing protectionism was not bad enough, COVID-19 engulfed the world in early 2020. The world is still struggling to defeat the virus, which is proving to be an invisible, insidious, and intractable enemy. In fact, as of August 2020, the pandemic shows no signs of going away any time soon. At a broader level, the pandemic alerted the world to the huge risks and costs of globalization. After all, the virus which first emerged in the wet markets of Wuhan, China, spread like a wildfire across the world in a matter of weeks. It has spread from China to the rest of the Asia and the Pacific region to the Europe and Middle East to North America and Latin America. We are living in a highly inter-connected world, but the spread of the coronavirus was a rude reminder that that is not necessarily a good thing. Border closures and flight bans meant that what we took for granted until as early as January 2020, namely freedom to travel to other countries, will not return for some time. Large multinational companies may bring some of their production home to protect themselves from the vulnerability of long and distant supply chains, painfully exposed by COVID-19. As a result of the pandemic, countries are likely to turn more inward and away from the world. COVID-19 may turn the retreat from globalization, which pre-dates the pandemic, into outright deglobalization.

How can Asian countries cope in a world that is deglobalizing and losing the leadership of a benign America? What are they to do?

The era of Pax Americana which served Asia so well in the past is coming to an end. The US government's disastrous mishandling of COVID-19, which turned the world's richest, most powerful, and technologically advanced country, into *the* global hotspot of the pandemic casts serious doubt on America's ability to lead the world. With just 4% of the world's population, America accounts for a quarter of the infections and deaths. Equally importantly, the Trump Administration's withdrawal from the Paris Agreement on climate change and the World Health Organization (WHO) at the height of the pandemic casts equally serious doubt on the willingness of America to lead. The US may have a new president and a new administration after the November 2020 elections, but the relative decline of America is set to continue. China's effective containment of COVID-19 stands in marked contrast to America's tragic ineptitude. However, the world is not even remotely ready to accept Chinese leadership in lieu of American leadership. Western countries will not fully embrace, let alone follow, an authoritarian China while developing countries, especially those in Asia, are apprehensive about an increasingly assertive China that is not afraid of flexing its muscles.

It is only natural that a region that gained so much from globalization is worried about its prospects in a deglobalizing world. However, there is no cause for undue pessimism. As noted earlier, geographically, the next wave of globalization is likely to be led by Asia, which is already the world's biggest economy and set to become relatively even bigger in the coming years. In other words, today's rich Asia is not yesterday's poor Asia which could not afford to buy what it produced. The stereotype of Asian countries producing parts and components shipping them to China, which produces some part and components on its own and puts together all parts and components and ships them to American and European consumers makes for a nice simple summary of the Asian production network, also known as Factory Asia, but it is an increasingly outdated picture. The emergence of Asia as a globally significant consumer as well as a globally significant producer means that global value chains that used Asian factories to produce final goods for Western consumers is giving way to regional value chains in which Asian factories produce final goods for Asian consumers. Asia's rising income is turning it into a self-sufficient economic bloc like North America or Europe, which consumes most of what it produces. Tellingly, intra-Asian trade is a growing share of Asia's trade and intra-Asian foreign direct investment (FDI) is a growing share of Asia's FDI. Geographically, the next wave of globalization will be characterized by the decline of globalization and the corresponding rise of regionalization. This trend will be especially evident in Asia.

No less significant than the geographical re-orientation of globalization from the distant world to the nearby region — i.e. from globalization to regionalization — in the coming fourth wave of globalization is the Fourth Industrial Revolution. Each earlier wave of globalization is accompanied by an industrial revolution, and the new wave will not be any different. The third wave of globalization was based on a physical supply chain built on face-to-face contact. But in the much more digital and smarter fourth wave of globalization, virtual global supply chains based on online contact will come to the fore. What makes possible the digitalization of global supply chains are the new technologies of the Fourth Industrial Revolution. These include AI, big data, cloud computing, smart sensor, digital platform, e-business, and FinTech. Big data generated by the Internet of Things (IoT) are stored in clouds and analyzed by AI. Manufacturing production will increasingly be performed by robots and 3D printers rather than workers. Online shopping, which dominated shopping during the pandemic, will continue to grow. The global supply chain will thus be smart and virtual. In the fourth wave of globalization, the key assets will be ideas, knowledge, and information, and they will generate economic activity and benefits across borders.

Going forward, the key for Asian countries to thrive and prosper in the fourth wave of globalization, just as they did during the third wave of globalization, is to adapt well to the Fourth Industrial Revolution of the more digital, smarter post-COVID world. The central feature of the Fourth Industrial Revolution is constant innovation. Innovation refers to not only new technologies but also new business models based on digital technology. New digital business models are not limited to advanced countries. Two examples of digital businesses in developing countries are Grab, Southeast Asia's top ride-hailing app, and Indonesia's Gojek, multi-service online platform that started out as a motorcycle-hailing app. Innovation is a fundamentally human endeavor. The key for Asian countries to do well in the Fourth Industrial Revolution and ride the fourth wave of globalization is to nurture creative human talent that can innovate. A strong education system that produces individuals with strong basic literacy, numeracy, and IT skills yet nimble, flexible minds that can think outside the box holds the key to nurturing creative human talent.

Besides a strong education system, high-quality entrepreneurship is associated with innovation.[19] Entrepreneurship matters for innovation, but it is quality that matters more than quantity. Only a very small minority of entrepreneurs account for the bulk of innovation and job growth while most entrepreneurs are neither innovative nor

19 Asian Development Bank (2020), Asian Development Outlook 2020: What drives innovation in Asia?

create jobs. Whether a country can foster such innovative, high-quality entrepreneurs is determined by institutional conditions such as property rights and rule of law. Finally, ICT has revolutionized the entrepreneurial ecosystem by sharply reducing the cost of innovative entrepreneurship, especially via new business models. Intellectual property rights (IPR) can promote innovation but different types of IPR matter more at different stages of national development. Evidence points to the importance of capital markets, especially equity markets, in financing innovation, and the importance of cities as engines of innovation. Above all, in light of the relentless technological change which will be triggered by the Fourth Industrial Revolution, developing a large pool of innovative entrepreneurs who can flexibly identify and capture new opportunities as they arise will determine a country's economic fate.

COVID-19 represents a once-in-a-lifetime global shock. As such, Asian countries should consider re-setting or re-configuring their economic and social paradigms. That is, it is high time for Asian countries to think up New Deals which will enable them to survive and thrive in the challenging post-COVID world. There is no single one-size-fits-all New Deal for all Asian countries, rather, each Asian country must design and pursue its own New Deal. Nevertheless, in light of the common strategic challenges facing all of Asia, the New Deal of all Asian countries should try to (1) make the necessary preparations to succeed in the Fourth Industrial Revolution and fourth wave of globalization, (2) promote inclusive growth that benefits broader segments of the population rather than a privileged elite, and (3) foster green growth which reconciles growth with environmental protection. While the New Deal of each Asian country will be unique and shaped by country-specific factors, the New Deals of all Asian countries will rest on the three axes of readiness for the Fourth

Industrial Revolution, inclusive growth, and green growth. COVID-19, which was rooted in mankind's relentless environmental destruction, served as a wake-up call to save our planet, and the pandemic has had a disproportionate effect on the poor, further strengthening the case for reducing economic inequality. We now explore the case of Korea to illustrate the specific mechanics of a New Deal based on three axes.

In July 2020, the Korean government announced the Korean New Deal as its centerpiece strategy for tackling the COVID-19 crisis. New Deal refers to the fiscal stimulus policies of the administration of US President Franklin D. Roosevelt to tackle the Great Depression. More specifically, "the New Deal was a series of programs, public works projects, financial reforms, and regulations enacted by the administration between 1933 and 1939. It responded to needs for relief, reform, and recovery from the Great Depression."[20] The New Deal had three major components — relief for the poor and the unemployed, recovery of economic activity, and reform of the financial system. As was the case with the much milder Great Recession which followed the global financial crisis of 2008–2009, the Great Depression was kicked off by a financial crisis — i.e. Wall Street stock market crash of the fall of 1929. Between 1929 and 1933, US GDP fell by 30%, industrial production declined by 47%, and unemployment surpassed 20%.

The New Deal, which lasted from 1933 to 1939, stopped the economic implosion and laid the foundation for recovery, although full-fledged recovery did not arrive until the Second World War, which was equivalent to a massive fiscal stimulus. While opinions differ on the effectiveness of the New Deal, there is universal consensus that it marked a revolutionary reset or reconfiguration of the American economic

---

20 *https://en.wikipedia.org/wiki/New_Deal#:~:text=The%20New%20Deal%20was%20 a,recovery%20from%20the%20Great%20Depression.*

paradigm. In the face of an unprecedented shock, the government intervened massively to save the economy. The US government made large investments in public infrastructure such as roads, ports, and railroads. Those investments generated much-needed jobs in the short term and built up infrastructure in the long term. Of course, the New Deal was costly, pushing up the US government debt by 50% from US$22 billion in 1933 to US$33 billion in 1936. However, overall, the massive bill for the massive government spending was money well spent, especially if we consider the alternative scenario of no New Deal.

The world is now facing another unprecedented shock, COVID-19. Since economies are currently mired in a deep downturn due to COVID-19, governments have launched a massive fiscal stimulus in an effort to revive their economies. This is why the Korean government has proposed the Korean New Deal, which consists of two axes. The core priority areas of the proposed program are DNA ecosystem, digital inclusion and social safety net, promotion of online industries, and digitalization of social overhead capital. The D in DNA refers to Data, N refers to Network, and A refers to AI. The Green New Deal consists of the three axes of (1) greening of infrastructure, (2) conducive ecosystem for innovative green industries, (3) and low-carbon, distributed energy. The government is planning to invest 76 trillion won in the Korean New Deal by 2025 and invest the first 31 trillion won by 2022.

The Korean New Deal can alleviate economic stagnation and unemployment in the short term while speeding up the advent of the Fourth Industrial Revolution, which is vital for Korea's long-term economic future. Since Korea is a small compact country, it may be possible to build a smart country rather than just smart Seoul and a few other big smart cities. Moreover, it would be desirable for Korea to lead the construction of a global digital network so that it can play a leading role in the coming age of digital globalization or the fourth wave of globalization.

It is a good thing that a Green New Deal is part of the Korean New Deal. The concept of the Green New Deal was first proposed by American journalist Thomas Friedman in his 2008 book *Hot, Flat, and Crowed.*[21] The essence of his proposal is that large-scale investments in renewable energy infrastructure will allow the world to tackle climate change *and* create new jobs. The United Nations Environment Programme (UNEP) proposed a Green New Deal as a new engine of growth in 2008. The EU announced the European Green Deal as a long-term roadmap for a green economy in December 2019. In the US, some Democrats are advocating a Green New Deal.

In principle, a Green New Deal can promote both economic growth and environmental sustainability. At a time when the world economy is mired in a downturn almost as bad as the Great Depression, concerted investment in environmental infrastructure can fight climate change and global warming while boosting the economy and employment in the short run and fostering new green industries in the long run. This can be a win-win partnership which benefits both economic growth and environment. While the promise is exciting indeed, in practice the devil is in the detail. More specifically, what is needed is a technologically and economically viable strategy that can actually deliver sizable economic and environmental benefits.[22] If the Korean green growth strategy is well designed and implemented, then it has a good chance of becoming a benchmark for the global community. That, in turn,

---

21 *T. Friedman (2008). Hot, Flat, and Crowed: Why We Need a Green Revolution – and How it can Renew America (New York: Farrar, Straus and Giroux).*

22 *In this connection, a blueprint such as the Sustainable Recovery Plan laid out in June 2020 World Energy Outlook and prepared by the International Energy Agency (IEA) in collaboration with the IMF, can show the way.*

would deepen political support for the Green New Deal so that a change of government does not affect it.

Social New Deal would be another good addition to the Korean New Deal. Income inequality and social polarization in Korea, which has been worsening steadily since the Asian financial crisis of 1998, grew even worse since the COVID-19 outbreak. Furthermore, Digital New Deal and Green New Deal will bring forth new regulations, such as regulations against thermal power plants. Such regulations will inevitably cause conflict and tension between different interest groups. FDR's New Deal in the 1930s not only built public infrastructure but also included social consensus building based on strengthening of labor unions and introduction of social protection systems. Korea too achieved a grand bargain among industry, labor, and government under President Kim Dae-Jung in the aftermath of the Asian financial crisis.

There must be a new grand bargain between industry, labor, and government in the aftermath of COVID-19. There must also be a grand bargain between large companies and small and medium enterprises (SMEs) and between different political forces, especially between conservatives and progressives. In sum, there must be a social grand bargain, or a Social New Deal, which encourages the disparate elements of society to work together and to share the pain. The many serious difficulties facing Korea include population crisis, slowdown of growth, social polarization, and environmental destruction. Global economic downturn due to COVID-19 and the US–China Cold War further darken the prospects of trade-dependent Korea.

But this is exactly why Korea urgently needs a New Deal. Digital New Deal to create growth and jobs in the Fourth Industrial Revolution, Green New Deal to foster coexistence of economic growth and the environment, and Social New Deal to promote harmony between the economy and the society collectively comprise the New Deal. This is the New Deal of three axes that Korea can offer the world. Of course, the real challenge is not just proposing this New Deal but actually making it work so that Korea can achieve economic growth, technological progress, social harmony, and a cleaner environment in the post-COVID world. If Korea manages to pull off this feat, COVID-19 could turn out to be a blessing in disguise that will transform Korea into an advanced economy and society where everybody can live in harmony with each other and pursue their own happiness.

Equality of opportunity will prevail in such a society so that everybody with talent and drive, even those from disadvantaged backgrounds, can aspire to become a dynamic, big-thinking, visionary entrepreneur like Steve Jobs, Elon Musk, or Boyan Slat. The bigger the pool of such innovative entrepreneurs, especially among the youth, the more likely the economy and society will thrive and successfully cope with the relentless economic and societal changes of the Fourth Industrial Revolution and fourth wave of globalization. There are some who argue that COVID-19 strengthens the case for a *permanent* expansion of the government's role in the economy and society. This is dangerous nonsense. For sure, tackling the health and economic crisis due to the pandemic requires unprecedented government intervention. In these exceptional times, massive and forceful government action is not only desirable but also necessary. However, once the pandemic recedes and the world returns to normal, it will be sensible for the government to withdraw to the background and let innovative entrepreneurs return to center stage. The best governments are those that create the most conducive environment for visionary entrepreneurs such as Elon Musk and Boyan Slat to flourish, so they can find innovative solutions to mankind's most urgent problems such as environmental destruction.

6.6. Final Thoughts: Toward Pax Asiana

To conclude, Asia is at critical crossroads amid the unprecedented global health and economic crisis of COVID-19. The pandemic, which was rooted in mankind's destruction of nature, alerted us to the urgency of protecting the environment. It also painfully exposed the unacceptably high levels of inequality that prevails in Asia and around the world. COVID-19 thus strengthens the case for inclusive, environmentally sustainable development. At the same time, the dawn of the Fourth Industrial Revolution will herald a new wave of globalization based on regionalization and digitalization. In this technological revolution, the most valuable assets are ideas, knowledge, and information which will drive economic activity and create value, both domestically and across borders. If Asian countries manage to lead the Fourth Industrial Revolution and the fourth wave of globalization, while blazing the trail for inclusive and environmentally sustainable development, they will be in pole position to preside over a Pax Asiana of global prosperity.

The advent of Pax Asiana will not only benefit Asia but the whole world. The reason is that Pax Americana, or America's benign leadership of the Third Industrial Revolution and the third wave of globalization, is coming to an end. Pax Sinica led by China is not yet a realistic option because China is neither strong enough to replace America nor does it have a large enough following in the community of nations. Furthermore, the growing conflict between US and China puts other Asian countries in a difficult dilemma. However, Asian countries need not look far for a practical solution to their predicament. Asia is now the world's biggest economy, and intra-Asian trade and investment flows are on the rise. In short, Asia is becoming a viable independent economic bloc that can stand on its own without undue dependence on America or Europe. While Asian countries, especially those in East Asia, are rapidly evolving into a de facto economic bloc on the ground, institutional arrangements for regional integration lag far behind.

However, institutional and inter-governmental regional integration is a pre-condition for Asia to be able to punch its weight on the global stage. Therefore, the first step toward turning the vision of Pax Asiana, or Asia's benign leadership of a new golden age of globalization, into reality is for Asian countries to work together to set aside their political differences and work closely together to build common institutions similar to the EU, although that would be purely a long-term goal. The elephant in the room is China, which is disproportionately big relative to other Asian countries. However, it is also in China's self-interest to forge closer official links with its Asian neighbors, which are individually small but collectively big. At a time when China finds itself in the middle of a bitter conflict with America, China also needs friends. Therefore, now is an opportune time for East Asian countries to institutionalize their close and growing economic links through a historic grand bargain. The grand bargain must include a commitment to resolve all major outstanding geopolitical, territorial, and historical disputes through peaceful means.

East Asia, which consists of China, Japan, Korea, the three smaller newly industrialized economies, and the Southeast Asian countries of ASEAN, already form a powerful economy. The region's GDP accounted for 18% of global GDP in 1998, and this share grew to 24% by 2018. Furthermore, they trade heavily with each other and invest heavily in each other. There are also heavy flows of people within East Asia, as millions of East Asians travel to other East Asian countries for business and pleasure. De facto, on-the-ground regional integration is thus well under way, but it will be further cemented by institutional regional integration. By opening their borders wide to cross-border flows of goods and services, capital, and people within the region, East Asia can become the standard bearer for globalization and economic openness. Pax Asiana will be grounded in open regionalism, which means that East Asia will keep its markets open to the rest of the world even as it promotes trade and investment within the region.

This last point is an important one. Pax Asiana will not be an exclusive Asian economic bloc that promotes more cross-border economic activity among Asian countries at the expense of cross-border economic activity between Asian countries and non-Asian countries. To the contrary, in the Pax Asiana age, Asia, the region that benefited the most from the third wave of globalization, will forcefully champion and spearhead globalization on the global stage. In addition to spreading the gospel of globalization, East Asian countries must gradually extend the bloc to other parts of Asia, especially India. They may also invite Australia and New Zealand to join. The essence of the benign nature of Pax Americana was that it was largely based on fair and impartial rules of the game. Pax Asiana will build upon and improve this regime by explicitly targeting inclusive and environmentally sustainable development. In this way, Pax Asiana will not only revive economic globalization but help the world confront income inequality and climate change.

Index

CPSIA information can be obtained
at www.ICGtesting.com
Printed in the USA
FSHW021213091220
76569FS